"FOR VALOUR"
            THE "V. C."

"It is held that valour is the chiefest virtue, and most dignifies the haver."
SHAKESPEARE (*Coriolanus.*)

"A LIVE SHELL DROPPED AMONG THE GUARD OF THE TRENCHES."
Frontispiece.]

"For Valour"
The "V. C."

A record of the Brave and Noble Deeds for which Her Majesty has bestowed the Victoria Cross, from its Institution to the present date

Compiled and Edited from the State Papers

BY

J. E. MUDDOCK

AUTHOR OF

"MAID MARIAN AND ROBIN HOOD," "FROM THE BOSOM OF THE DEEP," "FOR GOD AND THE CZAR," "STORMLIGHT," ETC.

WITH ILLUSTRATIONS BY G. H. EDWARDS

LONDON
HUTCHINSON & CO.
34 PATERNOSTER ROW
1895

TO

GENERAL LORD ROBERTS V.C., G.C.B.

WHOSE

SPLENDID MILITARY SERVICES HAVE PLACED HIM

IN THE

VERY FRONT RANK OF ENGLAND'S DISTINGUISHED SOLDIERS :

AND WHOSE

NOBLE DEEDS OF DARING AND DEVOTION

HAVE INDELIBLY STAMPED HIS NAME

ON THE DEATHLESS ROLL OF HIS COUNTRY'S HEROES

THIS BOOK IS DEDICATED

BY

THE AUTHOR

IN TOKEN OF HIS RESPECT AND ADMIRATION.

PREFACE.

Deeds of heroism and Acts of Bravery have always possessed the deepest interest for the British People; and it is to be hoped that the day is far distant when we shall cease to thrill with enthusiasm as we read of Duty and Devotion done and shown in the face of difficulty and death. At no other period of our national history have we needed so much as we do now, examples of unselfishness, and contempt for danger and death, where the country is to be served and suffering relieved. We live in a sordid, bustling age which tends to some extent, to show us the meaner attributes of human nature while suppressing the nobler ones. It is therefore desirable that our youth of both sexes should have some object lessons before them of high courage, fidelity to duty, and the tenderest regard for those who have suffered and been stricken in the hour of mortal peril. Since the institution of the Victoria Cross, there has been an official record kept of the magnificent deeds done by sea and land—by soldiers and sailors who have earned the cross;

but the records have not been readily accessible to the general public, and in compiling the little book I have been actuated by a feeling that these splendid stories of noble manhood are worthy of greater prominence than they can have in the dry-as-dust pages of state documents. In putting my materials together I have carefully refrained from adding anything that might seem to be in the nature of exaggeration. Perhaps it will be said I have erred on the side of terseness; but better that than to lay myself open to a charge of over-colouring. A story of an act of heroism is best told in simple, ungarnished language and I have studiously endeavoured to bear that in mind, with what result I must leave my readers to judge. At the same time I am conscious that nearly all, if not quite all, the cases referred to in this work would have gained in effect to a large extent by some elaboration of detail. But there were many difficulties in the way of carrying that out. Accuracy was of the first importance, and the necessary accuracy could only have been attained by taking the details down from the lips of the men themselves. But a large number of those who have had the honour of wearing the Victoria Cross, and who alone could have given reliable particulars of the scenes and conditions amidst, and under which their heroic deeds were performed, have laid down the burden of life and passed to the eternal silence. And I shrank from even seeming to wish to glorify our living heroes at the expense of our dead ones. Brave men are invariably modest and I am sure that those whose names figure in the following pages would rather that I said too little than too much.

While I do not suppose that the work is flawless I have striven to make it reliable; and I would humbly venture to express a hope that it may be regarded as " The Golden Book of Valour " to which men and women may turn and read with pleasure and profit by the lesson each story teaches.

Excerpt from the London Daily Telegraph.

January 4th, 1894.

"It is a pity we think, that, although all Englishmen honour this high decoration of the Victoria Cross and admire its heroic recipients, too little is known or remembered of the splendid deeds of "derring-do" which are registered against their worthy names. The modesty that always accompanies true manhood combines with the military brevity of the official description of each incident to render that a dry chronicle of facts which might be made, without exaggeration or extravagance, into a chapter of gallantry and devotion almost as good for English boys to learn by heart as their Church Catechism. We should like to have English girls and boys as familiar with the details of each brave deed as with the localities of the Cathedrals of the Kingdom, or the names of the Queen's ships of war.... It is well, we repeat, that each and all of the gallant deeds attached to the names of those figuring, or who have figured in this Golden Book of Valour should be more fully described and commemorated. The last men in the world to want their brave acts embellished are those who accomplished them; but it is good and useful for the Army and Navy first, and then for men and women of all sorts and conditions, to know what brave things have been done and are being done for the Queen and the Country. We do not say, like the Roman Senator, that mere physical courage is the highest of all the virtues. It depends a good deal upon bodily temperament, the excitement of the moment, and other circumstances. Nor is it even in any sense a rare gift among men of the English breed, high or low. When, however, to the disregard of death, which in itself is so noble a lesson to a selfish and timid time, there is added the beautiful impulse of humanity, when not merely for fame and praise, but from compassion, comradeship and commanding sense of duty a servant of the Queen does before the enemy such deeds, the example is surely one to be written in letters of gold, and not simply with the brief and stilted sentences of a paragraph in the London Gazette. When the Roman conferred the "Civic Crown" upon their very bravest "*Ob civem servatum*", because of a citizen's life saved, they inscribed his name upon the marble wall in the Capitol. Our Governments, less careful of the glories of the national story, hang upon these manly bosoms the red or blue ribbon with the bronze cross, sign an order upon the Treasury for an annual ten pound note, and straightway forget all about the matter."

INTRODUCTION.

THE ORIGIN OF THE "V. C."

The first announcement of the Institution and Creation of the Victoria Cross, appeared in the "London Gazette" of February 5th 1856. It was expressly pointed out that up to that time there had been no means of adequately rewarding the individual gallant services, either of officers of the lower grades in the naval and military services, or of warrant of the petty officers, seamen and marines in the navy, and non-commissioned officers and soldiers in the army. The Queen, therefore, expressed her gracious intention of instituting the new decoration to be called the "Victoria Cross," and her Majesty stated that she hoped the decoration would be eagerly sought after and highly prized by the officers and men of the military and naval services. The new decoration, it was further stated, should consist of a Maltese cross—made of neither gold nor silver—but bronze, with the Royal Crest in the centre and underneath which an escrol bearing this inscription:

FOR VALOUR.

It was ordained that the cross should be suspended from the left breast by a blue riband for the navy, and by a red riband for the army.

It was further ordained that anyone who, after having received the cross should again perform an act of bravery which if he had not already received the cross would have entitled him to it, such further act was to be recorded by a bar attached to the riband suspending the cross, and for every additional act an additional bar.

It was also determined that the decoration could only be awarded to officers and men who had served their Country in the presence of the enemy, and had there and then performed some signal act of valour and devotion.

In order that every man in either branch of the service, irrespective of rank or station, should be eligible, it was set forth that neither long service, wounds, nor any circumstance or condition whatever, should entitle anyone to the honour unless he had performed some conspicuous act of bravery. These conditions have been rigidly adhered to, and the man lives not who dares to breathe a hint that bias or partiality has been shown in the awardment of the Victoria Cross. It is above suspicion. It is perhaps the one order in the whole world which a man cannot obtain by influence or a side issue. Nor does an order exist which is more coveted by brave men.

Where the act of daring is performed under the eye and command of an admiral or general officer, the cross can be awarded on the spot. Where not so performed the claimant has to make good his claim and the claim is most jealously inquired into. In the first case the decoration is made publically before the naval or military force to which the claimant belongs, and his name is to be recorded in "a general order," while the cause of his special distinction is to be set forward. In the second instance the decoration is to be conferred as soon after the claim is proved as possible, and the name of the recipient must also appear in a general order.

In the case of conspicuous bravery on the part of a body of soldiers or sailors, not under fifty in number, where no special selection can be made, the officers engaged shall have the privilege of selecting one of their number for the honour; and one petty officer or non-commissioned officer shall be selected by the petty and non-commissioned officers engaged, while two seamen or private soldiers may be selected by their comrades.

Every warrant officer, petty officer, seaman, marine, non-commissioned officer or soldier who receives the cross is entitled to a special pension of ten pounds a year, dating from the date of the act of bravery; while each additional bar entitles the recipient to a further five pounds a year.

In order that the decoration might be kept free from taint, it was particularly ordained that anyone who received the cross being subsequently convicted of treason, cowardice, felony or any infamous crime was to have his pension stopped and his name erased from the Register of Honour. The first distribution of the cross took place in February 1857, there cipients being soldiers and sailors who had performed valorous acts during the terrible Crimean War.

INAUGURATION OF THE ORDER.

The inauguration of the order took place on the 26th June 1857, and was certainly one of the most imposing and touching military ceremonies that the Metropolis had ever seen. The Memorandum of the arrangements was dated from the Horse Guards, June 17th and ran as follows :

" The whole of the troops assembled to be under the command of Lieutenant-General Sir Colin Campbell G.C.B. The Cavalry, namely, 1st and 2nd Regiments of Life Guards, 6th Dragoons and 11th Hussars, under Major-General the Earl of Cardigain, K.C.B. The Royal Artillery, namely, one troop and two field batteries, under Major-General Sir William Williams K.C.B. One Company of Royal Engineers, under Colonel Chapman C.B. Three Battalions of Foot Guards, under Major-General Lord Rokeby, K.C.B. One Battalion of Royal Marines, the 79th Regiment, and 2nd Battalion Rifle Brigade, under the command of Major-General Lord William Saulet, C.B. The troops to be formed at ten o'clock a.m. in contiguous quarter distance columns right in front, facing Park Lane, in one or two lines as the ground may admit. The officers, warrant officers, non-commissioned officers, and men who are to receive the Victoria Cross will be assembled in front of the line of columns, and after passing by Her Majesty, and receiving the decoration, they will be formed opposite to the Queen, and there remain until the troops have marched past. The ground to be kept by detachments of Cavalry to be detailed for the purpose. The troops to march in slow and quick time.

By command of

H.R.H. The General Commanding in Chief,

   G. A. Wetherall, Adjutant-General."

In accordance with the foregoing order, the troops began to assemble about half past eight on the morning of the 26th of June. The weather was fine, and an enormous crowd had assembled to testify by their numbers and their cheers how much and highly they appreciated the services of the brave fellows who that day were to be the chief actors in the imposing scene, the stage of which was the noble Park that has witnessed so much that is great as well as humiliating in our National history.

When the troops had all been got into position, they certainly made a grand show, and Londoners evinced the pride they felt in their war-worn soldiers and sailors, by cheering lustily as the men were wheeled into their respective positions. The heroes of the hour were drawn up in single line facing the troops.

A few minutes before ten, a flash of fire and a heavy boom from the right of the field batteries told the densely packed masses of human beings that the royal party were approaching, and very soon they appeared in the following order:

CAPTAIN SAYER.

Deputy Assistant-Quartermaster General.
Detachment of Royal Horse Guards.
The Queen's led horses.

AIDES-DE-CAMP TO THE GENERAL COMMANDING IN CHIEF.

Lieutenant-Colonel Maude (Extra).
Lieutenant-Colonel Lord Burghersh.
Colonel Tyrwhitt.
Lieutenant-Colonel Clifton.
Hon. Colonel Macdonald.

AIDES DE-CAMP TO THE QUEEN.

Colonel Marquis of Ailesbury.
„ Duke of Buccleuch.
„ Marquis of Donegal.
Colonel Lake.
„ J. W. Gordon.
Deputy Quartermaster-General to the Forces.
Hon. Colonel A. Gordon.
Colonel Satten.
Colonel Lord Dynevor.
„ Holloway.

Colonel His Serene Highness Prince
W. A. of Saxe Weimar.
Colonel Sir I. Tronbridge.
Deputy Adjutant-General to the Forces.
Colonel Forster.

EQUERRIES TO THE QUEEN, AND TO HIS ROYAL HIGHNESS PRINCE ALBERT, IN WAITING.

Military Secretary.
Major-General Sir. C. Yorke.
Adjutant-General Royal Artillery.
General Sir H. D. Ross.
Quartermaster General.
Major-General Sir R. Airey.
Adjutant-General of the Forces.
Major-General Sir G. Wetherall.
His Royal Highness the General Commanding in Chief

Her Majesty THE QUEEN.

Prince Albert.
Gold Stick.
Lady Churchill.
Lady Codrington.
Prince Frederick William of Prussia.
Master of the Horse.
Prince of Wales.
Prince Alfred.
Royal Carriages.
Conveying Members of the Royal Family, and each attended by an Equerry.

General Officers.
Foreign General Officers
and
Equerries and Attendants upon Foreign Princes.
Two and Two.
Assistant-Adjutant.
General to the Forces.
Assistant-Adjutant.
General Royal Artillery.
Assistant-Quartermaster.
General to the Forces.
Lieutenant-Colonel Pipon.
Colonel Palliser.
Colonel O'Brien.
Lieutenant-Colonel Bingham.
Lords Lieutenants of Counties in Uniform.
Two and Two.
Royal Carriages, if empty.
Detachment of the Royal Horse Guards.

The Queen, who appeared mounted on a magnificent charger, rode between Prince Albert and Prince Frederick William. She wore a round hat, with a gold band round it, and on the right side a red and white feather. Her dress consisted of a scarlet body, made like a military tunic, but open from the throat. Over her shoulder she wore a gold, embroidered sash, while a dark blue skirt completed the costume. Like all the members of the Royal family who were in military costume, she had a band of crape round the left arm.

The Prince of Wales and Prince Alfred were

mounted on ponies, and were dressed in plaid trousers and Scotch caps. The Princess Royal, Princess Alice, the Duchess of Cambridge, and the Princess Mary rode in a carriage.

As soon as they arrived on the ground, the officers, composing the Queen's *Cortége*, formed in front of and facing Her Majesty; those preceding Her Majesty on the proper left; and those following on the right and at the distance of the front of the columns. As soon as this was done the distribution of the Victoria Cross commenced. The Queen took up her position with Prince Albert on her left, and Prince Frederick William on her right. The Duke of Cambridge, Lord Panmure, and other officers of rank were in close attendance to read the name of each hero as he appeared.

The officers who were entitled to the cross had assembled in Hyde Park, opposite Grosvenor Gate, at nine o'clock. Each officer had a loop of cord attached to the left breast of his tunic to facilitate the fastening on of the cross as Her Majesty presented it.

The non-commissioned officers and privates who were to receive the order had assembled at Portman Street Barracks, and marched thence to the Park, under the command of Lieutenant Knox of the Rifle Brigade.

When everything was ready the recipients advanced one by one in the order as given below. As each man came up Lord Panmure handed a cross to the Queen, who, stooping from her saddle, fixed it on the breast of the man entitled to it. The recipient at once passed on and formed again in line behind Her Majesty.

THE NAVY.

Commander Henry James Raby.
  „   John Bythesed.
  „   Hugh Talbot Burgoyne.
Lieutenant Charles Davis Lucas.
  „   William Nathan Wright Hewett.
Mr. John Roberts, Gunner.
Mr. John Kellaway, Boatswain.
Mr. Henry Cooper,   „
Joseph Trewavas, Seaman.
Thomas Reeves,   „
Henry Curtis, Boatswain's Mate.
George Ingoueville, Captain of the Mast.

ROYAL MARINES.

First Lieutenant George Dare Dowell, Royal Marine Artillery.

Thos Wilkinson, Bombardier, Royal Marine Artillery.

ARMY.

Sergeant-Major John Grieve	2nd Dragoons.
Private Samuel Parkes	4th „
Lieutenant Alexander R. Dunn	4th Hussars (Late).
Troop Sergeant-Major, J. Berryman	17th Lancers.
Colonel C. Dickson C.B.	Royal Artillery.
Capt. A. Henry, Quartermaster} Late Land Transport Corps }	„ „

Captain Gronow Davis	Royal Artillery.
Sergeant Daniel Cambridge	,, ,,
Gunner and Driver T. Arthus	,, ,,
Lieutenant Gerald Graham	Royal Engineers.
Corporal John Ross	,, ,,
,, Wm. J. Lendrim	,, ,,
Sapper John Perie	,, ,,
Colonel Hon. H. H. M. Percy	Grenadier Guards.
Brevet-Major Sir C. Russell Bart	,, ,,
Sergeant Alfred Ablett	,, ,,
Private Anthony Palmer	,, ,,
Brevet Major G. L. Goodlake	Coldstream Guards.
,, ,, J. A. Conolly Late 49th Regiment	,, ,,
Private George Strong	,, ,,
Brevet Major R. J. Lindsay	Scots Fusilier Guards.
Sergeant James McKechnie	,, ,, ,,
Private William Reynolds	,, ,, ,,
Private Thomas Grady	4th Regiment.
Lieutenant William Hope	7th Regiment (Late).
Assistant Surgeon J. E. Hale, M.D.	7th ,, ,,
Private Matthew Hughes	7th ,, ,,
,, William Norman	,, ,, ,,
Ensign Andrew Mognihan	8th Regiment.
Private Samuel Evans	19th ,,
,, John Lyons	,, ,,
Lieutenant Luke O'Connor	23rd ,,
Corporal Robert Shields	,, Reg. (Late).
Private William Coffey	34th Regiment.
,, John Sims	34th Reg. (Late).
Sergeant William McWheeney	44th Regiment.

Sergeant George Walters	49th Reg. (Late).
Corporal James Owens	,, ,, ,,
Brevet Major C. H. Sumley	97th Regiment.
Sergeant John Coleman	,, ,,
Brevet Major Hon. H. H. Cliffort	Rifle Brig. 1st Batt.
Private Francis Wheatley	,, ,, ,,
Captain Wm. J. Cummingham	,, ,, 2nd Batt.
Lieutenant John Knox	,, ,, ,,
Private Roderick McGregor	,, ,, ,,
Private Robert Humpston	,, ,, ,,
Private Joseph Bradslaw	,, ,, ,,
Brevet Major G. J. Bouchier	,, ,, 3rd Batt.

THE ORIGIN OF THE CRIMEAN WAR.

[It was in connection with this war that the first awards of the Cross took place].

In the short space at our disposal in a work of this nature it is impossible to do more than take a hurried glance at the history of the Crimea, and of the events which led up to England and France undertaking the stupendous war against Russia.

The history of Crimea extends over two thousand years; it commences with the earliest annals of Greece, and is associated with the proudest periods of Roman history. It is curious to reflect that while savages roamed through the forests of England, the Crimea was the seat of an advanced civilisation. When Rome herself had fallen a prey to barbarian hordes, the inhabitants of the Crimea had a precarious existence. At last, from the elevated plateau of Central Asia, the Turk began to make his way. The date of his first arrival in the Crimea it is impossible to fix but it is certain that during the seventh century the greater part of it was held by a Turkish tribe called Khazars, and was then known as Khazaria. During the next two or three centuries the Turkish rulers—Khans as they were called—lived in a state of dazzling splendour. But in the tenth century the Russians and a race called Pichengues broke the power of the Khans, and the Pichengues established themselves in the Crimea where they remained master for nearly two hundred years. Then they fled before the Mongol Tartars led by the Conqueror, Ghenis-Khan. In 1280 or thereabout the Genoese were permitted to found a settlement which they named Kaffa. So powerful did the Genoese ultimately become that they extended their settlements, and built strong fortifications. They obtained possession of Soldaid, now called Soudak, and also made themselves masters of Cembalo, which was destined to become known later as Balaklava. As the centuries rolled by a Turkish sovereign sat on the throne at Constantinople where the Cæsars had formerly ruled. Then the Tartars of the Crimea, who had been crushed by the Genoese, sent an embassy to Sultan Mohammed inviting his protection. The Sultan was flattered by this and at once fitted out an expedition consisting of 400 ships with an army of 20,000 men. The Genoese soon succumbed, and as Sultan Mohammed was not in the habit of restoring his conquests the Crimea became part of the Ottoman empire. The ambition of the Turks, being inflamed by their new possession, carried the conquering sword into Russia, and for a long while the Russian had to struggle with the powerful Turk for bare existence. But at last things changed.

XXVIII   THE ORIGIN OF THE CRIMEAN WAR.

Oppression aroused the Russians to desperation, and the oppressed arose in their might to smite the Oppressor. Very gradually they began to push southward, every league of the way being paid for with a delugué of blood. In 1736, under Marshall Munich, a Russian army 50,000 strong outwitted the Turks, and forced their way to the banks of the Alma. But in the wild barren country the Russians suffered terribly and at last Marshall Munich beat a retreat with the loss of half his army. Nevertheless the Russians were now bent on gaining a permanent hold of the Crimea, and this was virtually done in 1771 by the troops under the leadership of Prince Dolgorouki. The following year, by what is known as the treaty of Kainardji, the Crimea was nominally rendered an independent state under its ancient race of Khans. But in 1783 the Khanat which had become a mere farce was put an end to by the Empress Catherine, who announced her intention of uniting the Crimea to her Kingdom of Russia. This was a shameful violation of the treaty of Kainardji but the Turks were then too weak to offer opposition, and the Russians were thereby emboldened to aim at the throne of Constantinople. The passage of the Balkan, which was succeeded by the peace of Adrianople, showed the Russians that if they chose to make a supreme effort they could realise their desire. Europe, however, became alarmed, for the Russian nation, hitherto looked upon as a barbarous state, was a power to be reckoned with. Fortresses had risen on the banks of the Vistula thereby threatening Germany, and in the south in the most commanding position in the Black Sea at the extremity of the Crimean Peninsula the Great Naval Arsenal of Sebastopol sprang into existence. There is no doubt this arsenal was intended to be a standing menace to Turkey, and to render the conquest of Constantinople easier when the time came for the final blow. When the Emperor Nicholas, who was one of the ablest and most ambitious of Russian rulers, ascended the throne he believed that the moment had arrived for seizing the city on the Golden Horn. A French Revolution had placed Louis Napoleon on the throne of France, and it appeared as if France and England would be involved in hostilities. As these were the only two nations the Czar had to fear, he picked a quarrel with the Sultan, sent an army across the Pruth, and seized on the Danubian principalities.

This aggressive movement opened the eyes of Europe, and France and England could no longer remain indifferent to the common danger. They therefore sank their differences and presented a united and bold front to Nicholas who, when too late, recognised his error, and saw that he had been premature in the step he had taken. But his pride and vanity would not permit him to confess the wrong he had done, and retire to his own territory, and the result was England and France declared war against him. He himself selected the Danubian principalities as the theatre of war, but he reckoned without his host, for in September 1854, the conbined fleets of Great-Britain and France—forming the mightiest armament ever conveyed by sea, appeared off the west coast of the Crimea, less than thirty miles north of Sebastopol. The great army was disembarked on the 16th of September. On the 19th it began its march southward and early on the morning of the 20th it approached the banks of the Alma. The Russians had established themselves here under Prince Menschikoff, and they believed that their position was impregnable. But after a tremendous and sanguinary struggle, the heroic troops of France and England scaled the heights, and gained a victory which will be known for all time as the Battle of the Alma. The Russians had not anticipated this tremendous check at the very onset of the campaign, and it so demoralised them that had the Allies at once pushed on to Sebastopol that stronghold would probably have fallen at once, for the Czar, never dreaming of a land attack, had concentrated all his formidable powers of resistance on the sea face, and the landward side was practically without defence. For some inscrutable reason, however, the Allies did not follow up their victory as they should have done. This gave the Russians time to make preparations for the stupendous struggle, and a siege was consequently commenced which figures as one of the most remarkable in the annals of war. From the first the besiegers had the advantage, for being able to keep open their sea communications enormous supplies of munitions of war were forthcoming, though the sufferings the troops had to endure are almost without parallel. Contrary to the usual order of things the number of troops in the town, at one time greatly exceeded the besiegers. The consequence was defensive works arose like magic, until at last the besieged were able to assume the aggressive, and on the 5th of November they made an attack in force, and the great battle of Inkermann was the result. The Russians in the end, however, were repulsed, but the Allies suffered so much, and the outlook seemed so gloomy, that it was seriously proposed to abandon the siege.

But this was rejected, and recognising now that they had a stupendous struggle before them France and England set to work in real earnest, resolved to crush the foe. While the siege operations were thus being pushed forward with great vigour, despite the awful winter weather, other positions were won, and the Russian communications were threatened. So alarmed did the Russians become that they sank a large number of ships across the mouth of the harbour thereby rendering an attack on the sea front extremely difficult; while their fleet behind the sunken barrier had to be reckoned with. Notwithstanding this, however, the English and French fleet rendered good service, and the besiegers pushed on their saps and mines, gradually extending their outworks, and advancing their trenches, until on the 7th of June 1855, the Mamelon, a commanding height was captured, and on the 8th of September, the flag of the Allies floated proudly on the tower of the Malakoff. That night the Russians recognised that further defence was impossible and they withdrew to the northern side of the harbour, after they had sunk their ships and blown up the defences of the town which was taken possession of by the troops of the two great nations. There is little doubt whatever, that the Russians now could have been driven clean out of the Crimea, but they made overtures for peace and these overtures were listened to, with the result that, despite all the expenditure of our blood and treasure, they were allowed to retain the Crimea, and at the present day a new Sebastopol has arisen, compared to which that of 1854-5 was a toy, and it is doubtful if Russia could now be driven from the Crimea by any combination of nations that could be brought to bear against her.

THE DEEDS OF "DERRING-DO."

Cecil William Buckley

was a junior Lieutenant, serving on board Her Majesty's ship *Miranda* during hostilities in the Crimea. At a place called Genitchi the Russians had accumulated great quantities of stores upon which the troops in that quarter were dependent for sustenance for themselves and beasts. To destroy those stores was an act justified by the usages of warfare, since their destruction might lead to defeat or retreat of the enemy. Young Buckley, being no less desirous of serving his country than he was of distinguishing himself, landed in presence of a superior force and set fire to the stores.

The town of Genitchi had been shelled by the fleet on the 29th of May 1855; but it was subsequently found that the enemy was drawing his supplies from an immense accumulation of stores which had escaped, and in fact could not be reached from the sea. The destruction of these stores was of the highest importance in a military and naval sense. The task of carrying out this operation was recognised by everyone to be not only fraught with the greatest possible difficulty; but was in the nature of the forlornest of forlorn hopes. Nevertheless young Buckley, Lieutenant Hugh Burgoyne, and Mr. John Roberts, gunner, volunteered to land alone and fire the stores. The offer was accepted by Lord Lyons, and the three brave fellows, scorning the tremendous risk they ran, went forth staring Death in the face fearlessly. They landed in a boat quite out of reach of the protection the ships could afford them. With stealth and caution they crept towards their objective point and most effectually carried out their duty. In returning they had a desperate fight with the Cossacks who beset them and who all but succeeded in cutting off their retreat. But after many perils they gained their boat and pulled off under fire to their ship.

This young officer rendered a similar service at Taganrog while the town was being bombarded by the boats of the fleet. Buckley in a four oared gig, accompanied by Henry Cooper, Boatswain, the boat being manned by volunteers, repeatedly landed and fired different stores and government buildings. The service thus performed was described as being of the most desperate nature. The town was occupied by three thousand of the enemy's troops, and every effort was made to capture the daring fellows who managed, however, to return to the ship having rendered eminent service to the fleet.

HUGH TALBOT BURGOYNE, who was senior Lieutenant of the *Swallow* :—

JOHN ROBERTS (Gunner) and

HENRY COOPER (Boatswain) were all decorated with the Cross for the part they took in the affair.

Joseph Trewavas

was an able seaman on board the *Beagle* which was lying in the Straits of Genitchi. In these straits there was a floating bridge which much interfered with the operations and movements of the invaders. It could not be supposed that the Russians would remove this bridge in order to accommodate the foe; so bold Trewavas thought he would see what he could do as he had no particular reason for respecting the susceptibilities of the enemy. The consequence was, at Trewavas' instigation two boats were lowered from the *Beagle* and manned with volunteers. He pulled off under a tremendous musketry fire at a distance of eighty yards. The shore was lined with troops and the adjacent houses filled with riflemen; but in spite of these odds, Trewavas and his brave companions rowed as hard as they could to the bridge, and notwithstanding the difficulty attending the operation, Joseph with his own hand cut the main hawser of the bridge, and it went adrift. In returning the noble fellow was severely wounded. But he was mentioned in despatches and lived to receive the Cross.

Joseph Kellaway

was Boatswain of the *Wrangler* in the Sea of Azoff. A detachment had landed consisting of Mr. Odewaine (Mate), Mr. Kellaway and three seamen.

Their orders were to burn some boats, fishing stations, and haystacks on the opposite side of a small lake. They had nearly reached the spot when a party of fifty Russians who had been lying concealed suddenly rushed from their ambush, and endeavoured to seize the little party. One of the sailors fell into the enemy's hands, but Kellaway, the other two seamen, and Mr. Odewaine made good their escape pursued and fired upon by the Russians. While running Odewaine tripped and fell. Brave Kellaway forgot all about himself then for he thought his officer had been wounded, so he immediately stopped and at the imminent peril of his life he attempted to rescue him. He raised the mate up, but before he could get him away the enemy surrounded them. Kellaway made a tremendous resistance, but it proved useless; and though the Russians might have killed them it is to their honour and credit that they took them prisoners instead. At the close of the war Kellaway was released and decorated with the Cross. The other two seamen who took part in the expedition managed to get back to their ship.

George Fiott Day,

Commander, performed an act of great enterprise and gallantry while lying with his ship off Genitchi. He wished to make a personal reconnaissance of the enemy's lines in order to ascertain the practicability of reaching the Russian gunboats which were anchored in the Straits close to the town; he therefore decided at every risk to gain the knowledge he wished. So one dark but fine night he provided himself with a pocket compass and matches; stuffed some biscuits into his pockets, and was pulled to the shore. And no doubt when his crew took leave of him they thought they would see him no more, for it was a very desperate and daring enterprise beset with the most deadly peril. Nothing daunted the brave commander set off in the (to him) utterly unknown country. He found it was necessary to traverse a swamp into which he occasionally sank up to the knees. For five weary miles he went through that desolate quagmire not knowing the moment when he might plunge overhead and so meet with a dreadful death by suffocation. It required pluck and endurance of no ordinary kind to persevere under such circumstances; for he was utterly cut off from all assistance. His friends were far away; the enemy near. But he actually got within two hundred yards of the vessels, and as perfect silence prevailed he was led to believe there were no crews on board, so hastened back to report the feasibility of seizing the ships. On the following day, however, he saw reason to suppose he had made a mistake, and resolved on a second attempt to get at the facts. He landed again at night, but this time it was wild and squally, and the dangers of the journey thereby greatly increased. On reaching the spot from whence he had surveyed the ships on the previous night, he convinced himself that the vessels were fully manned and the crews on the alert. So he returned once more to report that any attempt to seize them would be useless, and might even be attended with disaster. He nevertheless had won his Cross, and deserved it.

John Edmund Commerell,

Commander. This hero was in command of the *Weser* in the Sea of Azoff when he resolved on a most hazardous expedition. On the Western side of the Sea of Azoff is a long narrow isthmus known as the *Arabat Tongue,* Genitchi, and Straits of same name being at the northern end of the Tongue. Between the western side of the Tongue and the Crimean coast is an inlet with a much indented shore. This inlet is called *The Sivash;* and on the Crimean side of it the Russians had accumulated a very large quantity of forage, which was of the utmost value to the enemy, while without it he would be driven to desperate straits. Commander Commerell made up his mind that he would destroy that store of forage and so harass his country's foe. It was a very ticklish venture indeed, fraught with imminent peril; while if it was to be successful pluck, coolness and powers of endurance of no ordinary kind would have to be exercised. But Commerell was equal to his self-appointed task, and selecting two trusty companions in the persons of William Richard, Quartermaster, and George Milestone A.B. he set off in a small boat one night. They hauled their boat over the narrow Tongue of Arabat, and launched her on the Sivash, and steadily and silently pulled to the Crimean shore of the Putrid Sea. The magazine where the forage was stored was then two and a half miles inland, in the enemy's country, mark you. In order to reach the point they aimed at, the three brave fellows—having first hidden their boat, were compelled to ford two rivers, the Kara-su, and the Salghir. This in itself was a most dangerous undertaking, for they were nearly up to their necks in the water with a rapid current threatening to wash them away if they made one false step; and encumbered as they were with their weapons it was no easy matter to keep their feet. The forage was stacked on the bank of the latter river and amounted to 400 tons. Close to it was a guardhouse, and a very short distance off was a little village in which a body of Cossacks were encamped. Commerwell and his companions got out of the water like dripping spaniels, and holding their very breath lest they should alarm the guard before their purpose was accomplished, they crept yard by yard towards the magazine. Reaching it at last they prepared their combustibles, which they had managed to keep dry, and in a very short time the great store-house of hay and corn was blazing in several different places. The crackling and glow of the flames alarmed the guard who turned out at once, and pursued the daring incendiaries, sending volley after volley of musket bullets after them, and all but succeeding in capturing them. But through the rivers and over the land sped the fugitives, their way lighted by the flames from the burning store-house. They gained their boat, sprang in, and spent and exhausted, but elated with their work, they reached their ship as the grey dawn was breaking and the sky was still encrimsoned with the blazing store-house.

William Richard,

Quartermaster, who took part in the forage firing expedition with Commander Commerell displayed great devotion to his companion, Milestone, who in his headlong flight, became so exhausted that he fell into the mud of the swampy ground between the rivers. Although Richard was almost done up himself, he nobly stayed in spite of the bullets that were flying around to help his shipmate, who but for this friendly assistance must have perished miserably or have been taken prisoner.

William Peel,

Captain, of the Naval Brigade, was in a battery near Inkermann on the 18th of Oct. 1854. Suddenly a huge shell shrieked through the air, and with the fuze still burning plumped amongst a heap of powder cases. At tremendous risk to himself, Peel dashed at the burning shell, seized it and hurled it over the parapet. It burst as it left his hands. Had it burst amongst the powder cases the battery must have been destroyed, and probably every soul in it would have perished.

Again, on the 5th of November, at the Battle of Inkermann, gallant Peel joined the Officers of the Grenadier Guards, and rendered most valuable assistance in defending the Colours of that regiment, which were all but captured at the sandbag battery. And lastly, on the 18th June 1855, having escaped a hundred and one perils and passed through most of the phases of the great war, he volunteered to lead the Ladder Party at the Assault of the Redan. He bore the first ladder, and was at the head of his company when he fell wounded.

Edward St. John Daniels,

Midshipman, was decorated with the coveted prize for great gallantry. This young fellow was in a battery when the horses drawing a waggon, ladened with much required ammunition, were shot outside. Although the waggon was a target for a tremendous fire from the enemy's guns, he volunteered to go out and secure the ammunition. This he succeeded in doing amidst the cheers of his comrades and shipmates.

At the Assault of the Redan on the 18th of June 1855, Daniels acted as aide-de-camp to brave Captain Peel who was at the head of the Ladder Party. When Peel fell terribly wounded on the glacis of the Redan, his aide-de-camp saved his life by tying a tourniquet on his arm. This was done under a heavy fire, and having stopped the bleeding he got his leader removed to a place of safety.

William Nathan Wright Hewett,

Lieutenant. This officer was acting mate of her

Majesty's ship *Beagle*, but when on shore with the Naval Brigade. On the 26th October 1854, Mr. Hewett was in command of the Right Lancaster Battery before Sebastopol. A Russian sortie took place, and the battery was placed in great jeopardy, as the enemy got within 300 yards of it, and poured in a most deadly fire from their Minie rifles. The guns in the battery were disabled with the exception of one, when an order was brought to Hewett that he was to spike that gun and retreat with the remnant of his shattered garrison. But the brave seaman did not understand what retreat meant. He said he was not going to spike the gun nor retreat for he did not believe the order had come from his commander (Captain Lushington). And to show that he was not beaten he set to work to pull down the parapet of the battery. Then with the assistance of some soldiers who stood by him, he slewed the gun round in such a way that he was enabled to sweep the advancing Russians with round shot. For a moment they stood firm as the iron messengers of death tore through their ranks; then they wavered, and fled at last in confusion. The battery was saved. For this act of heroism Hewett was promoted to be Lieutenant and received the Cross. On the 5th of November 1854 Lieutenant Hewett again greatly distinguished himself and was prominently brought under the notice of the Commander-in-chief.

John Sullivan,

Boatswain's Mate. This brave fellow was also on shore with the naval Brigade. He was in what was known as No. 5 Battery before Sebastopol. A concealed Russian battery had been doing terrible execution in one of our advanced works, and No. 5 was ordered to open fire, but it was impossible to find out the exact position of the concealed battery and so get its range. But Sullivan was equal to the occasion. He went forth with a flag; found out the range, then advanced to a mound on which a storm of shot and shell was beating. On this mound he planted his little flag as a guide for the gunners in his battery. As he beat a retreat No. 5 opened its iron jaws, and belched forth a furious hurricane of iron wrath on the concealed enemy who soon became silent. For his brave act Sullivan was spoken very highly of; and in the report it was mentioned that his gallantry had always been conspicuous.

John Shepherd,

Boatswain. On the night of the 15th of July 1855, Mr. Shepherd was serving as Boatswain's mate on board the *St. Jean d'Acre* attached to the naval Brigade. A Russian line of battle ship of formidable dimensions was lying at anchor in the Harbour of Sebastopol. John was annoyed by her appearance, and thought that she ought to be under not on top of the water. So providing himself with an exploding apparatus he pushed off in an ordinary punt right into the Harbour and in the very midst of the enemy. He had to pull past the steam boats at the entrance of Careening Bay, and would certainly have carried out his purpose, had it not been that he was prevented doing so by a long string of boats that were carrying troops from the south to the north side of Sebastopol. Recognising that he was baffled, he beat a leisurely retreat. But on the 2nd of August he was determined to have another try, and though he did not succeed, his gallantry and pluck were so conspicuous, and he had so fearlessly risked his life in his country's cause, that he was recommended for and received the Cross.

Thomas Reeves }
James Gorman } Seamen.
Mark Scholefield }

These three men were at the Battle of Inkermam on the 5th of November 1854, and were with their brigade stationed in the Right Lancaster Battery which was subjected to a fierce attack on the part of the enemy. In company with two other brave fellows, our three heroes mounted on to the *banquette* armed with the muskets of the disabled soldiers. As fast as the muskets were discharged at the advancing foe they were reloaded by wounded men lying under the shelter of the parapet. By this means the dauntless three kept up such a murderous fire on the enemy that he could not stand it and beat a retreat. The other two poor fellows were killed, but the three came through the fiery ordeal and lived to wear the decoration.

**Henry James Raby, Commander,
John Taylor, Captain of the Forecastle,
Henry Curtis, Boatswain's Mate.**

Immediately after the tremendous assault on Sebastopol by the allied forces on the 18th of June 1855, a soldier of the 57th Regiment was observed to have been shot through both legs, and was evidently suffering terribly. He was sitting up in the open crying aloud for help; but it seemed as if in that region of awful fire and death no human help could possibly reach him, and that he must perish miserably, for the enemy's guns from all sides were belching forth tons of metal. Gallant Commander Raby, however, saw the wounded soldier, and the seaman's heart went out towards him in great compassion. Raby at this time was safe within the Sap where he was stationed, and to go forth into that shot-harrowed space was like going into the wide-open jaws of Death. But Raby's tender heart would not allow him to remain inactive, so he called for assistance. Instantly two men sprang to his side—Taylor and Curtis. The three leapt the breastwork of the Sap, and proceeded across an open space for upwards of seventy yards, towards the salient angle of the Redan. They literally had to dodge the ponderous missiles, that hurtled through the air and tore up the ground in great furrows. But those three noble men never thought of turning back; onward they went and succeeded in rescuing the wounded soldier, whom they bore to a place of safety where his misery was alleviated until death terminated his sufferings.

IN THE BALTIC.

George Ingouville,

Captain of the Mast, was serving on board the saucy *Arrogant* on the 13th of July 1855, while the boats of his ship were engaged in a desperate encounter with the enemy's gun boats, and batteries off the town of Viborg. The *Arrogant's* second cutter fell into difficulties. Her magazine blew up and in consequence she swamped and was drifting under a battery. Now this was too much for the intrepid Ingouville. He wasn't going to see one of his ship's boats, even though she was a wreck, fall into the enemy's hands. Not a bit of it. He was a British sailor, and the Russians shouldn't have anything belonging to his country if he could possibly help it. The fact that he had a severely wounded arm counted for nothing with gallant George, nor was he going to wait for orders. So from the deck of his ship he dived into the sea, his disabled arm notwithstanding, and like a duck with one wing, while bullets were rained at him, he swam to the cutter, seized the painter which was hanging over the side, and towed the derelict back to his ship. It was a singularly heroic act; defiantly carried out in spite of the Russian fire, and performed in full view of his shipmates, who greeted his hazardous exploit with ringing cheers such as British sailors know how to give.

John Bythesed,

Commander. The act which secured the Cross for

Commander Bythesed reads almost like the creation of some romance writer. He was commander of the *Arrogant* which numbered amongst her crew that splendid sailor George Ingouville. By some means, which were not made known, Commander Bythesed became aware that on the 9th of August 1854 a special aide-de-camp from the Emperor of Russia had landed on the Island of Wardo, having come in charge of a mail and most important despatches for the Russian General then in charge of the Island. As soon as the intelligence reached Bythesed he conceived the daring project of trying to get possession of those despatches which might afford information of the very greatest moment to his country's commanders and generals who were conducting the war against Russia. He consequently applied for and obtained permission for himself and a stoker, named William Johnstone, to proceed on shore with a view to intercepting the aide-de-camp before he could reach the General. Such an enterprise must have seemed to many who heard of it at the time a very foolhardy undertaking. But Bythesed and his lowly companion had their own views. So they set about disguising themselves, and armed to the teeth they were rowed to the shore, not far from where the despatch vessel was lying. Bythesed managed to find out that the important mail had not been landed. He and his companion, therefore, concealed themselves amongst some bushes in swampy ground close to the spot where the mails must pass when brought on shore.

For three nights and days did those brave fellows remain at their post, suffering the greatest possible discomfort, and running the most tremendous risk of their lives, for had they been discovered they would have been shot immediately as spies.

On the night of the 12th, the mail bags were landed, and were accompanied by a military escort of five soldiers fully armed. They were allowed to proceed a little way on their road when up jumped the Commander and the stoker, and fell upon the astonished escort who were five to two. Three were placed *hors de combat*, before they could recover from their surprise, the others were taken prisoners, the mail bags seized, and Bythesed and the stoker proceeded with their prisoners to a boat which the Commander had ordered to be concealed in a creek that was indicated. The boat was there all right. The victors bundled their prisoners in, and, with the precious mail bags, pulled off to the ship, where, as may be supposed, they received a tremendous greeting. When the mail and despatches were examined they were found to be even more important than was anticipated, and a service that could not possibly be overrated was thus rendered to the allied forces.

William Johnstone,

Stoker, was Commander Bythesed's companion and was duly decorated with the Cross.

Charles D. Lucas

who was not only awarded the Cross but was

promoted to a Lieutenancy, was on board the *Hecla* when, on the 21st of June 1854, she attacked the batteries of Bomarsund. While thus engaged a live shell, the fuze still burning fiercely fell plump on to the deck of the ship, and had it exploded not only would many lives have been lost, but in all probability the ship would have been destroyed. The keen eye of Mr. Lucas, however, has seen the iron messenger coming, and with remarkable coolness he went to it, picked it up and hurled it overboard.

THE ROYAL MARINES.

George Dare Dowell,

Lieutenant, R.M.A. During the attack on some of the posts near Viborg in July 1855, an explosion occurred in one of the rocket boats of the *Arrogant*. Dowell at the time was on board of the *Ruby*, and he immediately jumped into the quarter boat of that vessel with three volunteers, he himself pulling stroke oar. Under a heavy fire of musketry and grape he went to the assistance of the disabled boat, in spite of every attempt on the part of the Russians to prevent him doing so. He succeeded in saving three of the boats crew whom he placed in safety on board the Ruby. Then he returned to the disabled cutter and prevented her from falling into the enemy's hands.

John Prettyjohn,

Corporal, R.M. At the Battle of Inkermann this

man was observed to display great gallantry. He
placed himself in a very advanced position, and
kept a body of Russian at bay, four of whom he
shot. He was mentioned in despatches and duly
decorated with the Cross.

Thomas Wilkinson,

Bombardier, R.M.A. Received very special mention for remarkable coolness and bravery under
a galling fire. On the 7th of June 1855, he was
in one of the advanced batteries before Sebastopol,
when the works were partially destroyed. With
heroic devotion he exposed himself to the chance
of instant death, and was mainly instrumental in
placing sandbags to repair the breaches made by
the enemy's cannon, having to work the whole time
under a hail of bullets. His commander strongly
recommended him for the Cross.

THE ARMY.

John Grieve,

Sergeant-Major of the 2nd Dragoons. During
the heavy cavalry charge at Balaklava an officer
of the regiment was in imminent peril, being
surrounded by Russian Cavalry who would in
another minute have cut him down. But Grieve
observed the situation and, in spite of the tremendous
odds against him, he swooped upon the group of
horsemen, absolutely decapitating one of them, and
scattering the others by the fury of his onslaught.

By this heroic act he saved the officer's life and won the Cross for himself.

Samuel Parkes,

Private No. 635, 4th Light Dragoons. During the charge of the Light Brigade at Balaklava Trumpet-Major Crawford's horse stumbled and threw his rider who lost his sword at the same time. Two Cossacks at once furiously attacked him in spite of his defenceless position. It seemed as if his life was not worth half a minute's purchase; nor would it have been so had Parkes not been near the spot. His horse had just been shot under him, and with one great leap he fearlessly flung himself between the disarmed man and the cowardly foe. With such vigour did private Parkes use his sword that he sent the Cossacks flying. He and the Trumpet-Major then endeavoured to follow the retreating Brigade when six Russians bore down upon them. For some time Parkes defended his companion and kept the Russians at bay, and they found it impossible to subdue him. At last, however, a shot actually carried his sword out of his hand. There was then nothing for it but to surrender to the foe. They were both taken prisoners, but subsequently released, when private Parkes had the satisfaction of receiving the Cross as an acknowledgement of his valour, and of his devotion to his unarmed companion.

Alexander Robert Dunn,

Lieutenant, 11th Hussars. In the Light Cavalry

charge on the 25th Oct. 1854, this officer saved the life of Sergeant Bentley of the same regiment. Bentley had been attacked from the rear by three Russian Lancers, two of the three Dunn cut down, and the third, deeming discretion the better part of valour, and wishing to live to fight another day—bolted. Subsequently the same young officer noticed that private Levett, also of the same regiment, was being furiously attacked by a Russian Hussar who had the best of it. Dunn at once dashed forward and ran his sword through the Russian thereby preventing Levett's name from appearing amongst the list of the dead.

John Berryman,

Troop Sergeant-Major, 4th Lancers. This heroic fellow, who seemed to be made of cast iron and to have nerves of triple steel, served with his regiment during the whole of the Crimean campaign. He was present at the Battle of Alma, and was also engaged in the pursuit at "Mackenzie's Farm," where he succeeded in taking prisoner three Russians who were close to their own guns. At the Battle of Balaklava his horse was shot under him and it seemed as if he were doomed. But he had no thought for self, for seeing a wounded officer—Captain Webb—lying on the ground amidst a shower of shot and shell, brave Berryman ran to his aid. His officer repeatedly told him to go away as he would only sacrifice his life to no purpose. But in this instance he disobeyed the orders of a superior officer. He stood by Webb administering such comfort as he could, while round shot and conical shell screeched and roared on all sides. Presently trooper sergeant John Farrall came within hailing distance and Berryman called him. He responded to the call, and the two Ser-

The two Sergeants carried the Officer to a place of safety.

geants carried the officer to a place of safety. For this magnificent devotion under the most trying circumstances Berryman was decorated with the Cross.

Andrew Henry,

Sergeant-Major, 2nd Division Land Transport Corps, Royal Artillery. This gallant officer defended the guns of his battery against overwhelming numbers of the enemy at the Battle of Inkermann; and it was not until he had received no fewer than twelve bayonet wounds that he was forced to own defeat, but only then because he was physically incapable of moving. He was promoted to a captaincy and lived to be decorated with the V. C.

Matthew Charles Dixon,

Brevet Lieutenant-Colonel, Royal Artillery. On the 17th of April 1855, this splendid officer was in command of a battery when an enemy's shell burst into the magazine, blowing it up, destroying the parapets, killing and wounding ten men, rendering five guns useless, and bringing a sixth under a mass of earth. The enemy seeing the destruction they had wrought sprang on to their own parapets, cheering frantically. Any man might have been pardoned for being daunted by the appalling disaster such as that which had overtaken Dixon's Command. But he was made of the stuff that heroes are made of, and the Russians found to their cost that they had cheered a little too soon. In the wrecked battery one gun and some ammunition yet remained intact, and so did Dixon. He had escaped the fury of the hell of fire, and the shock of the explosion. He loaded up that gun; he trained it at the jeering foe who quickly got under shelter.

On that gun and its magnificent gunner the enemy's batteries concentrated their fire; but some charm must have hung around him, for Dixon worked his gun till sunset and darkness put an end to the unequal duel. It was a deed of splendid valour, and England might well be proud of such a son as Brevet Lieutenant-Colonel Matthew Charles Dixon.

Thomas Arthur,

Gunner and driver, Royal Artillery. On the 7th of June 1855, Arthur was in charge of one of the Left Advanced Batteries of the Right Attack. Some quarries which had been gallantly held by the enemy were at last rushed and taken. Then Arthur of his own accord carried barrels of ammunition during the evening to the 7th Fusiliers who were fighting the quarries. To do this he had to cross backwards and forwards, over an open space that was exposed to a deadly fire. But with the utmost coolness he performed his work, rendering invaluable service, for it is probable that but for his timely aid in supplying them with stores of ammunition, the Fusiliers would have had to surrender their captured position. Gunner Arthur was also one of the volunteers who formed the spiking party of Artillery at the assault on the Redan on the 18th of June 1855.

Gerald Graham,

Lieutenant, Royal Engineers. During the assault on the Redan, just mentioned, this officer was placed in command of a ladder-party. He displayed the most determined bravery, and an utter fearlessness of death. He also rendered humane and heroic service by sallying out of the trenches on numerous occasions and carrying in wounded officers and men.

D. Lennox,

Lieutenant, Royal Engineers. This Officer established a lodgement in what was known as Tryon's Rifle Pit, whereby he rendered incalculable service by repelling the repeated and furious assaults of the enemy. For this gallantry a special order was drawn up by General Canrobert, and Lennox duly received the Cross.

John Ross,

Corporal No. 997, Royal Engineers. On the 21st of July 1855, Corporal Ross greatly distinguished himself by connecting what was termed—in military parlance—the 4th Parallel, Right Attack with an Old Russian Rifle Pit in front, which proved of enormous advantage to the attacking party. On August the 23rd 1855 he was in charge of the Advance from the 5th Parallel Attack on the Redan. Under a very heavy fire he filled and placed in position 25 gabions; and finally, on the night of the 8th of September, he crept fearlessly up to the Redan and found it deserted. He immediately returned and reported the fact, whereupon it was taken possession of by the English.

William J. Lendrim,

Corporal No. 1078, Royal Engineers. This was another man who added largely to the honour and glory of his regiment. It was on the 11th of April 1855, that the top of a magazine in which he was placed, was set on fire. He at once mounted under a storm of bullets, extinguished the flames and made good the breach, thereby preventing the magazine from blowing up. He had previously rendered himself conspicuous by his bravery; for on the 14th of the preceding February he had superintended 150 French Chasseurs in building a battery; and he himself replaced the gabions as they were capsized by the galling fire of the enemy. He also formed one of the party of volunteers who destroyed the farthest rifle pit on the 20th of April.

John Perie,

Sapper No. 854, Royal Engineers. This regiment had certainly cause to feel proud of the number of its heroes. The Redan was stormed on the 18th of June 1855, and Perie got his chance. He gallantly led a party of sailors with ladders, and rendered great service, not only by his own acts, but by his example of coolness and intrepidity in the face of danger and death. At last he was wounded by a bullet in the side; but notwithstanding his own wound he nobly rescued a comrade who was lying in the open and must have been killed had he not been carried off at once.

Sir Charles Russell, Bart.

Brevet Major, Grenadier Guards. A party of Russians were in charge of a sand bag battery which was causing not only great annoyance but havoc amongst our troops. Sir Charles volunteered to dislodge them if anyone would follow him. At once there sprang to his aid Sergeant Norman, and privates Anthony Palmer, and Bailey. Forth went the fearless four and rushed that battery. The attack was so desperate that the Russians probably thought there were overwhelming numbers of the foe at hand. Any way they fled in disorder, leaving wounded and dead behind them, and the battery was silenced. Poor Bailey paid for his intrepidity with his life.*

Anthony Palmer.

Private No. 3571, 3rd Battalion Grenadier Guards, was one of the little party who with Sir Charles Russell at their head, dislodged the Russians from the sandbag battery.

Alfred Ablett.

Sergeant No. 5872, 3rd Battalion Grenadier Guards. This man was in a trench. It was the 2nd of September 1855, when a screaming shell all aflame dropped into the very centre of a number of ammunition cases and powder barrels. Without a moment's hesitation Sergeant Ablett grappled with

---

* NOTE. Sergeant Norman was probably killed soon afterwards as no mention is made of his having been rewarded with the Cross.

that shell, and with a mighty swing of his strong arms he hurled the unwelcome intruder over the parapet and it burst as it touched the ground. By this fearless act he not only saved the stores but many lives.

Gerald Littlehales Goodlake,

Brevet Major, Coldstream Guards. This gallant officer was in command of a contingent of sharpshooters furnished by his regiment on the 28th of October 1854. He was ordered to hold a position known as "The Windmill Ravine", below the Picquet House, against a very superior force of the enemy. Making a "powerful sortie", he attacked the Russians with such fury that thirty-eight of them were slain, including an officer. He took prisoner one officer and three privates. Goodlake was the only officer in command of his party. In November he performed another gallant feat. He surprised a picquet of the enemy at the bottom of the Windmill Ravine, and succeeded in capturing all their rifles and knapsacks.

William Stanbock,

Private No. 3968, Coldstream Guards, was employed as one of the sharpshooters at the Windmill Ravine. It was highly important that the enemy's position should be reconnoitred. It was a work of extreme danger and difficulty but Stanbock was equal to the occasion. He undertook to crawl up to within six yards of a Russian sentry and gain the information that was so much desired. He was told it was all but impossible he could escape with his life. But this trifle did not weigh with the brave soldier. He had made up his mind to go, and go he did; and he not only succeeded in getting precisely the information required, and which enabled Major Goodlake to deliver his attack and carry the position, but he escaped without a scratch.

George Strong,

Private No. 4787, Coldstream Guards. In 1855 in the month September, private Strong was doing duty in the trenches when a live shell fell close to him. He did not bolt and leave it there to burst and spread death and destruction around, but he at once seized it, and hurled it outside, where it exploded without doing any harm.

Robert James Lindsay,

Brevet Major, Scots Fusilier Guards. During the Battle of Alma the formation of the line of his regiment was disordered by the tremendous fire to which it was exposed. Lindsay, with extraordinary coolness, stood firm by the colours, and by his example and his bravery he greatly tended to restore order, and prevented the men from becoming demoralised. At Inkermann, during a most trying moment when it seemed as if his party would be overwhelmed, he, with a few men only, fearlessly charged a large body of Russians and drove them back.

McKechnie,

Sergeant No. 3234, Scots Fusilier Guards. When

his regiment was disordered at Alma, as recorded in the foregoing, he behaved with conspicuous bravery, and rallied his comrades round the colours.

William Reynolds,

Private No. 3368, Scots Fusilier Guards. This man also helped to save the colours by rallying his comrades and setting them an example of dauntless bravery.

Joseph Prosser,

Private No. 1672; 2nd Battalion, 1st Regiment. On the 16th of June 1855, he was doing trench duty when he observed a soldier in the act of deserting to the enemy. Prosser at once pursued him under a heavy fire from two sides, and seizing him brought him back. On the 11th of August 1855, the same gallant fellow was in the most advanced trench before Sebastopol when he saw a man of the 95th lying outside severely wounded. Without a moment's hesitancy Prosser leaped from his position of relative safety, and though a tremendous musketry fire was at once opened upon him from the enemy, he went forward, lifted up the wounded man and carried him in.

Frederick Francis Maule,

Brevet Lieutenant-Colonel, 3rd Regiment. This officer distinguished himself by most devoted and conspicuous bravery on the 8th of September 1855. He was in command of the covering and ladder party during the assault of the Redan when, in spite of a tremendous fire and many obstacles, he urged his men forward. By his coolness and example his men were stimulated to perform the most valuable services. He succeeded at last in getting on to the Redan with only nine followers; yet with this little force he heroically held for some time a most dangerous position between traverses. At last, when it became painfully apparent that there was no hope of support coming to him, he was forced to retire, but did not do so until after he had been terribly wounded.

John Connors,

Private No. 2649, 3rd Regiment. During the assault on the Redan on the 8th of September 1855 Connors made himself conspicuous by his courage and devotion. He got inside of the Redan at great personal risk, and seeing an officer of the 30th Regiment surrounded by the enemy he rushed to the officer's assistance. He immediately shot one of the Russians, ran his bayonet through another, and then for some time carried on a hand-to-hand encounter against great odds, until support came. Besides being decorated with the Cross he was selected by his company to become the recipient of the French war medal.

Matthew Hughes,

Private No. 1879, 7th Regiment—Royal Fusiliers. It was on the 7th of June 1885, that the Russian position before Sebastopol, known as the Quarries, was stormed. The Quarries had been tenaciously held by the enemy, as they were of great strategical importance. During the assault many acts of personal bravery were noticed, and Hughes made himself particularly conspicuous. He was observed to twice cross the open ground, upon which a fierce storm of shot and shell was beating, and bring back from the supply store much needed ammunition. He next went to the front to bring in private John Hannington who was lying severely wounded in an exposed position. And some days later he gallantly went out to rescue an officer of his own regiment, named Hobson, a lieutenant who was seriously wounded; and while engaged in this meritorious act Hughes himself fell severely wounded. He happily lived, however, to enjoy the honour of the Cross.

William Norman,

Private No. 3443, same regiment as the foregoing. On the night of the 19th of December 1854, this brave man occupied one of the most trying positions a soldier is called upon to experience. It was a cold, dark, bitter night, and Norman was posted as a lonely sentry in front of the advanced sentries of an outlying picquet in what was known as the white Horse Ravine. His post was one of extreme peril, and not only demanded extraordinary vigilance on the part of the sentry, but great presence of mind and coolness of nerves. Norman, however, was quite equal to the occasion. He had his wits about him, his eyes open, his ears on the alert. He knew how much depended upon him, and though only a humble private he was a hero. In front of him, and only 300 yards away was a Russian picquet guarding the enemy's lines. Presently as Norman kept his weary watch with the cutting wind whistling shirlly through the scrub, he heard sounds that were not due to the wind; and straining his eyes, he made out that three dark objects were creeping towards him. Many men would at once have fallen back and given the signal of alarm; but Norman did nothing of the kind. He fell upon those three moving objects, which proved to be three Russian soldiers. One of them he disabled at once, and the other two he actually took prisoners, without so much as alarming the Russian picquet, and be trotted his two prisoners back to his own lines.

It was an act of the highest heroism, for in the darkness he had no means of ascertaining how many of his foes surrounded him, and almost any man might have been pardoned if he had lost his nerve in such a trying moment. The act well merited this high honour it gained for the performer.

Andrew Mognihan,

Ensign, 90th Regiment. At the time this man performed the service which won him the Cross he was a sergeant in the 90th Light Infantry, and took part in the assault on the Redan, 8th of September 1855. Being surrounded by the enemy he fought and killed five of them single-handed. And a little later he advanced under heavy fire to the rescue of a wounded officer whom he succeeded in carrying to a place of safety. He received promotion as well as the decoration.

Philip Smith,

Corporal, Lance Sergeant, 17th Regiment. It was before the great Redan, which played such a conspicuous part in the Crimean war, that Smith brought himself into prominent notice as a brave and humane man. The date was the 18th of June 1855. After the tremendous assault on the fort, Philip Smith, while the column was retiring or had retired, left the shelter of the trenches in order to save and assist wounded and dying men. He did this under heavy fire; and not only did he relieve much suffering; but was the means of saving numerous lives.

John Lyons,

Private No. 1051, 19th Regiment. On the 10th of June 1855, while John Lyons was doing duty in the trenches, a live shell dropped among the guard of the trenches. Had it burst dozens of lives would have been sacrificed; but Lyons hurled it over the parapet and it burst without doing harm.

Edward W. D. Bell,

Brevet Lieutenant-Colonel, 23rd Regiment. This officer was recommended for general gallantry, but it was at the Alma he specially distinguished himself.

One of the enemy's guns was limbered up and being carried off when Bell thought he might as well have it as the Russians, so he went for it, seized it in spite of desperate opposition, and brought it into his own lines. A little later all his senior officers having been killed he succeeded to the command of the regiment which he brought out of action in splendid style.

Luke O'Connor,

Lieutenant, 23rd Regiment. This noble fellow set an example of fortitude and heroism well calculated to arouse the martial ardour of youth who are ambitious of making their names favourably known. He was one of the centre sergeants at the Battle of the Alma, and advanced between two officers who bore the precious colours. When close to the redoubt, Lieutenant Anstruther, one of the colour bearers fell mortally wounded, while O'Connor himself received a bullet in the breast and fell; but by a tremendous effort he sprang up, seized the colour which was lying on the ground, waved it triumphantly aloft, and bore it to the end of the action. He was repeatedly told by his captain (Captain Granville) to relinquish the colour and retire to the rear so that his wound might be dressed. But he resolutely declined to do so. He was recommended for and received a commission; and later on he displayed remarkable gallantry at the assault on the Redan when he was shot through both thighs.

THE "V. C." 35

Robert Shields,

Corporal No. 2945, 23rd Regiment. After the attack on the Redan on the 8th of September 1855, he volunteered to go to the front from the 5th Parallel and bring in Lieutenant Dymley who was lying dangerously wounded. This he succeeded in doing though the unfortunate officer succumbed to his wounds.

William Coffey,

Private No. 3837, 34th Regiment. On the 29th of March 1855 he saved many lives by throwing over the parapet a live shell that fell into the trench where he was on duty. Although this feat is one of great risk, and requiring unusual nerve and presence of mind, it was frequently accomplished during the war.

John J. Sims,

Private No. 3482, 34th Regiment. After the assault on the Redan, the 18th of June 1855, when his regiment had retired to the trenches, Sims in broad daylight went out into the open, upon which a withering fire was still being kept up, and with the most dauntless courage, and a touching devotion he carried in many wounded soldiers, and thereby saved lives which otherwise would have been sacrificed. In this self-appointed task Sims ran unusual risk of meeting with instant death; but coolness never once deserted him, and his bravery called forth the admiration of his comrades. His noble work very properly gained him the V. C.

Hugh Rowlands,

Brevet Major, 41st Regiment. This officer greatly distinguished himself by rescuing Colonel Haly, who had been seriously wounded and was surrounded by Russian soldiers who were doing their best to kill him. Rowlands—although there were fearful odds against him—rushed into the fray, and attacked the Russians with such fury that they were scattered, and before they could rally he had lifted up his comrade and carried him to a place of safety. This was one of his heroic deeds. Another was at the battle of Inkermann, when he was in charge of an advanced picquet, which was attacked over and over again. It was of the very highest importance to the carrying out of the plan of attack, that Rowlands' picquet should retain its position, and the importance of that position being fully recognised by the Russians they threw themselves on the little band in overwhelming numbers. But Rowlands did not know the meaning of the words 'retire' or 'yield'; he fought like a lion, and so inspirited his men that the position was retained, and the incalculable service thus rendered was freely acknowledged in despatches and otherwise.

Ambrose Madden,

Sergeant-Major, 41st Regiment. This brave fellow headed a party of men of his own regiment, and encouraged them to attack a superior number of Russians, who, by a bold movement executed with great strategical skill, were cut off from their regiment, by Madden. One officer and fourteen privates were taken prisoners, three of the men being captured by Madden himself.

William McWheeney,

Sergeant No. 2802, 44th Regiment. At the commencement of the great siege of Sebastopol McWheeney volunteered as a sharpshooter, and was placed in charge of a party from his own regiment. He displayed great vigilance and activity, and by his example and fearlessness, he stimulated his men to acts of great daring. On the 20th of October 1854, one of his men, Private John Keane, was dangerously wounded while on duty in the Worowzoff Road, at the time the sharpshooters had been repulsed from the (oft-mentioned) Quarries by overwhelming numbers of the enemy. Despite the rain of rifle bullets that was poured upon the little band McWheeney lifted his wounded comrade upon to his back and running the gauntlet of flying missiles he carried him to safety. Nor was this all; for on the 5th of December of the same year, another of his men—Corporal Courtney, of the Sharpshooters— was severely wounded in the head and must have died had it not been for McWheeney, who carried him from the front under fire. And as it was impossible to proceed to the rear then, he threw up a mound by the aid of his bayonet. Behind this mound he placed the wounded man, protecting him and comforting him. He remained with him for hours, until darkness fell. Then he hoisted him on to his back and bore him safely to the rear, where surgical aid was forthcoming. Many months later, that is on the 18th of June 1855, McWheeney having so far escaped all the dangers of the terrible war, volunteered for the advance guard of General Eyre's Brigade in the Cemetery, a very trying position that was only held by dauntless courage. It is a remarkable fact that despite his daring, and the many hardships and trials he was called upon to endure, McWheeney was never absent one day from his duties throughout the prolonged war.

John McDermond,

Private No. 2040, 47th Regiment. On the 5th of November 1854, Colonel Haly was lying on the ground disabled, and surrounded by a party of the enemy who were about to kill him, when McDermond, who was near, attacked the Russians, killed the one who had wounded the Colonel, and driving the others off saved the officer's life.

George Walters,

Sergeant, 49th Regiment. This brave fellow performed a similar feat to the foregoing, at the Battle of Inkermann. Brigadier General Admans, C.B., was surrounded, when Walters rushed to the fray; bayonetted one man, wounded others and got the officer away.

James Owens,

Corporal, 49th Regiment, greatly distinguished himself on the 30th of Oct. 1854 in a personal encounter with the Russians, and he rendered eminent service to Major Conolly of the Coldstream Guards who would probably have lost his life but for the timely aid given by Owens.

Thomas Beach,

Private, 55th Regiment. At the Battle of Inkermann, 5th of November 1854, Thomas Beach was on picquet duty when he observed several Russians plundering Lieutenant-Colonel Carpenter of the 41st Regiment, who was lying on the ground terribly wounded. Beach at once sprang to the rescue. He killed two of the Russians, and stood guard over the wounded officer until some men of the 41st came up and bore him off.

Frederick C. Elton,

Brevet Major, 55th Regiment. On the night of the 4th of August 1855, Major Elton was in command of a working party in the advanced trenches in front of the Quarries. A dreadful fire was being poured upon the men who showed signs of wavering. Elton, however, encouraged them by voice and example, and seizing a pick and shovel he went into the open and worked bravely away while a perfect storm of bullets fell about him. His men were so inspirited by his pluck that they got over their nervousness and proceeded steadily with their appointed duty. One of his own soldiers said of Elton—"There isn't another officer in the British army who would have done what Elton did that night." That perhaps was an unwarranted assertion, but it testified in a marked degree to the officer's popularity, and the enthusiasm he had kindled amongst his own men. In the course of the month of March 1855, the Major volunteered with a small party of men to drive off a body of Russians who were destroying one of the new detached works of the English. He carried out his duty most valiantly, and with his own hands brought in a prisoner. On the 7th of June of the same year he was the first of his party to leave the trenches and attack the Quarries. He succeeded in getting inside and by his example he kept his men together when they were disposed to waver and retreat.

T. De Courcy Hamilton,

Captain, 68th Regiment. It was the 11th of May 1855, and a dark night. The Russians had managed to obtain possession of a small battery which was of great importance to us. Although the enemy were there in great numbers Hamilton with a small force swept down upon them, and after a brilliant fight he drove the foe out and recovered the battery. His conduct on this occasion was described as of the most daring and gallant nature, while his bravery and heroism greatly inspired his men, who waged an unequal strife against superior numbers and yet came off victorious.

Charles McCorrie,

Private No. 1971, 57th Regiment, threw a live shell out of the trench where he was on duty, just as it was in the act of exploding.

John Byrne,

Private, 68th Regiment. At the Battle of Inkermann the 68th was ordered to retire, and while doing so Byrne saw that a wounded soldier had been left behind. He at once went back alone towards the enemy who were pouring a galling fire on the retreating regiment; but Byrne showed no wavering. He boldly carried out his self-appointed task and carried his wounded comrade to the rear. On the 11th of May 1855, he fearlessly engaged in a hand-to-hand encounter with one of the enemy who had succeeded in gaining the parapet of the work Byrne was charged to defend. He killed the Russian, took his weapons, and displayed such heroism and activity that he kept a host at bay until assistance was sent to him.

John Park,

Sergeant, 77th Regiment. It was at the Battle of the Alma that Park gave proof of the heroism that was in him. On the night of the 19th of April 1855, at the taking of the Russian Rifle Pits, his valour was so remarkable that it called forth the approbation of Colonel Egerton who was in command of the regiment. His conduct was no less daring at the two attacks on the Redan in which he took part. At the last attack he was severely wounded.

Alex Wright,

Private, 77th Regiment, was awarded the Cross for conspicuous bravery throughout the whole of the Crimean Campaign. On the night of the 22nd of March 1855, he was mainly instrumental in repelling a determined sortie. He also distinguished himself at the taking of the Russian Rifle Pits on the night of the 19th of April; and by his fearless example he encouraged his comrades who were exposed to a tremendous fire. He was wounded in this affair, but was in action again on the 30th of August 1855, when he was again wounded.

John Alexander,

Private 2932, 90th Regiment. After the attack on the Redan 18th of June 1855 he left the trenches under a heavy fire and brought in several wounded men. On the 6th of September same year, he was with a working party in the most advance trench, when he heard that Captain Buckley, Scots Fusilier Guards, was lying dangerously wounded. Without hesitation, and notwithstanding that a heavy fire was being kept up on the spot, he ran forward and brought the wounded officer in. This act of daring and devotion was performed under circumstances and conditions that were well calculated to daunt even a bold man. But private Alexander was evidently deeply imbued with a spirit of altruism, and he forgot himself and the risks he ran in his desire to save a fellow man.

Charles Henry Lumley,

Brevet Major, 97th Regiment. It was during the tremendous assault on the Redan, on the 8th of Sept. 1855 that this gallant officer so nobly distinguished himself. The many battles that were fought about the Redan were all of the most desperate nature, and served to prove the stuff of which the soldiers on both sides were made. The Redan was a position of great strength, and from the first the Allies saw how necessary it was that it should be carried. The Russians on their part were no less conscious of the importance of their works, and with extraordinary stubbornness they contested every inch of ground, and fought with heroic bravery. On the date named our troops seemed bent on achieving their object, and the most elaborate plans had been drawn up for the guidance of the storming parties. Charles Henry Lumley was among the very first to get inside of the works and as he jumped down from the embarkment, he alighted in the midst of three Russian gunners who were in the very act of reloading a field piece. As soon as they beheld the foreigner amongst them they left their gun and attacked him with the fury of desperation: nothing daunted by the overwhelming odds he was thus suddenly called upon to face, Lumley defended himself, and shot two of his assailants. The third hurled a large stone at him which striking him on the head, felled him to the ground. He lay stunned for some moments. Then recovering, he took in the situation, and springing up he waved his sword, and cheered on his men who were all engaged in a deadly struggle with the foe. His bravery and example so encouraged them, that they redoubled their efforts and pressed the enemy back, while Lumley, by words and actions, urged them forward. While doing this he was struck full in the mouth by a bullet, and so severely wounded that he had to be carried off.

John Coleman,

Sergeant 97th Regiment. This man proved himself also to be a hero of no common mould. He was one of a working party who had been told off to construct a new sap on the night of the 30th of August 1855. Suddenly without any warning the party were surprised by the enemy who fell upon them in great force, driving them in. Coleman, like many others, however, did not understand the word retreat, and standing his ground even against the enemy's fire, he fought with such stubborn obstinacy, that it might with little exaggeration be said that he kept a host at bay. He saw his friends and comrades go down before the onslaught of the Russians, until he was almost left alone. Recognising then that it was hopeless for him to continue the unequal struggle he commenced to slowly retire under a tremendous fire from the enemy's Rifle Pit, and as he did so he observed one of his officers lying on the ground mortally wounded. Stooping down he raised him to his shoulders and carried him out of action. For his conspicuous bravery and devotion on this notable occasion he was very deservedly decorated with the bronze prize.

Hon. Henry. H. Clifford,

Brevet Major, 1st Battalion Rifle Brigade. The Battle of Inkermann was fought with desperate valour by the soldiers on both sides, and the fight was prolific in individual acts of heroism. Clifford greatly distinguished himself; displaying an utter disregard for all personal considerations. In the face of tremendous odds he led a charge and scattered the enemy right and left, thereby rendering great service. Seeing a private soldier surrounded and about to be cut down he rushed to the rescue, killing one of the enemy, disabling another, and bringing the man out of the peril in which he was placed.

William James Cuninghame,

Captain, 1st Battalion Rifle Brigade. At the capture of the Rifle Pits on the 20th of November 1854, this officer rendered himself peculiarly conspicuous by his gallantry and devotion. His example of fearless bravery inspirited and ennerved his men who, in spite of difficulties and a galling fire, would not yield an inch of their ground. Cuninghame's gallant conduct was recorded in the French general orders, and led to his being subsequently decorated with the Cross.

Claude Thomas Bourchier,

Brevet Major, 1st Battalion Rifle Brigade. This

officer also greatly distinguished himself at the same time as the foregoing, and in much the same way. He, too, was recorded in the French general orders.

F. Wheatley,

Private, 1st Battalion Rifle Brigade. Wheatley was occupied in trench duty, and was hard at work with a party when a live shell came tearing in amongst them. The men scattered in consternation but probably not one would have escaped alive had the shell exploded. Before it could do that, however, Private Wheatley was down upon it; with great effort he raised it in his hands and hurled it over the parapet. It exploded in the air, but its deadly fragments fell outside of the trench and not a man was hurt.

John Knox,

Lieutenant, 2nd Battalion Rifle Brigade. The daring deed for which this gallant fellow received the Cross was performed at the Battle of the Alma while he was serving as a sergeant in the Scots Fusilier Guards. During a terrific charge of the enemy. The ranks of his regiment were broken, and his men seemed demoralised. By supreme effort, however, and by setting an example of utter fearlessness he not only stayed their retreat, but reformed them, and inspiriting them by voice and act, he succeeded in repelling a second charge of the enemy and drove them back. Subsequently when he had been transferred to the Rifle Brigade, he volunteered to conduct a ladder party during the attack on the

Redan on the 18th of June. The service he rendered was of the most heroic character, and not until he had been twice seriously wounded did he go out of action.

R. McGregor,

Private No. 2074, 2nd Battalion Rifle Brigade. This man who had all the qualities of a most excellent soldier was employed as a sharpshooter in the advanced trenches in the month of July 1855. During this time he displayed the utmost fearlessness, and inspired his comrades with the spirit of emulation. A short distance from where he was posted there was a rifle pit occupied by two Russians who kept up a fire of extraordinary rapidity and deadly aim. They seemed never to miss their mark, and they picked off man after man, and galled our troops tremendously. As they were well sheltered they could not be reached by our fire, and it appeared as if a whole company would be held at bay by these two hidden men, who had given painfully practical proof that they were no ordinary marksmen. In Private McGregor, however, they had their match. This intrepid fellow resolved to dislodge them or perish. So forth he went into the open, thus fully exposing himself to their fire. But without a moment's hesitation he went on and succeeded in reaching a piece of rock which not only afforded him shelter, but enabled him to command the Russians, both of whom he shot dead, and with a cheer he rushed in and took possession of the pit. This signal act of service proved of immense advantage to his party, and he was very properly decorated with the Cross.

Robert Humpston,

Private, 2nd Battalion Rifle Brigade. Amongst the rocks overhanging the Woronzoff road, between—to use military terms—the 3rd parallel Right attack and the formidable Quarries then strongly held by the enemy, was a Russian rifle pit, very artfully concealed and affording perfect protection to those whose duty it was to retain it. Every night a large number of Russians were placed in the pit, and their position enabled them to command a portion of the Left attack, whereby they not only greatly impeded the work in a new battery which was then being erected by the English on the extreme Right front of the 2nd parallel, but they created great havoc by their deadly fire. Humpston chafed at this, until at last he resolved to try and exterminate the nest of scorpions which were such a source of danger to his party. To this end he induced a comrade to join issues with him. And in the early dawn of day on the 22nd of April 1855, the two brave fellows crept out of their shelter, and in spite of the sudden death which stared them in the face and dogged their footsteps, they stealthily proceeded towards the pit, when with a sudden cheer and wild rush, they fell upon the Russians and at the point of the bayonet actually drove them out. Before they could rally and recapture the lost position the English threw in support to the two noble fellows, and in a very short time they had utterly demolished the pit and thus did away with the deadly danger. The desperate nature of the service and its invaluable results could not pass unnoticed, and Humpston was quickly promoted, received a reward of £5 and in due time was decorated with the Cross.

Joseph Bradshaw,

Private, No. 3471 2nd Battalion Rifle Brigade. This man was the comrade who joined Humpston in the daring attack on the Russian rifle pit, as mentioned in the preceding case. Bradshaw's services were also well recognised, and in addition to the Victoria Cross, he was also rewarded with the French war medal.

Charles Teesdale, C.B.,

Lieutenant, Royal Artillery. This officer throughout the whole of his service displayed the most intrepid gallantry. On the 25th of September 1855, he was acting as aide-de-camp to Major General Sir William Fennick Williams, Bart., K.C.B., at Kars, and he volunteered to take command of the force engaged in the defence of the most advanced part of the works— the key of the position against the attack of the Russian Army. His services were accepted, and at that time the enemy had actually penetrated into the redoubt, and it seemed as if the position must be lost. But Teesdale very speedily proved he was the right man in the right place. By means of that magic which a brave soldier can exert, he so stirred the garrison, and inspired them with such courage, that led by him they made a terrific onslaught on the Russians and after a sanguinary fight they expelled them and drove them back, thereby saving the position. A little later, Teesdale again greatly distinguished himself. During the hottest part of the action, which was everywhere being carried on with the most pitiless fierceness, the enemy's tremendous fire drove the brave Turkish artillery men from their guns. Teesdale saw in an instant the danger this was to the allied army, for it was of the highest importance that the Turkish battery should keep playing on the Russians and thus help to hold them in check. So he threw himself amongst the retreating Turks and rallied them with such effect, that he led them back to their post where with renewed vigour they worked their guns and aided in bringing about the final victory which the allies were to score. In the last great charge which decided the victory, Teesdale led on his men in the face of a storm of shot and shell; and when the fight was practically done, his splendid manhood was displayed in the noble desire to save instead of destroy, for at the very greatest personal risk, he rescued from the fury of the maddened Turks a considerable number of disabled Russians who were lying wounded outside of the works. This act of devotion to his country's enemies, was witnessed by the Russian General Mowravieff, and by him most gratefully acknowledged before the whole of his staff. Teesdale's conduct was well calculated to inspire brave men with admiration whether they were friends or foes, and in honouring her brave servant by bestowing the Victoria Cross upon him, the Queen honoured herself.

Joseph Malone,

Sergeant, 13th Light Dragoons. On the 25th of October 1854, this brave Irishman was in action during the great charge of the Light Brigade at the Battle of Balaklava. His horse was shot under him, and he was thereby compelled to follow the retreating army as best he could on foot. A tremendous and murderous fire was being poured by the Russians into the harassed troops, but notwithstanding this, Malone left the ranks which afforded him relative protection, in order that he might render some assistance to Captain Webb of the 17th Lancers, who was lying on the ground terribly wounded. Webb told him that he was doomed, and he urged Malone to save his own life, and hurry after the troops, otherwise he was certain to be killed. But Malone was too brave and heroic to be influenced by any such consideration. He put aside all thoughts of self and remained with the wounded officer, stanching his blood and comforting him as well as he was able. Presently some stragglers came up and with their aid Malone carried the officer to the rear. Poor Webb, however, was too terribly shattered to survive, and he breathed his last very soon afterwards. But Malone's noble devotion, and tender-heartedness displayed as they were under the most trying circumstances, and when it was, so to speak, every man for himself, placed him in the ranks of the heroes who have worn the Victoria Cross, and his name will continue to live.

Henry Mitchell Jones,

Captain, 7th Fusiliers. At the storming of the death-dealing quarries before Sebastopol on the 7th of June 1855, Captain Jones greatly distinguished himself. These quarries had been a source of terrible suffering and loss to the Allies. The Russians had so fortified them, and posted themselves so strongly, that it was feared they could not be dislodged. Nevertheless it was determined to storm the fatal quarries at all cost and risk. Captain Jones was placed in command of a section of the storming party, and displayed the most extraordinary coolness. So skilfully did he keep his men in hand, that they repelled again and again the continued assaults of the enemy during the darkness of the terrible night. In the early part of the evening he had been wounded and was counselled and urged to retire, but resolutely declined to do so. He had a duty to perform; he believed he was capable of performing it, and nothing could make him swerve. Hour after hour during that hellish night he stuck unflinchingly to his post, inspiring his men with his own dauntless courage in the face of carnage and death. When the daylight fully dawned, and it was seen that victory was with the English, though at a dreadful cost, brave Captain Jones consented to retire. He was then worn out with exhaustion and suffering greatly from his wound. It was admitted on all sides that his heroic attitude and noble bearing had contributed in no small measure to bring about the result which was so disastrous to the Russians. They had pinned their faith to those quarries, which while affording them admirable shelter, had enabled them to inflict cruel punishment on the foe; and they knew that so long as they retained possession of the quarries, Sebastopol could never be reduced. But the Allies were also aware of this, and those responsible for the conduct of the war, saw that unless the Russians could be driven out, the siege might be prolonged indefinitely. The assault was therefore agreed upon, and no one could be indifferent to the deadly nature of the work each man was called upon to do. In such a case much, very much, depended on individual effort, and as the odds were all against the attacking force, men were very apt to lose their nerve unless inspirited by brave example. Nobody knew this better than Captain Jones, and recognising to the full the responsibility resting on him as a leader, he did his duty to his country nobly and unselfishly. And when by the rules of war he was by reason of his wound entitled to retire to a place of safety, he scorned to take advantage of his privilege, knowing that his presence exerted an influence over his men. Such bravery and devotion in the hour of mortal peril and suffering are certainly worthy of reward.

Thomas Esmonde,

Captain, 18th Regiment. This officer also greatly distinguished himself by his humanity, skill and bravery. On the 18th to the 20th of June 1855, he was engaged on the attack on the Redan, when at very great personal risk, for he had to do it under a heavy fire of shot and shell which reduced the chances of life to almost nothing, he rescued many wounded men from exposed positions, thereby not only relieving cruel suffering, but prolonging many a brave life. Two days later, he performed another daring feat. He had charge of a working party before the enemy who were most anxious to determine the exact position of the party. To this end they sent a fire ball into the works. Instantly —although it seemed certain death to do so—Captain Esmonde rushed forward and with considerable difficulty extinguished the blazing ball, and at once with coolness and tact drew off his men from the spot which immediately became the focus for a murderous fire of shell and grape. It fell harmlessly, for Captain Esmonde had placed his men under shelter.

John Farrell,

Quarter Master Sergeant, 17th Lancers. This brave fellow was one of the men who under a storm of shot and shell remained with Captain Webb of the 17th Lancers on the 25th of October 1854. It will be remembered (see page 50), that Sergeant Joseph Malone of the 13th Light Dragoons, had been unhorsed during the magnificent charge of the noble six hundred, and during the retreat, when he was making his way out of action on foot, he left the ranks to attend to Webb who was lying on the ground. Farrell and a comrade—Sergeant-Major Berryman—had carried Webb for some distance, and they subsequently helped Malone to bear him off the field. Farrell was also on foot, his horse having been killed under him during the charge. In rendering assistance to his captain he knew perfectly well that he was risking almost certain death; but he seemed not to care for himself while it was in his power to help another who was helpless.

George Symons,

Lieutenant, Military train, 5th Battalion. On the 6th of June 1855, Symons was a sergeant in the Royal Artillery when he undertook to perform a military feat which not only demanded daring of no ordinary kind, but was dangerous to death. This feat consisted in what is known as "unmasking" the embrasures of a five-gun battery in the Advanced Right attack. On the opening of the first embrasure the enemy commenced a terrific fire, but nothing daunted Symons persevered in his deadly work. As each embrasure was opened the enemy's storm of shot and shell increased. In uncovering the last the noble fellow experienced very great difficulty, and he was compelled to fully expose himself by mounting the parapet to throw down the sandbags which concealed the gun. While doing this a shell burst close to him and wounded him severely; but his gallant task was accomplished; he had fully opened the battery, thereby enabling his comrades to reply with tongues of flame and a voice of thunder to the enemy's death-dealing roar. After much suffering Symons recovered from his terrible wound, and received promotion and the Cross.

James Craig,

Ensign and Adjutant, Sergeant, Scots Fusiliers. Promoted to Ensign, Military train, 3rd Battalion. It was on the 6th of September 1855, that this brave young fellow performed the deed which placed him on the roll of Victoria Cross heroes. He was on night duty in the Right Advanced Sap in front of the deadly Redan. A report was suddenly circulated that Captain Buckley of the Scots Fusiliers was missing, and there was every reason to believe he was lying outside of the Sap terribly wounded. The air was full of the fierce roar of shot and shell from the enemy's batteries, and the heavens were aglow with the flame from the bursting missiles which were tearing up the earth all around. It seemed as if nothing animate could possibly survive if exposed to that hellish storm, for the enemy knowing the importance of the Sap were bent upon rendering it untenable. Young Craig, however, in spite of the danger was resolved to render his captain assistance if it was in the power of mortal man to do so. He therefore collected two or three volunteers as brave as himself, and leaving the shelter of the trench forth they went into the open upon which with pitiless fury the iron hail and the sulphurous fires beat. Craig and his comrades searched about, and ultimately found Buckley. He was lying all indifferent then to the awful passions of men, for he had passed to where beyond these voices there is peace. But Craig had done a noble act inspired by the most humane of motives, and though he could not save his captain's life he saved his body, for he and a drummer carried it into the works where in due time it received military burial.

Henry Thomas Sylvester,

Assistant Surgeon, 23rd Regiment. On the 8th of September 1855, this gentleman went out under a heavy fire in front of the 5th Parallel Right Attack, to a spot near the Redan where Lieutenant and Adjutant Dyneley was lying mortally wounded. At the imminent peril of his life the Surgeon dressed the poor officer's wounds, and during all this time he was exposed to a tremendous fire. Surgeon Sylvester was also mentioned in Sir James Simpson's despatch of the 18th of September 1855, for conspicuous bravery and coolness in going to the front under heavy fire to assist the wounded.

Henry Ramage,

Sergeant, 2nd Dragoons. At the Battle of Balaklava, 24th of October 1854, Ramage galloped out to the assistance of his comrade, Private McPherson of the same regiment. Mac was surrounded by

Russians who were bent on cutting him up, and the odds were so great he must have fallen had it not been for Ramage who went for those Russians and scattered them. Then he and his comrade rode triumphantly back. On the selfsame day when the Heavy Brigade was rallying and the enemy retreating, Ramage could not get his horse to go forward. The animal had either been seized with funk or stubbornness, but any way he refused to budge in the direction his rider desired him to go. Ramage did not approve of this. He wanted some fight and wasn't going to be deprived of it through the capers of a perverse beast. So he dismounted, left the horse to his own devices, and rushing over to the Russian lines, he actually seized a man and brought him away as a prisoner. It was a plucky and daring act and must rather have astonished the enemy. Again on the same day, he performed a still nobler deed. The Heavy Brigade were covering the retreat of the Light Brigade, when Ramage observed Private Gardiner in a terrible plight on his horse, the man's leg having been shattered by a round shot. Forth rushed Ramage again, lifted the suffering man down, and then, under a cross fire specially directed at him he carried the wounded soldier to the rear. Immediately afterwards the very spot where this deed of heroism was performed was covered by Russian Cavalry. Ramage's record for that day alone was no mean one and proved that he was made of the right stuff, and his heroism being brought under the notice of the authorities Her Majesty was pleased to signify her appreciation of his conduct by awarding him the Cross.

Mark Walker,

Brevet Major, 30th Regiment. In the full presence of his regiment at Inkermann, this gallant officer jumped over a wall in the face of two battalions of Russian Infantry who were marching towards it. His object was to encourage his comrades who needed inspiriting for the odds opposed to them were excessively great, and it seemed almost a hopeless task to stand up against them. The men were so impressed, however, by their officer's example that they hesitated no longer, but sprang over the wall, threw themselves with a wild cheer and resistless energy against the foe and drove the Russians back. It was freely admitted that this was a brilliant feat of arms, and it was so evident that the victory might have been entirely the other way but for Walker's example, that he was mentioned in despatches and the Cross awarded him. The date of his heroic performance was the 5th of November 1854.

George Gardiner,

Colour-Sergeant, 57th Regiment. On the 22nd of March 1855, Colour-Sergeant Gardiner was doing duty as orderly sergeant to the Field officers of the trenches of the Left attack upon Sebastopol. A strong "covering party" had had an encounter with the Russians and been driven in disorganised. This gave Gardiner his opportunity. Displaying the utmost coolness and gallantry he inspirited the men to such an extent that they rallied, and turning like lions at bay they went for the Russians who by this time were close to the trenches which would soon have been in their possession. But now the tables were turned and the enemy were so beaten that they wavered and fled and the trenches were saved. On the 18th of June 1855, during the attack on the Redan, Gardiner again displayed the most devoted and heroic courage. The party to which he belonged in the attack had been subjected to a heavy and merciless fire, and the ground about them was strewn with their dead. Huge holes had also been ploughed by shells, and when the men showed signs of wavering, Gardiner induced them to screen themselves in the shell holes, and by making a parapet of dead bodies they were enabled to keep up such a galling fire on the Russians that they cleared the walls of them and thus greatly aided the attack. The act of heroism was performed under such a tremendous hail of shot and shell that half the officers and a third of the rank and file of the attacking party had either been killed or grievously wounded.

James Monat, C.B.,

Surgeon, 6th Dragoon Guards. After the splendid charge of the Light Brigade at the Battle of Balaklava, and while the cavalry were retreating, Surgeon Monat voluntarily proceeded to the assistance of Lieutenant Colonel Morris, C.B., of the 17th

Lancers who was lying dangerously wounded in a most exposed position. Notwithstanding the very heavy fire that was still being kept up, Monat went forth, though at any moment he was liable to be struck down. Reaching the spot where the officer was lying, he proceeded to attend to him as coolly as if he had been in the operating room, and by stopping the hemorrhage he saved Colonel Morris's life. This noble act of heroic self-devotion was performed on the 26th of October 1854.

Howard Crawford Elphinstone,

Captain, Royal Engineers. On the 18th of June 1855, after an unsuccessful attack on the Redan, Captain Elphinstone went out at night with a party of volunteers to search for and bring back the scaling ladders which had been left behind after the repulse. He performed this task most successfully, and in addition he rescued trophies from the enemy, and also brought in under very great difficulty twenty wounded men who otherwise must certainly have perished. The service thus rendered was of a very daring character, and during the whole time that Elphinstone and his party were engaged on their self-imposed task they were exposed to the greatest peril.

Henry McDonald,

Colour-Sergeant, Royal Engineers. This officer was engaged on duty with his party in the Left advance of the Right attack before Sebastopol. All the Engineer officers had been disabled, and the command thus devolved upon McDonald, who thereupon determined to drive the enemy in front of him from the rifle pits. In spite of a galling fire that was poured upon him, he persisted in carrying on the Sap, and by the most daring and gallant conduct he retained his position against attack after attack of the enemy, and thus rendered invaluable service to the British forces who were then engaged in the arduous work of reducing Sebastopol. The date was the 19th of April 1855.

Peter Leitch,

Colour-Sergeant, Royal Engineers. The tremendous struggle that took place during the assault on the Redan tested to the fullest possible extent the powers and quality of every man engaged. The Redan was a series of military works which the Russians considered impregnable. There was the great Redan and little Redan, which allied and in touch with the Malakoff presented most formidable obstacles to the advance of our troops and the capture of Sebastopol, for the enemy had twelve battalions of soldiers in the Malakoff, eight in the small Redan, and nine in the great Redan. While these forts remained intact the allies were kept at bay and their destruction or capture therefore became imperatively necessary. Preparations for the assault were carefully made, and it was arranged that the French should storm the Malakoff, while the English were to direct their attention to the great Redan. When all was ready a deafening roar of artillery broke upon the ear. It was said that since gunpowder was invented such a thundering discharge of it had never been heard before, nor such a flashing of fire, or hurricane of iron seen. Between the trenches and the fort was a space of 200 yards of open ground and across this the storming party had to make their way. Shot and shell, and grape shot were poured upon this open in a murderous storm, and men were mowed down like corn before the sickle. It was known to be a forlorn hope, owing to the assaulting party being too few in numbers, but not a man flinched; not one shirked his duty. Leitch particularly distinguished himself. He was amongst the leading ladder party who suffered terribly. With dauntless bravery Leitch formed a *caponnière* across the ditch, as well as a rampart by fearlessly tearing down gabions from the enemy's parapet, and placing and filling them so as to afford shelter to his comrades. He continued this work until he was disabled by wounds. Nevertheless he lived through that terrible time, and his services were recognised by the Cross being awarded to him. The date of his gallant exploit was the 18th of June 1855.

Frederick Miller,

Major, Royal Artillery. This officer at the Battle of Inkermann performed what may without exaggeration be described as prodigies of valour. He proved himself to be not only fearless but courageous even to recklessness; and the Russians on more than one occasion had reason to remember his individual powers. The deed which won him the distinguished and coveted honour of the Victoria Cross was performed on the 5th of November 1854. A battery in his division had all but fallen into the hands of the foe. Indeed, the Russians surrounded it and for a brief space it almost seemed as if the Royal Artillery would have to bear the humiliation of knowing that a whole battery had fallen into the hands of the enemy. But Major Miller was there. He knew how to die but not how to accept defeat. That was a lesson he had been slow to learn. So inspiriting his men with cheering words, he himself fell upon three Russians and smote them hip and thigh. His comrades caught his spirit of enthusiasm, and turning like lions at bay they drove the Russians from their position and the threatened English guns were saved. The value of this feat may be estimated when it is stated that part of a Regiment of English Infantry had previously retired through the Battery in front of this body of Russians; and but for Major Miller's splendid efforts and indomitable pluck the Battery would have been sacrificed.

For some reason or other the decoration was not conferred upon the gallant Major until five years later.

Charles Wooden,

Sergeant-Major, 17th Lancers. After the retreat of the Light Cavalry at the Battle of Balaklava on the 16th of October 1854, Wooden together with Dr. James Monat, C.B. helped to save the life of Lieutenant-Col. Morris, C.B., of the 17th Lancers, who was lying dangerously wounded in a most exposed position. It seemed like certain death to go to him but Wooden having no fear proceeded under a heavy fire, and was thereby instrumental in preserving the officer's life.

INDIA.

Joseph P. H. Crowe,

Lieutenant, 78th Regiment. Promoted and made Captain in 18th Regiment. On the 18th of August 1857, Major General Havelock telegraphed to the commander-in-chief in India. The telegram was dated Cawnpore and was to the effect that Lieutenant Crowe had been the first to enter the redoubt at Bourzekee Chowkee. This was an entrenched village in front of the Busherut Gunge and had been desperately defended by the mutineers. It was stormed by Havelock's troops on the 17th of August, and after heavy fighting fell into the hands of the English. Crowe greatly distinguished himself, and was the very first man to force his way into the enemy's position during the severest of the fighting.

Francis Cornwallis Maude, C.B.,

Captain, Promoted to Major, Royal Artillery. This officer received the Cross for most gallant conduct in face of the enemy. Sir James Outran in his despatch said, the attack that this officer made on the enemy appeared to him to indicate no reckless or foolhardy daring, but the calm heroism of a true soldier who fully appreciates the difficulties and dangers of the task he has undertaken, and that but for Captain Maude's nerve and coolness on this trying occasion, the army could not have advanced.

William Olpherts,

Captain, Promoted Lieutenant-Colonel, Bengal Artillery. On the 25th of September 1857, the British troops under Major General Havelock penetrated after hard fighting into the city of Lucknow. Olpherts charged on horseback with Her Majesty's 90th Regiment which was headed by Colonel Campbell. Through Olpherts' energy and daring two guns were captured in spite of a storm of grape shot. He afterwards returned, under a heavy fire, to bring up limbers and horses to carry off the captured guns. He was successful in accomplishing this task which was performed under conditions of great danger and difficulty.

Herbert Taylor Macpherson,

Lieutenant, Promoted Captain, 78th Regiment. On the same date and at the same place as the foregoing officer, Lieutenant Macpherson, so encouraged and inspirited his men during the hottest of the fighting, that they captured two brass nine pounders at the point of the bayonet. This daring deed was directly attributable to Macpherson's daring who throughout the fighting displayed the utmost bravery. His gallant conduct being brought under the notice of the authorities he was duly awarded the Victoria Cross.

Valentine Munbee McMaster,

Assistant Surgeon, 78th Regiment. During the dreadful carnage at Lucknow on the 25th of September, Mc Master fearlessly exposed himself to the fire of the enemy in his efforts to succour the wounded. By his gallantry he saved many lives, and succeeded in bringing into a place of safety many men who were lying on the ground suffering terribly from their wounds.

George Lambert,

Sergeant-Major, 84th Regiment. This gallant fellow won his Cross by intrepidity and distinguished conduct at Onao on the 29th of July; at Bithoor, on the 16th of August; and at Lucknow on the 25th of September.

Patrick Mahoney,

Sergeant, 1st Madras Fusiliers. Mahoney was doing duty with the volunteer Regiment of Cavalry at Mungulwar on the 21st of September 1857, when he greatly distinguished himself. He together with a number of comrades whom he inspired with his own bravery rushed for the Regimental colour of the 1st Regiment Native Infantry, and succeeded in capturing it after a desperate struggle during which he displayed absolute fearlessness.

Abraham Boulger,

Lance Corporal, 84th Regiment. This man received the Cross for very conspicuous bravery and forwardness as a skirmisher in no fewer than twelve actions fought between the 12th of July and the 25th of September 1857. His courage was remarkable and not only stimulated his comrades, but drew forth expressions of admiration from his superior officers.

Joel Holmes,

Private, 84th Regiment. During an engagement with the enemy Captain Maude's Battery had been exposed to a continuous and heavy fire, with the result that nearly the whole of the artillerymen had been killed or seriously wounded. The position of affairs was desperate when Private Holmes volunteered to work a gun. And he displayed so much energy and fearlessness that in a large measure he was the means of saving the battery.

James Hollowell,

Private, 78th Regiment. On the 26th of September 1857, a party of Europeans was besieged and shut up in a house in the city of Lucknow. Amongst this party was brave James Hollowell. The enemy seemed so bent upon reducing the house to ruins and killing every one in it, that most of the besieged lost heart as they seemed to feel that defence was hopeless. But Hollowell rose equal to the occasion. He recognised that it was time for someone to bestir himself and prove to the rebels that Englishmen would fight while breath remained, and when fighting was no longer possible, die as became heroes. He therefore set to work by force of example to put new hope into his unfortunate companions, and hour after hour he behaved in such a manner that the others were encouraged to make a most desperate resistance to the efforts of the enemy to destroy them. Over and over again Hollowell exposed himself fearlessly, and when he saw any one of his party faltering he persuaded and cheered him on, and was the means of inducing nine weary and broken men to show such courage that though the house was on fire, and the rebels were firing through four of the windows, the defenders kept them at bay until help came and the party was saved.

James McManus,

Private. This man also distinguished himself as a hero on the same occasion as Hollowell. Private Peter McManus even scorned to be inside the house, and from the shelter of a pillar he succeeded by an incessant fire in keeping the sepoys from making a rush on the building. At last McManus was wounded and had to be taken in, but his spirits were not crushed nor his energy subdued. And noting that Captain Arnold of the 1st Madras Fusiliers was in a dooly and likely to fall into the hands of the enemy, he rushed out in spite of his wound, in company with Private John Ryan, and lifting Captain Arnold from the dooly bore him into the house, notwithstanding a storm of bullets that was directed at them, and which caused Arnold to be wounded a second time, but, owing to the bravery and devotion of the two privates, his life was spared.

John Ryan,

Private, 1st Madras Fusiliers. In addition to the act of bravery mentioned in the foregoing case, whereby Ryan helped to save the life of his superior officer, the noble fellow greatly distinguished himself through the whole of that eventful day by issuing forth and rescuing the wounded in the neighbourhood who would otherwise have been barbarously massacred by the rebels. His energy seemed untiring, and he displayed a fearlessness which greatly inspirited and encouraged his comrades.

Thomas Duffy,

Private, 1st Madras Fusiliers. This man won his Cross by a most heroic and daring deed. By a display of coolness, intrepidity, and remarkable skill he saved a 24-pounder from falling into the hands of the enemy.

Henry Ward,

Private, 78th Regiment. On the night of the 25th

and morning of the 28th of September 1857, this heroic fellow remained by the dooly in which lay Captain H. M. Havelock, 10th Regiment, Deputy Assistant Adjutant General, Field Force, severely wounded. In the morning he escorted that officer and Private Thomas Pilkington, 78th Highlanders, who was also terribly wounded and had taken refuge in the same dooly, through a heavy cross fire of musketry and ordnance. In spite of what seemed the risk of certain death he ran, Ward would not quit the dooly, and by his fearlessness and devotion he inspirited the dooly bearers and prevented them from dropping their double load. It is stated that throughout this trying and terrible ordeal Ward preserved the same steadiness and coolness that he would have done on parade, and by his noble exertions he managed to get both the wounded men to the Baillie Guard, and thereby saved their lives. For this splendid service he was mentioned in despatches, and was duly decorated with the Victoria Cross.

Anthony Dixon Home,

Surgeon, 90th Regiment. Surgeon Home received the Cross for persevering bravery and admirable conduct while in charge of the wounded men left behind the column when the troops under Major-General Havelock forced their way into the Residency of Lucknow, on the 26th of September 1857. The escort which had been left to protect the wounded had by casualties been reduced to a few stragglers. Being entirely separated from the column, this little party with their wounded whom they were charged to protect to the best of their ability, were forced to take shelter in a house where they bravely defended themselves until the house was set on fire. They then retreated to a shed a few yards from it, and in this place they presented such a heroic face to the enemy, and defended themselves so well that they kept the foe at bay for upwards of twenty-two hours. In the end only six men, and Surgeon Home remained able to fire. Of four officers who were with the party all were badly wounded, three of them ultimately dying. In these desperate circumstances the command devolved upon Home and nobly did he acquit himself. In his active exertions previously to being forced into the house, and to his splendid conduct throughout the whole of the dreadful time, the safety of the wounded, and the successful defence were attributable. It was indeed a gallant service, for which he was very properly decorated with the Cross.

William Bradshaw,

Assistant Surgeon, 90th Regiment. This gentleman received the Cross for intrepidity and good conduct when ordered with Surgeon Home to remove the wounded men who had been left behind the column that forced its way into the Residency of Lucknow on the 26th of September. The dooly bearers had all bolted and left the doolies with the wounded lying in them and liable to be massacred by the rebels who surrounded them. With a display of utter indifference to his own safety, Bradshaw set to work to get some dooly bearers together and though he was separated with twenty doolies from the rest, he succeeded by tact and skill in reaching the Residency by the river bank.

George Forrest,

Captain, Bengal Veteran Establishment. This officer displayed the most heroic conduct during the defence of the Delhi Arsenal on the 11th of May 1857. The mutiny had declared itself on the previous day at Meerut forty miles off. Having been successful in Meerut the rebels swarmed into Delhi, and at once attacked the magazine where an enormous quantity of war stores was kept. But owing to the bravery and splendid fighting powers of the handful of men who had charge of this great arsenal, the stores were prevented from falling into the hands of the enemy.

William Raynor,

Captain, Bengal Veteran Establishment. This officer also won his Cross for gallant conduct in defending the magazine at Delhi on the 11th of May.

John Buckley,

Deputy Assistant Commissary of Ordnance, Commissariat Department (Bengal Establishment.) This man was also one of the noble little band that defended the Arsenal.

Robert Blair,

Lieutenant, 2nd Dragoon Guards. This young officer was the hero of a most gallant feat. He was ordered to take a party of one sergeant and twelve men and bring in a deserted ammunition waggon. As he and his party approached, a body of between fifty and sixty of the enemy's horse swept down upon them from a neighbouring village where they had been concealed. Without a moment's hesitation Blair formed up his men, and regardless of all risks and consequences, boldly led them on, and making a dash through the rebels, he effected his retreat without losing a man, but he left nine of the enemy dead on the field. Four of these fell to his own sword, and having run a native officer through the body, he himself was desperately wounded, his shoulder being nearly severed from his body. Nevertheless he kept his horse and took his troop out of action. Date, 28th September 1857.

Alfred Stowell Jones,

Lieutenant, 9th Lancers, Promoted to be Captain of 18th Hussars. A despatch from Major-General James Hope Grant, K.C.B., dated 10th of January 1858, reads thus: "The cavalry charged the rebels and rode through them. Lieutenant Jones of the 9th Lancers, with his squadron, captured one of their guns, killing the drivers, and with Lieutenant-Colonel Yules' assistance turned it upon a village occupied by the rebels who were quickly dislodged. This was a well-conceived act gallantly executed."

THE "V. C." 75

Dighton Macnaghten Probyn,

Captain, 2nd Punjaub cavalry. This officer greatly distinguished himself throughout the Campaign. At the battle of Agra, when his squadron charged the rebel infantry, he was for some time separated from his men, and surrounded by five or six sepoys. He defended himself from the various cuts made at him, and before his own men were able to rejoin him, he killed two of his assailants. At another time in single combat with a sepoy, he was wounded in the wrist by the bayonet, and his horse also was slightly wounded, but though the sepoy fought desperately he went down before Probyn's blows. The same day he singled out a standard bearer, and in presence of a number of the enemy he killed him and captured his standard. On other occasions he displayed no less bravery and he was mentioned in despatches in terms of very high praise by Major-General James Hope Grant, K.C.B.

John Watson,

Lieutenant, 1st Punjaub Cavalry. This officer on the 14th of November 1857, with his own Squadron and that of Lieutenant Proby, came upon a body of the rebel cavalry. The Ressaldar in command of them—who was described as "a fine specimen of the Hindustani Mussulman" and backed up by half-a-dozen equally brave men, rode out to the front. Watson at once went for the imposing looking Commander and attacked him. The Ressaldar aimed his pistol at Watson's breast from a distance of only a yard, and fired. But from some unexplained cause the shot failed to take effect. Indeed it is supposed that the bullet must have fallen out while the weapon was being loaded, for it is difficult to understand how, if there had been a bullet, it failed to go through the officer's body, seeing that the weapon was aimed pointblank, Watson without flinching, attacked the man with his sword and dismounted him. Nothing daunted, the brave Ressaldar drew his tulwar, and with some of his sowars made a fierce onslaught on the young lieutenant who defended himself with remarkable skill and lion-like courage, until some of his men came to his assistance, and the native soldiers were put to flight. In the fight Watson was struck on the head with a tulwar and received another cut on the left arm, which severed his chain gauntlet glove; he was also struck on the right arm by a blow which divided the sleeve of his jacket, and though the arm was not wounded it was for the time disabled. A bullet also went through his coat, and he received a terrific blow on the leg which lamed him for some time.

MEMORANDUM.

Lieutenants Duncan Charles Home and Philip Salkeld, of the Bengal Engineers rendered splendid service in the performance of their desperate duty of blowing open the Cashmere Gate of the Fortress of Delhi in broad daylight, under a tremendous musketry fire on the morning of the 14th of September 1857, preparatory to the general assault. They were both desperately wounded and the Victoria Cross was provisionally conferred upon them by Major-General Sir Archdale Wilson, Bart, K.C.B., but they did not survive their wounds.

Henry Tombs, C. B.,

Lieutenant Colonel, Bengal Artillery; and Lieutenant

James Hills.

For very gallant conduct on the part of Lieutenant Hills before Delhi, in defending the position assigned to him in case of alarm, and for noble behaviour on the part of Lieutenant Colonel Tombs in twice going to the rescue of his subaltern, and on each occasion killing his man. Date, 9th of July 1857.

William Alexander Kerr,

Lieutenant, 24th Bombay Native Infantry. On the breaking out of the Mutiny in the 27th Bombay Native Infantry in July 1857, a party of the rebels took up a position in the stronghold, or paga, near the town of Kolapore, and defended themselves with great bravery and determination. Lieutenant Kerr, of the Southern Mahratta Irregular Horse, took a prominent part in the attack on the rebel position, and at the moment when its capture was of the greatest public importance, he made a dash at one of the gateways with some dismounted horsemen, and forced an entrance into the stronghold by battering in the gate. The daring of this attack seemed to paralyse the defenders who in the rush that followed were killed, wounded, or captured. This result was entirely due to Kerr's devotion and bravery in conjunction with remarkable skill and tact. The service he thus rendered was of the greatest moment, and the Cross was duly conferred upon him. The date of the heroic act was the 10th of July 1857.

John Smith,

Sergeant, Bengal Sappers and Miners. For conspicuous gallantry on the 14th of September in conjunction with Lieutenants Home and Salkeld in the performance of the terrible duty of blowing open the Cashmere Gate at Delhi, to prepare the way for the general assault.

Robert Hawthorne,

Bugler, 52nd Regiment. This man was also one of the explosion party, and not only performed his duty with conspicuous gallantry, but attached himself to Lieutenant Salkeld when he was desperately wounded, whose wounds he bound up under a heavy musketry fire, and had him removed to a place of safety.

Henry Smith,

Lance Corporal, 52nd Regiment. On the morning of the assault on Delhi, on the 14th of September 1857, Smith most gallantly carried away a wounded comrade from the Chaundee Chouck, while a storm of grape and shell was being poured upon it, and thereby he saved his comrade's life.

Bernard Diamond, Sergeant, and Richard Fitzgerald, Gunner.

These two brave fellows were awarded the Cross for an act of valour performed in action on the 28th of September 1857. They were engaged with the Mutineers at Boolundshur, when in spite of tremendous difficulties they evinced the most determined bravery in working the gun they were placed in charge of, and this notwithstanding that a hail of bullets was poured upon them. Their pluck and endurance, coupled with the skill they displayed in handling the gun after every other man belonging to it had been either killed or wounded, cleared the road of the enemy, and enabled the British to score a triumph where otherwise they must have chronicled a defeat.

Frederick Robertson Aikman,

Lieutenant, promoted to Captain, 4th Bengal Native Infantry. On the 1st of March 1858, this gallant officer was in command of the 3rd Sikh Cavalry, on the advanced picquet with one hundred of his men, when he obtained information, just as the force marched on the morning of the 1st of March, that three miles off the high road a body of Rebel Infantry was posted, consisting of 500 men, together with 200 horses and two guns under a notorious rebel named Moosahib Ali Chuckbdar. As soon as Aikman came to this knowledge he resolved to attack the rebels notwithstanding his own numerical weakness which gave rise amongst his followers to a belief that the risk was so great as to render the enterprise foolhardy. But Aikman was one of those individuals who do not pause to consider odds. To him his duty seemed plain. Here was a considerable force of the enemy in close proximity, and it was highly important that they should not only be dispersed, but rendered incapable for further mischief. He therefore put his little body of troops in motion, and fell suddenly and swiftly on the rebels. A fierce fight ensued, but the bold Lieutenant and his men were made of the right stuff, and they fought with such stern determination that they not only routed their foe, but they cut up one hundred of them, captured the two guns, and drove the demoralised survivors over the Goomtee river. This gallant feat of arms was performed under every possible disadvantage of singularly broken ground and subject to a galling cross fire from an adjoining rebel fort. Aikman performed various personal deeds of valour, and in an encounter he had with one of the enemy, who seemed resolved not to yield or be beaten, he received a terrible sabre cut in the face.

William Connolly,

Gunner, Bengal Horse Artillery. This brave soldier was in action with the enemy at Jhelum on the 7th of July 1857. From the report of Lieutenant

Cookes, of the same regiment, we extract the following particulars:—

"About daybreak on the 7th, I advanced my half troop at a gallop and engaged the enemy within easy musket range. The spongeman of one of my guns having been shot during the advance, Gunner Connolly assumed the duties of second spongeman and he had barely assisted in two discharges of his gun when a musket ball through the left thigh felled him to the ground. Nothing daunted by the pain or loss of blood he was endeavouring to resume his duties, when I ordered a movement in retirement, and though so severely wounded he was mounted on his horse in the gun team, and rode to the next position which the guns took up. He was then informed that owing to his wound he must retire to the rear. But this he resolutely and manfully declined to do, saying that he preferred to stick to his post.

"About eleven o'clock a.m. when the guns were still in action, the same gunner, while sponging, was again knocked down by a musket ball striking him on the hip, thereby causing great faintness and partial unconsciousness, for the pain was excessive and the blood flowed fast. On seeing this I gave instructions for his removal out of action, but this brave man hearing the order staggered to his feet and said, 'No sir, I'll not go there whilst I can work here', and shortly afterwards he again resumed his post as a spongeman.

"Late in the afternoon of the same day my three

guns were engaged at one hundred yards from the walls of a village with the defenders, namely the 16th Native Infantry—Mutineers—amidst a storm of bullets which did great execution. Gunner Connolly though suffering severely from his two previous wounds, was wielding his sponge with an energy and courage which attracted the admiration of his comrades, and while cheerfully encouraging a wounded man to hasten in bringing up ammunition a musket ball tore through the muscles of his right leg; but with the most undaunted bravery he struggled on; and not till he had loaded six times, did this man give way, when through loss of blood he fell into my arms and I placed him on a waggon which shortly afterwards bore him in a state of unconsciousness from the fight."

John Adam Tytler,

Lieutenant, 66th (Ghoor Kla) Bengal Native Infantry. It was the 10th of February 1858, when an attacking party approached the enemy's position under a heavy fire of round shot, grape and musketry on the occasion of an action at Choorpoorals. Lieutenant Tytler dashed on horseback ahead of all, and alone up to the enemy's guns, where he remained engaged hand to hand until the guns were carried by us. He was shot through the left arm, had a spear wound in his chest, and a ball through the right sleeve of his coat.

M. Rosamond,

Sergeant-Major, 37th Bengal Native Infantry. On

the 4th of June 1857, this non-commissioned officer volunteered to accompany Lieutenant-Colonel Spottiswoode—commanding the 37th regiment of Bengal Native Infantry, to the right of the lines in order to set them on fire with a view to driving out the Sepoys, on the occasion of the outbreak at Benares. He also volunteered with Sergeant-Major Gill of the Loodiana regiment to bring off Captain Brown, Pension Paymaster, his wife and infant, and also some others from a detached bungalow into the Barracks. His conduct was highly courageous and greatly inspired his comrades. In addition to the Cross he received promotion.

Peter Gill,

Sergeant-Major, Loodiana Regiment, non-commissioned. This officer also conducted himself with great gallantry at Benares on the same date as Rosamond. He volunteered with his comrade to bring off Captain Brown, and he also saved the life of the Quartermaster-Sergeant of the 25th Regiment of Bengal Native Infantry in the early part of the evening, by cutting off the sepoy who had just bayonetted him. Sergeant-Major Gill states that on the same night he faced a guard of 27 men with only a sergeant's sword; and further than that he twice saved the life of Major Barrett, of the 27th Regiment of Bengal Native Infantry, when attacked by sepoys of his own Regiment.

William Gardner,

Colour Sergeant, 42nd Regiment. On the morning

of the 5th of May 1858, this man distinguished himself by most gallant and heroic conduct. His commanding officer, Lieutenant-Colonel Cameron, on that day during the action at Bareilly came within an ace of losing his life. He was knocked from his horse and as he lay on the ground three fanatics rushed upon him, bent on despatching him. But Gardner had noted their coming; he rushed out with his bayonet fixed, and pinned two of them, and was in the act of attacking the third when he was shot down by another soldier of the Regiment. He had saved his commanding officer's life, however, and assistance coming up they were both rescued from their perilous position.

Edward Robinson, A.B.,

Naval Brigade. At Lucknow on the 13th of March 1858, this brave fellow while under a heavy musketry fire within a range of fifty yards, jumped on to the sand bags of a battery and extinguished a fire amongst them. He was dangerously wounded while performing this important service.

John Harrison,

Lieutenant, promoted to Commander,

Nowel Salunor,

Naval Brigade. These two brave men were also at Lucknow on the 16th of November 1857, and they climbed a tree touching the angle of the Shah Nujjiff in order that they might reply to the fire of the enemy. This act of dangerous service was performed in response to a call from Captain Peel for volunteers.

W. Goat,

Lance Corporal, 9th Lancers. The Cross was awarded to Goat for very conspicuous gallantry and distinguished service also at Lucknow on the 6th of March 1858. In the presence of a number of the enemy he dismounted from his horse, and took up the body of Major Smith, 2nd Dragoon Guards, and endeavoured to take it off the field. He was obliged, however, to relinquish it, being surrounded by the enemy's cavalry. Nevertheless he went out a second time under a heavy fire and recovered the body.

R. Newell,

Private, 9th Lancers. For conspicuous gallantry at Lucknow on the 19th of March 1858, in going to the assistance of a comrade whose horse had stumbled on bad ground. The comrade under these circumstances must certainly have fallen into the hands of the enemy, had not Newell with unselfish devotion ridden out to him under a heavy musketry fire and assisted him in getting his horse up and remounting.

Spence,

Troop Sergeant-Major, 9th Lancers. On the 17th of January 1858, this brave non-commissioned officer was at a place called Shumsabad when he saw a comrade named Kidd lying on the ground wounded and his horse disabled. He was surrounded by rebels who were about to despatch him when

Spence sprang to his rescue and at the imminent risk of his life he brought him safely out of the fray.

Rushe,

Troop Sergeant-Major, 9th Lancers. On the 19th of March 1858, at Lucknow this man in company with one private of the troop attacked eight of the enemy with such desperate energy, that three of them were killed and the others put to flight. They had posted themselves in a nullah and being sheltered were a menace and a danger.

Alfred Kirke Ffrench,

Lieutenant. The date of this officer's act of bravery was the 16th of November 1857, at the taking of the Secundra Bagh Lucknow, when he was in command of the Grenadier Company. He fought with magnificent heroism, displaying an utter disregard of himself and an unfaltering devotion to duty. He was one of the very first to enter the well-defended building, and by his splendid example and heroism he greatly encouraged his comrades. His conduct was very highly praised by the whole company; and he was unanimously elected by the officers of the regiment for the honour of the Cross.

Charles Pye,

Sergeant-Major, promoted to ensign, 53rd Regiment, was awarded the Cross for steady and fearless conduct under fire at Lucknow on the 17th of November 1857, when bringing up ammunition to the

Mess House; and on every occasion when his regiment was engaged he very greatly distinguished himself. He was elected by the non-commissioned officers of his regiment for the honour of being decorated.

J. Kenry,

Private, 53rd Regiment. During the attack on the Secundra Bagh at Lucknow, which was so long and obstinately defended by the mutineers, Kenry displayed an astonishing coolness, no less than devoted courage. And he volunteered to bring up ammunition to his company, although in so doing he was subjected to a galling cross fire, which placed him in the extremest peril. But without once faltering or flinching he manfully performed his duty, thereby rendering invaluable service to the troops and contributing in a measure to the capture of the stronghold. He was elected by the private soldiers of his regiment as a worthy recipient of the Cross.

C. Irwin,

Private, 53rd Regiment. This man also displayed conspicuous heroism at the assault on the Secundra Bagh on the same date. Although he was severely wounded through the right shoulder he was one of the first men of his regiment to enter the building under a tremendous fire. He also was elected by the private soldiers of his regiment.

V. Bambrick,

Private, 10th Regiment 1st Battalion. For conspicuous bravery at Bareilly on the 6th of May 1858, when in a serai he was attacked by the Ghazees, one of whom he cut down. He was twice wounded on this occasion.

P. Mylott,

Private, 84th Regiment. This man was in frequent engagements and on every occasion displayed the most gallant conduct. On the 17th of July 1857, he rushed across the road under a shower of bullets, together with some comrades to take an opposite enclosure, he being the foremost. This service proved of great advantage, and was duly recognised.

The Hon. Augustus Henry Archibald Anson,

Captain, 84th Regiment. On the 28th of September 1857, this officer was at Bolmudshahur on active service. The 9th Light Dragoons had charged through the town, and were reforming in the Serai. The enemy thereupon endeavoured to close the entrance by drawing their carts across it so as to shut in the cavalry, and form a shelter for themselves so that they might be able to pour in a galling fire on the troops who would thus be caught, as it were, in a trap. Captain Anson seeing this, and recognising the peril the soldiers would be in if the movement succeeded, seized a lance and without a moment's hesitation, he dashed out of the gateway, and commenced such a furious onslaught on the drivers that many of them fell from their carts. Owing to a wound in his left hand, which he had received at Delhi he could not stop his horse which carried him into the middle of the enemy, who at once emptied their muskets at him, one ball passing through his coat. He succeeded, however, in getting clear and was rescued by his comrades. At Lucknow, during the assault on the Secundra Bagh, he was one of the first to enter with the storming party as soon as the gates were burst open. He had his horse killed under him, and he himself was slightly wounded on that occasion. Throughout his service he displayed dauntless courage, and rendered most valuable services, and a large number of the enemy fell to his sword.

Sinnott,

Lance Corporal, 84th Regiment. On the 6th of October 1857, Sinnott displayed conspicuous gallantry at Lucknow in going out with Sergeants Glim and Mullins, and Private Mullins to rescue Lieutenant Gibant, who in carrying out water to extinguish a fire in the breast-work, had been mortally wounded and lay outside. They succeeded after much difficulty in reaching the body, and had to bring it in under a very heavy fire which threatened to annihilate them. Sinnott was twice wounded. He had repeatedly accompanied Gibant to carry the water for the purpose of putting out the fire. Sinnott was unanimously elected by his comrades as in every way entitled to the honour of the Cross which was duly awarded to him.

John Christopher Guise,

Major, 90th Regiment, received the Cross for very

conspicuous gallantry in action on the 16th and 17th of November 1857, at Lucknow.

S. Hill,

Sergeant, 90th Regiment. For devoted and gallant conduct on the 16th and 17th of November at Lucknow during the storming of the Secundra Bagh, during which he saved the life of Captain Irby by warding off with his firelock a tulwar cut made with terrific force at the officer's head by a Sepoy. Subsequently Hill went out into the open under a heavy fire to help two wounded men. Throughout the whole of the operation, undertaken for the relief of the Lucknow garrison, Hill greatly distinguished himself, and by his brave example encouraged and ennerved his comrades under the most trying and disheartening circumstances.

P. Graham,

Private, 90th Regiment. This brave man at the risk of his own life brought in a wounded comrade under a heavy fire, on the 17th of November 1857, at Lucknow.

William George Drummond Stewart,

Captain, 93rd Regiment. For distinguished personal gallantry at Lucknow on the 16th of November 1857, in leading an attack upon and capturing two guns, by which service the position of the mess house was secured.

J. Paton,

Sergeant. For distinguished personal bravery and

"MACKAY CAPTURED ONE OF THE COLOURS OF THE ENEMY."

[*page* 91.

heroism on the 16th of November at Lucknow, in proceeding alone and at great risk round the Shah Nujjiff under an extremely heavy fire, to see if a breach had been made in the walls. He found that on the opposite side there was a breach and returning safely he made his report, and afterwards conducted the regiment to the wall, and by that means the place was taken.

J. Dunley,

Lance Corporal, 93rd Regiment. He was one of the first men who on the 16th of November 1857, entered one of the breaches in the Secundra Bagh defences at Lucknow. His superior officer, Captain Burroughs, was at once surrounded by overwhelming numbers of the enemy and would have succumbed but for the heroism of Dunley who supported him without flinching, and drove the enemy off.

D. Mackay,

Private, 93rd Regiment. On the 16th of November 1857, a date on which numerous acts of devoted courage were performed, Mackay captured one of the colours of the enemy, after a most desperate resistance at the Secundra Bagh. Subsequently while rendering Trojan service at the capture of Shah Nujjiff he was severely wounded.

P. Grant,

Private, 93rd Regiment. This man also conspicuously distinguished himself at the Secundra Bagh. He attacked and killed five of the enemy with one of their own swords when they were following and trying to cut down Lieutenant-Colonel Ewart, when that officer had succeeded in capturing a colour and was carrying it off. Had it not been for Grant's noble conduct, the flag would have been recovered and the officer killed.

William McBean,

Lieutenant and Adjutant, 93rd Regiment. For distinguished personal bravery in killing eleven of the enemy with his own hand in the main breach of the Begum Bagh at Lucknow on the 11th of March 1858.

Henry Wilmot,

Captain, 2nd Battalion, Rifle Brigade. On the 11th of March 1858, this officer also rendered noble service. His company was engaged with a large body of the enemy near the Iron Bridge. Suddenly Wilmot found himself at the end of a narrow street, with only four of his men, and a large body of the enemy threatening them. One of the four men was immediately shot through both legs and became utterly helpless: the two men lifted him up; and Private Hawkes, although severely wounded himself carried him a considerable distance, exposed to the fire of the enemy. Captain Wilmot covered the retreat by keeping the enemy at bay with a galling fire from the rifles of his men.

David Hawkes,

Private, 2nd Battalion, Rifle Brigade. For the distinguished service to a wounded comrade recorded in the preceding case.

J. Smith,

Private, 1st Madras Fusiliers. On the 16th of November 1857, he was one of the first to try and enter the gateway on the north side of the Secundra Bagh. On the gateway being burst open he was amongst those who first rushed in, and he was at once surrounded by the enemy. He received a sword cut on the head, a bayonet wound on the left side, and a contusion from the butt end of a gun on the right shoulder. Notwithstanding all this he bravely fought his way out, and insisted on performing his duties during the rest of the day.

Lieutenant Hastings Edward Harrington
Rough Rider E. Jennings
Gunner J. Park } Bengal Artillery.
Gunner J. Laughnar
Gunner H. McInnes

All the above were elected under the 13th clause of the Royal Warrant of the 29th of January 1856, by the officers and non-commissioned officers generally and by the private soldiers of each troop of battery, for conspicuous gallantry at the Relief of Lucknow from the 14th to the 22nd of November 1857. Throughout those stormy days, when the fate of the suffering garrison of Lucknow trembled in the balance, these men by their individual and collective heroism, set such a worthy example to their comrades, and aided the cause of their country to such an extent that they helped in no small degree

Hugh Henry Gough,

Lieutenant, 1st Bengal European Light Cavalry. Lieutenant Gough while in command of a party of Hodson's Horse near Almbagh on the 12th of November 1857, particularly distinguished himself by his bravery and forward bearing in charging across a swamp and capturing two guns, although they were defended by a vastly superior body of the enemy. On this occasion he had his horse wounded in two places, and his turban cut through by blows from the sepoys whom he engaged single-handed. This officer further very greatly distinguished himself near Jellalabad, Lucknow on the 25th of February 1858, by setting a brilliant example to his regiment when ordered to charge the enemy's guns. By this example and his dauntless courage he so inspired the men that they effected their object and brought the guns in. While performing this service Gough engaged himself in a series of single combats, until at last he was disabled by a musket ball through the leg while he was in the act of charging two sepoys who opposed him with fixed bayonets. On this memorable day Gough had two horses killed under him, a shot through his helmet, and another through his scabbard; besides which he was severely wounded.

Frederick Sleigh Roberts,

Lieutenant, Bengal Artillery. "Lieutenant Roberts'

gallantry has on every occasion been most marked." So runs the despatch. On following up the retreating enemy on the 2nd of January 1858, at Khodagunge he saw in the distance two sepoys going off with a standard. This was more than Roberts could stand, so putting spurs to his horse, he went after them, overtook them just as they were about to enter a village, and engaged them. They turned immediately and presented their muskets at him. One of the men pulled the trigger of his musket, but the cap snapped, and before he could recover himself, Roberts had cut him down and seized the standard, which, in spite of the efforts of the second man to prevent him, he bore back in triumph. On the same day he had another personal adventure in which he distinguished himself as a hero. He rode at a sepoy who was standing at bay with musket and bayonet, keeping off a sowar. Roberts went full tilt at the sepoy and with a terrific blow across the face killed him on the spot.

P. Donohoe.

Private, 9th Lancers. On the 28th of September 1857, this man at Bolundshahur, went to the assistance of Lieutenant Blair who had been severely wounded, and with a few other men he safely conveyed the wounded officer through a large force of the enemy's cavalry.

J. Freeman,

Private, 9th Lancers. On the 10th of October 1857,

at Agra this brave fellow performed a similar service. He went to the assistance of Lieutenant Jones who had been shot. He killed the leader of the enemy's cavalry, and for a long time successfully defended Jones from the attacks of several of the enemy.

J. R. Roberts,

Private, 9th Lancers. On the 28th of Sept. 1857, Roberts was in action at Bolundshahur when he performed one of those feats of Christian charity and devotion which redeem our common nature from its sordid and selfish character. The fighting had been very hot, and men, dying and dead, were lying in the streets of the native village which had witnessed such agonising scenes. A comrade of Roberts, mortally wounded, had been stricken to the ground, and Roberts not knowing that he had been stricken to rise no more, was determined to try and save his life. So he assisted his friend on to his back, and bore him steadily and determinedly through a long narrow street which was swept by a storm of bullets. In performing this splendid deed of brotherly love he himself was severely wounded, but he succeeded in bringing his comrade to a place where such rough comfort as could be administered to him, was administered and tended to soothe his dying moments.

R. Kells,

Lance Corporal, 9th Lancers. On the same date and at the same place this brave man showed what gallantry is capable of in the hour of mortal peril, and how unselfish and devoted men may be on the battle-field, whereas it is generally supposed all the instincts of fellow feeling are crushed out, and only the fiercer passions of wrath and hate show themselves. But this, like a good many other things, is a popular fallacy. At least, if hatred and wrath make themselves manifested, and assuredly they do, Christian charity and brotherly love are by no means absent. In this case, Corporal Kells staked his own life to save that of his superior officer, Captain Drysdale who was lying in a street with his collar-bone broken, his horse having been disabled by a shot, and thrown him. To his assistance and defence went brave Kells, and fighting like a lion at bay he kept off a horde of rebels who were thirsting for blood and tried every means to kill the corporal and the captain. But in attempting this they did not count the cost, nor take into consideration the magnificent spirit of heroism which nerved and stimulated Kells and so man after man of their number fell before his unerring aim, until at last succour arrived, and Kells and his captain were saved.

James Leith,

Lieutenant, 14th Light Dragoons. At the battle of Betivah on the 1st of April 1858, Leith noticed that Captain Need of the same regiment was surrounded by the enemy and that his position was hopeless unless he was rescued. So never thinking of himself Leith charged alone, and sweeping down on the group like a whirlwind, he scattered the foe, saved his captain, and they rode back to the lines in triumph.

W. Napier,

Sergeant, 1st Battalion, 13th Regiment. His was another case of devotion and unselfishness where life was risked to save a comrade. It was at Azinghur on the 6th of April 1858, that Private Benjamin Miles of the same Regiment was severely wounded at the Baggage Guard and in mortal peril. So brave Napier went to his assistance and with courage that knew no shrinking he defended him against the howling sepoys who tried to reach him. But Napier scattered them although they charged over and over again. Then when a breathing moment came, and though bullets were raining upon the spot, he coolly and collectedly bandaged his friend's wounds, and finally carried him in safety to the convoy. It was a splendid deed, and Napier was fittingly rewarded with the Cross.

Richard Wadeson,

Lieutenant, 75th Regiment. On the 18th of July 1857, this Regiment was engaged in the Subgee Mundee at Delhi, when Wadeson saved the life of Private Michael Farrell who was fiercely attacked by a sowar of the enemy's cavalry. But the sowar had not counted the cost of his venture and as a result he bit the dust never to rise any more, and Farrell was saved to fight again. Later in the same day and at the same place the heroic lieutenant saved another private named John Barry under similar circumstances. Barry was wounded and helpless when a sowar bore down upon him. But forth went Wadeson to the rescue, killed the sowar, and brought away the wounded man.

Hugh Stewart Cochrane,

Lieutenant and Adjutant, 86th Regiment. No. 1 Company of this Regiment were ordered to take a gun near Jhansi on the 1st of April 1858. Cochrane heard the order, and at once dashed forward for the gun, attacked its defenders with irresistible fury, actually drove them off and kept the gun until his comrades rode up and made the capture certain. He further distinguished himself by attacking the rear guard of the enemy and harassing them. During this exploit he had three horses in succession shot under him.

William Rennie,

Lieutenant and Adjutant, 90th Regiment. Rennie was awarded the Cross for conspicuous gallantry during the advance on Lucknow under Major-General Havelock. It was the 21st of September 1857, and Rennie with a dash and courage beyond praise charged the enemy's guns which were doing great execution. He charged in advance of the skirmishers of the 90th Light Infantry and under a heavy musketry fire. The enemy were in the act of dragging the guns to a more advantageous position where they would have been able to still better command the advancing troops. But Rennie prevented this, and through his instrumentality one of the guns was captured. Again on the 25th of September at Lucknow he charged in advance of the 90th Column in the face of a heavy fire of grape, and forced the enemy to abandon their guns.

John James M'Leod Innes,

Lieutenant, Bengal Engineers. At the action at Sultanpore, Lieutenant Innes, far in advance of the leading skirmishers, was the first to secure a gun which the enemy were abandoning. Retiring from this they rallied round another gun further back, from which the shot in another instant would have ploughed through the advancing columm of English. But Innes was there. He dashed in amongst the gunners, shot dead the man who was in the very act of applying the port fire, and then scattered the others. All undaunted by the fact that he was a target for a hundred matchlock men who were sheltered in some adjoining huts, he kept the gunners at bay until assistance reached him.

J. Thomas,

Bombardier, Bengal Artillery, 4th Company, 1st Battalion. At Lucknow on the 27th of September 1857, Thomas brought off on his back under heavy fire, and under circumstances of the most difficult nature, a wounded soldier of the Madras Fusiliers, when the party to which he was attached were returning to the Residency from a sortie. But for this noble act the wounded man must of a certainty have fallen into the hands of the enemy who would have butchered him in cold blood.

J. McGuire,
Sergeant, 1st European Bengal Fusiliers.

M. Ryan,
Drummer, same Regiment.

At the assault on Delhi on the 14th of September 1857, the Brigade had reached the Cabul Gate, and the 1st Fusiliers, the 75th Regiment and some Sikhs were waiting for orders. The Regiments were getting ammunition served out when from some unknown cause, never yet explained, three boxes of the ammunition exploded, and two others were observed to be on fire. The panic and confusion were tremendous. Crowds of soldiers and camp-followers were rushing about not knowing where the danger lay or what the roar and rumble portended. McGuire and Drummer Ryan took in the terrible situation at a glance, they saw that unless a further explosion was prevented the loss of life would be fearful and the panic might develop into a stampede. So without thinking of the peril of being blown to pieces they themselves ran, they rushed at the burning mass, seized the blazing boxes, and tossed them one after the other over the parapet of the bridge into the water below. They thus averted a calamity, and by their heroism and coolness set such an example to those around that the panic was allayed and order restored.

Patrick Carlin,

Private, 13th Regiment. This man was recommended by his commanding officer, for that he did on the 6th of April 1858, rescue a wounded Naick of the 4th Madras Rifles in the field of battle, after killing with the Naick's sword a mutineer sepoy who fired at him as he was bearing off his wounded comrade on his shoulders.

Patrick Green,

Private, 75th Regiment. On the 11th of September 1857, Private Patrick Green was with his Regiment at the Koodria Baugh at Delhi when a picquet in which he was doing duty was very hotly pressed indeed by a large body of the enemy. It was a time when it was every man for himself, but Green was made of the stuff that heroes are formed of, and at the imminent risk of his life he stopped to rescue a wounded comrade who had fallen as a skirmisher, and in another few minutes would have been butchered by the enemy. Green, however, bore him to a place of safety.

Same Shaw,

Private, Rifle Brigade, 3rd Battalion. It was at Lucknow, and the date, the 13th of June 1858. An armed rebel bent on mischief was seen to enter a tope of trees. Some officers and men ran into the tope in pursuit of him. The rebel was a Ghazee. Shaw was amongst the men and was the first to find the Ghazee, and at once fell upon him. Shaw was armed with only a short sword, but fearlessly he attacked his foe and a terrific struggle ensued which ended in the Ghazee biting the dust, but not before he had with his tulwar given Shaw a terrible wound.

MEMORANDUM.

Cornet William George Harwtrey Bankes, 7th Hussars, upon whom the Commander-in-chief in India had reported that the decoration of the Victoria Cross had been provisionally conferred for conspicuous gallantry, in thrice charging a body of infuriated fanatics who had rushed on the guns employed in shelling a small mud fort in the vicinity of Moosa-Bagh, Lucknow, on the 19th of March 1858, when he was severely wounded and subsequently died. Had he survived he would have been recommended to Her Majesty for confirmation of the distinction.

Captain Clement Walker Hewage
Sergeant Joseph Ward No. 1584
Farrier George Hollis No. 1298
Private John Pearson No. 861
} 8th Hussars.

These men were selected by their comrades for the distinguished honour of the Cross, when during the gallant charge made by the Squadron of the Regiment at Gwalior on the 17th of June 1858, in company with a division of the Bombay Horse Artillery, and Her Majesty's 95th Regiment. They routed the enemy who were advancing against

Brigadier Smith's position. The men mentioned charged through the rebel camp into two batteries, capturing and bringing into their camp two of the enemy's guns under a heavy and converging fire from the Fort and Town.

Lieutenant Thomas James Young } Naval Brigade.
William Hall, A.B.

Lieutenant Young was gunnery officer on board of Her Majesty's ship *Shannon;* and William Hall was captain of the foretop of the same vessel. They marched with brave Captain Peel to Lucknow, and on the 16th of November 1857, they displayed conspicuous bravery by working under every possible disadvantage a 24-pounder gun which had been brought up to the angle of the Shah Nujjiff. This was done at imminent risk of their lives, and the service they rendered was incalculable.

Thomas Bernard Hackett,

Lieutenant, 23rd Regiment. The Cross was conferred upon him for daring gallantry at Secundra Bagh, Lucknow, on the 18th of November 1857. In company with others he rescued a corporal of the 23rd Regiment who was lying wounded and exposed to a heavy fire. Also for conspicuous bravery in having, under a heavy fire, ascended the roof and cut down the thatch of a bungalow, to prevent its being set on fire. This service was of the very highest importance at the time.

George Monger,

Private, 23rd Regiment. For daring gallantry at Secundra Bagh, Lucknow, on the 18th of November 1857, in having volunteered to accompany Lieutenant Hackett in his heroic attempt to rescue a corporal of the 23rd Regiment who was lying desperately wounded.

Stewart McPherson,

Colour Sergeant, 78th Regiment. On the 26th of September 1857, this brave man, while in the Lucknow Residency rescued at great personal risk, a wounded private of his Company who was lying in a most exposed situation. McPherson could only do this by running the gauntlet of a very heavy fire. On various other occasions the gallant soldier distinguished himself by coolness and bravery in action.

Thomas Flinn,

Drummer, 64th Regiment. For very conspicuous gallantry on the 28th of November 1857, in the charge on the enemy's guns when, although he was wounded, he engaged in a hand-to-hand encounter with two of the rebel artillerymen and slew them.

George Alexander Renny,

Captain, Bengal Horse Artillery. Lieutenant-Colonel Farquhar, commanding the 1st Belooch Regiment, reports that he was in command of the troops stationed in the Delhi Magazine, after its capture on the 16th of September 1857. Early in the forenoon of that day a most vigorous attack was made on the post by the enemy, being kept up with great violence for some time without the slightest chance of success. Under cover of a heavy cross fire from high houses on the right flank of the magazine, and from Selinghur and the Palace, the enemy advanced to the high wall of the magazine and endeavoured to set in flames a thatched roof, which, had the attempt succeeded, would have endangered the magazine. Indeed, the roof was partially set on fire but was extinguished by a sepoy of the Belooch Battalion, a soldier of the 61st Regiment having attempted in vain to do so. Almost immediately afterwards the roof was again set on fire, whereupon Renny with great coolness and gallantry mounted to the top of the wall and flung several shells with lighted fuzes over into the midst of the enemy, which caused such havoc amongst them that they were seized with panic and fled.

Patrick Roddy,

Ensign, Bengal Army. (Unattached.) This young officer greatly distinguished himself on several occasions and attracted the attention of his superior officers. The particular act for which he received the Cross was this:

On the return from Kuthirga of the Kuppur Thulla Contingent on the 27th of September 1858, he was in action when a rebel armed with a percussion cap musket kept a host at bay. Kneeling on the ground with his gun to his shoulder he threatened anyone who attempted to approach him with instant death. No one seemed bold enough to attempt to despatch the rebel until dauntless Roddy put spurs into his horse and dashed wildly at the man, who when his foe had got within six yards, fired, but missing the officer shot the horse, which immediately pitched over, entangling its rider in the stirrups. The rebel at once swooped upon him, but he had reckoned without his host. Roddy seized him, and a desperate struggle ensued, during which the officer managed to free himself from the horse and draw his sword, which he at once plunged into the fellow's body. The rebel turned out to be a subadar of the late 8th Native Infantry, and was known to be a most powerful and desperate man.

Thomas Adair Butler,

Lieutenant, 1st Bengal European Fusiliers. At the siege of Lucknow this young officer gave a practical illustration of the heroic stuff he was made of. A heavily fortified work of the enemy was playing havoc with our troops who were engaged in reducing it; and in order to encourage his men Butler swam across the river Goomtee under a storm of bullets; and climbing the parapet of the fortification there he remained in view of all, and in spite of a heavy musketry fire which seemed to render it impossible that he could live for five minutes. But he unflinchngly maintained his position as if he had been in possession of a charmed life, and the fact of his being there made it imperative that his men should exert themselves with might and main to win success, and they did win. The fortified work was captured and brave Butler lived to enjoy the honour of his well earned decoration.

Michael Murphy,

Private (Farrier), 2nd Battalion Military Train. This man was engaged with his regiment in pursuing the enemy consisting of Kooer Singh's Army from Azinghur, when he came across Lieutenant Hamilton, Adjutant, of the 3rd Sikh Cavalry, who was wounded, dismounted and surrounded by the enemy who were about to despatch him. But Farrier Murphy had to be reckoned with before they could put their intention into execution. He attacked them with such fury and courage that several men fell to his sword, and this so demoralised the others that they began to scatter. By this time Murphy was himself wounded and exhausted; but he still preserved a bold front, and would not quit the lieutenant's side. As the enemy did not care to face even a dying lion, they kept at a respectful distance, and shortly afterwards assistance arrived, and brave Murphy and the disabled officer were rescued and conveyed to a place of safety. It was a noble act of Murphy's and well deserved the reward that marked it, and gave him a place in the roll of his country's heroes. The date of the daring and brotherly deed was the 15th of April 1858.

Alexander Thompson,

Lance Corporal, 42nd Regiment. On the same date as the foregoing, Corporal Thompson, also made good his claim, to be honoured by Her Majesty. At the attack of the fort of Ruhya he volunteered to assist Captain Cafe, commanding the 4th Punjaub Rifles, bringing in the body of Lieutenant Willoughby of that corps from the top of the Glacis, where he lay in a most exposed position under a heavy fire. The service was one which was attended with imminent personal risk, and called for coolness, decisiveness and indifference to death. All these qualities Thompson possessed, and he came unscathed out of the storm of bullets which were hurled at him.

John Simpson,

Quartermaster-Sergeant, 42nd Regiment. This fine fellow also distinguished himself on the same date and the same occasion. The Fort of Ruhya was being desperately attacked, and many a brave fellow had fallen wounded and dead in his country's cause. Within forty yards of the parapet of the works lay Lieutenant Douglas dangerously wounded. Not only did it seem impossible that he could be rescued, but equally impossible that any living thing could go forth into that hell of fire and survive for a single minute. But Quartermaster-Sergeant John Simpson was another man who did not know the meaning of "impossible" and forth he went to the aid of the poor Lieutenant, whom he brought into a place of safety. And a little later noble Simpson sallied out again to rescue a private soldier who was lying desperately hurt, and with admirable coolness and courage he accomplished his self-imposed task.

James Davis,

Private, 42nd Regiment. On the same date and at the same place James Davis won his Cross. During the attack on the fort, when the fire was tremendous he went with an advanced party to point out the gate of the fort to the engineer officer. And while engaged in this duty he undertook to carry the body of Lieutenant Bramley, who had been killed at this point, to the Regiment. He performed this duty of danger and affection under the very walls of the fort.

Memorandum.

Private Edward Spence, 42nd Regiment, would have been recommended to Her Majesty for the decoration of the Victoria Cross, had he survived. But fate willed it otherwise and his heroism cost him his life. He and Lance Corporal Thompson of the Regiment volunteered at the attack of the Fort of Ruhya on the 15th of April 1858, to assist Captain Groves, commanding the 4th Punjaub Rifles, to bring in the body of Lieutenant B. Willoughby from the top of the Glacis. Spence dauntlessly placed himself in an exposed position so as to cover the party bearing away the body. And while in this position he was desperately wounded and passed away on the 17th of the same month.

Francis Edward Henry Farquharson,

Lieutenant, 42nd Regiment. On the 9th of March 1858, Lieutenant Farquharson was engaged with his regiment before Lucknow. Two guns on a bastion were pouring out a deadly and destructive fire on our troops who had gained an advanced position, which, however, was untenable while those terrible guns remained effective. So Farquharson took a portion of his company, stormed the bastion with an irresistible rush, gained the guns, spiked them, thus rendering them useless, and so enabled the position to be held. On the next morning— that is on the 10th of March—he himself was very severely wounded. He survived, however, to wear the Cross.

Private Walter Cook
Private Duncan Miller } **42nd Regiment.**

In the action at Maylah Ghaut on the 15th of January 1859, Brigadier-General Walpole, reported that the conduct of Cook and Miller deserved to be particularly pointed out. At the time the fight was severest, and the few men of the 42nd Regiment were skirmishing so close to the enemy, who were in great numbers, some of the men were wounded by sword cuts, and the only officer with the 42nd was borne to the rear severely wounded, while the colour sergeant was killed. At this momentous juncture of affairs, Cook and Miller gave evidence of the qualities that were in them, and going fearlessly to the front, they took a prominent part in directing the company, and displayed a courage, coolness and discipline which were the admiration of all who witnessed them.

William George Cubitt,

Lieutenant, 13th Bengal Native Infantry. During the retreat from Chinhut on the 30th of June 1857, this brave man exposed himself to the greatest danger, in order that he might save the lives of three men of the 32nd Regiment. This he succeeded in doing, though subjected to a tremendous fire.

Hanson Chambers Taylor Jarrett,

Lieutenant. 26th Bengal Native Infantry. At the village of Baroun on the 14th of October 1858, about seventy sepoys were defending themselves with despairing and desperate energy in a brick building. It was necessary they should be dislodged, and Jarrett made a bold try for it. The only approach to the building was up a very narrow street which was swept with bullets. Upon this street Jarrett dashed, followed by some four men only of his regiment. Making a rush at the narrow entrance of the house he pushed his way to the wall notwithstanding that a shower of bullets was hurled at him. Beating up the bayonets of the rebels with his sword, he endeavoured to get in, but was compelled at last to retire, but not before several of the enemy had fallen.

John McGovern,

Private, 1st Bengal Fusiliers. This man displayed

THE "V. C."

great gallantry during the tremendous struggle before Delhi; and on the 23rd of June 1857, when the fire from the enemy's battery was terrific, he went forth and carried into camp a wounded comrade.

Memorandum.

The Queen was graciously pleased by a warrant under Her Royal Sign Manual bearing date of the 13th of December 1858, to declare that non-military persons who as volunteers had borne arms against the mutineers both at Lucknow and elsewhere, during the operations in India, should be considered as eligible to receive the decoration of the Victoria Cross, subject to the rules and ordinances already made and ordained for the government thereof. Provided that it was established in any case that the person was serving under the orders of a general officer, or other officer in command of troops in the field when he performed the act of bravery for which the decoration was to be conferred. In accordance with this warrant Her Majesty was therefore pleased to signify her intentions to confer the high distinction on the undermentioned gentlemen:

Mr. Thomas Henry Kavanagh,

Assistant-Commissioner in Oude. On the 8th of November 1857, Mr. Kavanagh was serving under the orders of Lieutenant-General Sir James Outram in Lucknow, when he volunteered for the dangerous duty of proceeding through the city to the camp of the Commander-in-chief for the purpose of guiding the relieving force to the beleaguered garrison in the Residency. This task he performed with chivalrous gallantry and devotion, and thereby rendered the most eminent service to his distressed country people, who were suffering so cruelly in the Residency where they had been shut up by the rebels.

Mr. Ross Lowis Mangles,

of the Bengal Civil Service, Assistant Magistrate at Patna. Mr. Mangles volunteered for and served with the force consisting of detachments of Her Majesty's 10th and 37th Regiments and some native troops, despatched to the relief of Arrah in July 1857, under the command of Captain Dunbar of the 10th Regiment. The force unfortunately fell into an ambuscade on the night of the 29th of July 1857, and during the retreat on the next morning Mr. Mangles with signal gallantry and the most generous self-devotion, and notwithstanding that he himself had previously been wounded, carried for several miles out of action a wounded soldier of Her Majesty's 37th Regiment, after binding up his wounds under a murderous fire, which killed or wounded almost the whole of the detachment. Mr. Mangles, however, persevered with his task and bore his wounded companion in safety to the boats.

Charles John Stanley Gough,

Major, 5th Bengal European Cavalry. This gallant

officer performed many acts of the most conspicuous bravery, each one of which was sufficient to earn him the decoration. The first was in an affair at Khurdowdah near Rhotuck on the 15th of August 1857, in which he saved his brother who was wounded, and killed two of the enemy.

The second act was on the 18th of August— three days later—when he led a troop of the Guide Cavalry in a charge and cut down two of the enemy's sowars, with one of whom he had a desperate hand-to-hand encounter.

Thirdly on the 27th of January 1858, at Ghunshabad, during a charge he attacked one of the enemy's leaders and pierced him with his sword, which was carried out of his hand in the melée. He then defended himself with his revolver and shot two of the enemy.

Fourthly, on the 23rd of February of the same year at Meangunge, he went to the assistance of Brevet-Major O. H. St. George Anson and killed his opponent, inmediately after cutting down another of the enemy in the same gallant manner.

Robert Haydon Shebbeare,

Brevet-Captain, 60th Bengal Native Infantry. This officer distinguished himself very greatly at the head of the Guides with the 4th Column of assault at Delhi on the 14th of September 1857. When after twice charging beneath the wall or loopholed Serai it was found impossible owing to the murderous fire, to attain the breach, Captain (then a Lieutenant)

Shebbeare endeavoured to reorganise the men, but one third of the Europeans having fallen, his efforts to do so failed. He then conducted the rear-guard of the retreat across the canal most successfully. He was most miraculously preserved through the affair but he left the field with one bullet through his cheek and a bad scalp wound at the back of his head, caused by another bullet striking him.

Herbert Mackworth Clogstoun,

Captain, 19th Madras Native Infantry. This officer was decorated for conspicuous bravery displayed in charging the rebels into Chichunbah with only eight men of his Regiment (the 2nd Cavalry Hyderabad Contingent) and compelling them to re-enter the town, and finally to abandon their plunder. He was severely wounded himself and lost seven men out of the eight who accompanied him.

Harry Hammon Lyster,

Lieutenant, 72nd Bengal Native Infantry. Lieutenant Lyster charged and broke singly a skirmishing square of the retreating rebel army from Calpee, killing several sepoys in the conflict. This act of daring was witnessed by Major-General Sir Hugh Henry Rose, G.C.B. and Lieutenant Colonel Gall, C.B. of the 14th Light Dragoons.

Harry North Dalrymple Prendergast,

Lieutenant, Madras Engineers. On the 21st of November 1857, this brave and devoted officer saved the life of Lieutenant G. Dew 14th Light Dragoons at Mundisore. He attempted to cut down a Velaitee who covered Dew with his musket from only a few paces to the rear. Lieutenant Prendergast nearly lost his own life by the man's fire and was wounded; and he would in all probability have been cut down himself had not Major Orr who was near, killed the rebel.

Prendergast also greatly distinguished himself at Rahgurh and Betwa, where he was severely wounded. Major-General Sir Hugh Rose in forwarding his recommendation of this officer for the Cross said:

"Lieutenant Prendergast, Madras Engineers, was "specially mentioned by Brigadier, now Sir Charles "Stuart, for the gallant act at Mundisore, where "he was severely wounded. Secondly, he was "specially mentioned by me when acting voluntarily "as my aide-de-camp in the action, before besieging "Ratgurh on the Beena river, for gallant conduct. "His horse was killed on the occasion. Thirdly, at "the action of the 'Betwa' he again voluntarily "acted as my aide-de-camp and distinguished him-"self by his bravery in the charge which I made "with Captain Need's troop, Her Majesty's 14th "Light Dragoons, against the left of the so-called "Peishwa's Army under Tantia Topee. He was "severely wounded on that occasion also."

Frederick Whirlpool,

Private, 3rd Bombay European Regiment. On the 3rd of April 1858, he gallantly volunteered during the attack on Jhansi to return and carry away several killed and wounded, which service he performed twice under a heavy fire from the wall. At the Assault of Lohari on the 2nd of May 1858, he displayed devoted bravery by rushing to the rescue of Lieutenant Doune of the same regiment, who was dangerously wounded. In this service Private Whirlpool received no fewer than seventeen desperate wounds, and one of them nearly severed his head from his body. The gallant example shown by this brave man is considered to have greatly contributed to the success of the day.

Memorandum.

Ensign Everard Aloysius Lisle Phillips of the Regiment of Bengal Native Infantry would have been recommended for the Victoria Cross had he survived, for many gallant deeds which he performed during the Siege of Delhi, in the course of which he was wounded three times. At the assault of that city he captured the Water Bastion with a small party of men, and was finally killed in the streets of Delhi on the 18th of September.

Henry Edward Jerome,

Captain, 86th Regiment. On the 3rd of April 1858, he displayed conspicuous gallantry at Jhansi in having, with the assistance of Private Byrne, removed under a very heavy fire, Lieutenant Sewell of the same regiment, and who was lying severely wounded at a very exposed point of attack upon the fort. He further distinguished himself for very gallant conduct at the capture of the Fort of Chandairee, the storming of Jhansi, and in action with a superior rebel force on the Jumna, on the 28th of May, when he was severely wounded.

Aylmer Spicer Cameron,

Lieutenant, 72nd Regiment. This officer was decorated because on the 30th of March 1858, at Kotah he headed a small party of men, and attacked a large body of armed fanatic rebels who were strongly posted in a loopholed house, with one narrow entrance. Lieutenant Cameron stormed the house and killed three rebels in single combat. He was severely wounded, losing half of one hand by a tremendous cut from a tulwar.

Michael Sleavon,

Corporal, Royal Engineers. This man showed the most indomitable pluck during the attack on the fort of Jhansi, on the 3rd of April 1858. He maintained his position at the head of a sap in spite of all attempts to dislodge him, and he continued to work under a heavy fire with a cool and steady determination worthy of the highest praise, and which served to greatly encourage and inspire his comrades.

Joseph Brennan,

Bombardier, Royal Artillery. This brave soldier also won his Cross at Jhansi. He was instrumental in bringing up two guns of the Hyderabad Contingent manned by Natives. Under a heavy fire from the walls he laid the guns so accurately and blazed away with such persistency that he drove the enemy from a battery with which they had been doing terrible execution.

George Richardson,

Private, 34th Regiment. At Kewanie, Trans-Gogra, on the 27th of April 1859, this man was severely wounded, having one arm disabled. But notwithstanding this he closed with and secured a rebel sepoy who was armed with a loaded revolver and was about to fire at the troops.

Bernard McQuirt,

Private, 95th Regiment. On the 6th of January 1858, at the capture of the entrenched town of Rowa, this man showed great determination and spirit. In a hand-to-hand fight with three men, of whom he killed one and wounded another, he was terribly wounded. He received no less than five sabre cuts, and a bullet wound.

James Byrne,

Private, 86th Regiment. During the attack on the fort of Jhansi, on the 3rd of April 1858, Byrne carried Lieutenant Sewell, who was lying desperately wounded in a most exposed position, to a place of safety, with the assistance of Captain Jerome. In the performance of his act of devotion Byrne received a severe sword cut.

THE "V. C."

George Rodgers,

Private, 71st Regiment. Decorated for daring conduct at Marar Gwalior on the 16th of June 1858, in attacking alone a party of seven rebels, one of whom he killed. This was considered a valuable and remarkable service, as the rebels were well armed and strongly posted in the line of advance of a detachment of the 71st Regiment.

Samuel Hill Lawrence,

Lieutenant, 32nd Regiment. This officer performed many acts of devotion and courage. Notably on the 7th July 1851, during a sortie of the Lucknow Garrison. The object of the sortie was to examine a house strongly held by the enemy, and to try and find out if a mine was being driven from it. Major Wilson, Deputy-Assistant-Adjutant-General of the Lucknow Garrison, states that he saw the attack, and was an eye-witness to the great personal gallantry of Major Lawrence on the occasion, he being the first person to mount the ladder and enter the window of the house; in effecting this entrance he had his pistol knocked out of his hand by one of the enemy. Again on the 26th of September 1857, he made another sortie, during which he charged with two of his men in advance of his company, and captured a 9-pounder gun.

William Oxenham,

Corporal, 32nd Regiment, was awarded the Cross for distinguished service in perilling his own life to save the life of Mr. Cappar of the Bengal Civil Service, who was buried in the ruins of a verandah that had fallen upon him. From this position Corporal Oxenham rescued him. He was upwards of ten minutes engaged in the work, and during the whole of the time exposed to a heavy fire.

William Dowling,

Private, 32nd Regiment, distinguished himself on the 4th of July 1857, by going out with two other men, who were both killed, and spiking two of the enemy's guns. He had an encounter with one of the enemy, a Soubadar, but killed him.

On the 9th of the same month he again went out with three men, who were all killed, to spike a gun; but as the spike was too short he had to retire, and did so under a heavy fire.

On the 27th of September 1857, he spiked an 18-pounder during a sortie, he being under an exceedingly heavy fire from the enemy.

Alfred Spencer Heathcote,

Lieutenant, 60th Rifles. This officer was engaged on active service throughout the memorable siege of Delhi, and during the fateful four months, when our hold on India trembled in the balance, and brave men were pouring out their blood like water for the love of the flag they served, Lieutenant Heathcote showed that he had all the noble instincts of the true soldier, and the devoted and unselfish courage which distinguishes the hero. The

Siege occupied from June to September 1857, and not a day passed but what the handful of British troops engaged gave some evidence that the old fighting spirit of their race was as strong in them as it had been in their ancestors. Delhi was one of the most powerful strongholds in India. It was a huge city protected by a fortified wall which entirely engirted it. Entrance to the city was by numerous gates, but each of these gateways had been turned into a formidable battery. In this stronghold the rebels had shut themselves up with the civilian population; they numbered hundreds of thousands. A very large proportion were trained soldiers, who had been taught the use of arms in our own schools. That they were brave could not be gainsaid; and now being driven to bay they fought with the desperation of maddening despair, for they knew that this was the last stand they could make. If the hated Fernighees could not be beaten now they never would be beaten, and the mighty rebellion would not only be crushed but those who had promoted it and taken a prominent part would suffer an ignominious death. Consequently that huge army, assisted by a reckless and lawless population, who believed that for them a new era of boundless wealth had dawned, fought as they had never fought before. They had huge stores of ammunition, and a formidable array of heavy guns mounted on the crenulated walls, and from these guns they belched forth fire and destruction, but the thin ranks of the British, who though a mere handful as compared with the rebels, clung to their hold with bulldog tenacity, and neither fire, sallies, disease, suffering, danger nor slaughter could shake them off. It is necessary that these things should be remembered in reading of the Siege of Delhi for it serves to bring into greater prominence individual acts of heroism, and to strengthen our feeling of pride in our brave countrymen, who could not be daunted, and while ready to die, understood not the meaning of the word defeat. Seldom, indeed, in the history of our wars have our troops been called upon to face such fearful odds as were the soldiers of Queen Victoria when they invested Delhi. Ill-provided with the necessary siege trains and implements of war it seemed at first as if it was a forlorn hope, and the city of the Moguls might yet give a new race of rulers to India. But if anyone had that feeling it was never allowed to show itself, and the troops of Great Britain behaved as became their glorious traditions. They knew that in their far away homes where the summer sun shone on smiling and peaceful landscapes, and the busy whirl of industrial life was resounding from end to end of the kingdom, anxious eyes were strained in watching their movements and loving hearts were palpitating with yearning for the absent ones; therefore it behoved those upon whom the honour of their country rested to yield no point, and give no advantage to the pitiless enemy who had already deluged India's fair strand with the blood of white men, women and children; and up from the bloodstained soil arose a dumb but eloquent cry for vengeance on those who had shown no quarter and declined to spare even the babe at its mother's breast. It was this which nerved the arms of weary soldiers fainting under the sweltering sun, and gave them energy to persevere against the frightful odds. Lieutenant Heathcote proved a host in himself. Although severely wounded he would not give in. He was an officer wearing Her Majesty's uniform, and he knew how necessary it was that the officers should set examples of deeds of derring-do, which would fire their men with the spirit of emulation. When at last after weeks and weeks of awful suffering and magnificent endurance our soldiers battered in the gates of the rebel city and swarmed into the streets which were swept with a hellish fire of shot and shell, while from every window, every house-top, every loopoole, the furious natives poured forth a pitiless hail of musket bullets, Heathcote was in spite of his wounds still to the front, and he volunteered for services of the extremest danger and difficulty. So splendid was his daring, so conspicuous his soldierly qualities, that the officers of his own regiment selected him as a most fitting recipient for the Victoria Cross, knowing that in honouring him they honoured themselves.

James Champion,

Troop Sergeant-Major, 8th Hussars. This brave man won his Cross at Beejapore on the 8th of September 1857, during which he was wounded, and when both the officers attached to the troop were wounded. At the commencement of the action he received a bullet in his body, but this did not daunt him. He bore up unflinchingly, and joined his comrades in pursuit of the rebels, several of whom he shot with his revolver. He was also commended for distinguished conduct at Gwalior.

George Waller,

Colour Sergeant, 60th Rifles, 1st Battalion. The Cross was awarded to Waller for splendid behaviour at Delhi on the 14th of September 1857. He charged and captured the enemy's guns near the Cabul Gate, thus rendering incalculable service to the investing troops engaged in the assault. Again, on the 18th of September, he particularly distinguished himself by repulsing a sudden attack made by the enemy on a gun near the Chaudney Chouk. He was elected for the honour of decoration by the non-commissioned officers of his regiment.

Stephen Garvin,

Colour Sergeant, 60th Rifles, 1st Battalion. This man was also one of the many heroes of Delhi, and on the 23rd of June in the most memorable year he exhibited most gallant and daring conduct. In a place known as the "Sammy House" a body of the enemy's troops had taken up a position there, and harassed our men terribly. Volunteers were called for to dislodge these scorpions. It was recognised as desperate service, and that the hope of living through it was small indeed. But forth stepped Colour Sergeant Garvin and volunteered to turn the foe out of the Sammy House. Selecting a small party of men as brave as himself he started on his desperate errand. Possibly the enemy feeling secure in the shelter of his improvised fort laughed at what might have seemed to him a feeble effort; but soon his laugh must have changed, for Garvin and his comrades, though so few, were dauntless, and so full of heroic pluck that neither fire nor sword could keep them in check. On they went in the face of fearful odds; they rushed the Sammy House, they fell upon the defenders with the fury of bayed lions, and such as lived to tell the tale, fled from the terrible Feringhees, leaving everything behind them. In this little affair Garvin's individualism was strikingly conspicuous, and his comrades were inspired to feats of arms, that probably they had never dreamed of even in their wildest imaginings. It was deeds of this kind which created such a wonderful impression on the native soldiers, who said "These British are only a handful and yet every man is himself equal to a battalion." Throughout the whole of the siege operations Garvin distinguished himself and rendered magnificent service.

William Sutton,

Bugler, 60th Rifles, 1st Battalion. This was another of the Delhi heroes. The great assault was delivered on the 14th of September, and the city fell into our hands once more. The night previous Bugler Sutton volunteered to perform a most important, but desperate duty, from which any man not cast in heroic mould would have shrunk. He undertook to reconnoitre the breach where, when the bugles sounded at the break of day, our regiments were to be hurled. He carried out his self-imposed task with the greatest success and was enabled to carry back to his superior officers the most valuable information. All through the prolonged siege Sutton distinguished himself, and on the 2nd of August, when the enemy attacked the British trenches in force, Sutton rushed from his cover, and fell upon a native bugler who was in the very act of sounding the advance to his comrades. But the advance was never given, for Bugler Sutton smote the bugler rebel dead, and those who were following were demoralised and disordered, and ultimately driven back with tremendous loss. The privates of Sutton's Regiment, with the unselfishness of brave men recognised that in their bugler they possessed a hero of the true metal, and that he was well worthy of upholding the honour and dignity of their colours; therefore they selected him to be the recipient of the Cross.

John Divane,

Private, 60th Rifles, 1st Battalion. It will be seen that the 60th Rifles were rich in heroes during the fierce days of the rebellion. Private Divane distinguished himself on the 10th of September 1857, four days before the assault. One of the trenches occupied by the rebels had to be rushed, and Divane headed a charge made by the Beelooche and Seikh troops. He leapt out of the shelter of his own trench, cheered the men on, and as the soldiers swept like a whirlwind into the enemy's defences, Divane was shot down from the breastwork. He survived, however, to recount the story of how the trench was won, and to wear the cross of honour which would bear evidence to his children's children, how great his valour had been.

James Thompson,

Private, 60th Rifles, 1st Battalion. That first Battalion of the 60th Rifles must indeed have been a grand one, and the men might justifiably have been proud of each other. It was on the 9th of July 1857, that Captain Wilton of the same Regiment was in mortal peril for he was surrounded by a party of fanatical Ghazees who had rushed upon him from a serai. His life did not seem to be worth the value of a hair, notwithstanding that he defended himself desperately. But Private Thompson had his eye on those Ghazees as they were to learn to their cost. Sword in hand he went for them and two fell dead at his first rush. The others were thrown into confusion by this unexpected turn, for they had felt sure of their prey, but learnt now that they had reckoned without their host, and deeming discretion the better part of valour, they fled, and thus through the unselfish devotion of Private Thompson, Captain Wilton's life was saved. All through the siege, as did others of his regiment, Thompson distinguished himself, and was severely wounded. The privates of his corps elected him to bear the honour of the decoration.

Samuel Turner,

Private, 60th Rifles, 1st Battalion. The 60th Rifles as they read the record of their noble deeds must verily experience a thrill of exquisite pleasure, for the regiment rendered Trojan service during the dark period of the Mutiny. Private Turner was at Delhi on the 19th of June 1857, when the enemy in force attacked the rear of the British camp. The conflict was terrific, the camp for the moment was thrown into confusion. The enemy fought with savage fury, and not content with slaying, he mutilated too; hacking the dead to pieces, and subjecting the bodies of officers particularly to the most barbarous indignities. During the fight Lieutenant Humphreys of the Indian Service fell mortally wounded. He was seen to fall by Private Turner, who rushed to his aid in the face of a withering fire, and raising the dying officer on to his shoulders he bore him off fighting every inch of his way, and receiving a severe sabre wound during his splendid exploit. The poor officer's life was not preserved by this act of devotion, but his corpse was saved from mutilation. The next day the mangled remains of many officers and men were recovered, and the way in which they had been treated was ample evidence of the barbaric savagery of the rebel troops.

John Kirk,

Private, 10th Regiment. This man was at Benares,

on the 4th of June 1857, on the first outbreak into mutiny of the native troops stationed in that city. When the outbreak, of which there had been but little warning, declared itself, Captain Brown, the pension paymaster, together with his family, found himself shut up in his house which was surrounded by the rebels clamouring and howling for the life of himself and those he loved. Private Kirk, with two non-commissioned officers volunteered for the desperate service of rescuing the unfortunate captain and his family, and so well did he carry out his task, although his life trembled in the balance, that Brown and the rest were brought to a place of safety.

Mr. William Fraser McDonell,

of the Bengal Civil Service, Magistrate of Sarun. Although Mr. McDonell was a civilian he was entitled to receive the cross for gallant service in accordance with Her Majesty's Sign Manual of the 13th of December 1858. It was on the 30th of July 1857, that Mr. McDonell distinguished himself. The British troops were retreating from Arrah. He and thirty-five British soldiers were in a boat where they had taken refuge. The rudder of the boat, however, was securely lashed to the side and while it so remained the boat was useless, although it afforded shelter for the time, but being exposed to an incessant and pitiless fire it was obvious to the meanest intelligence that it must soon be wrecked, when every life would be sacrificed. For any one to show his face above the gunwale was to court almost certain death. But the situation was terrible and desperate. McDonell grasped the position, however, and felt that it was better for one man to die than for thirty-five, even though they were soldiers, and it was a soldier's duty to meet death with heroic fortitude. Having come to this determination the brave civilian armed himself with a knife; climbed outside of the boat, and though he became at once a target for a hail of bullets, he cut the lashing, and thus released the boat, with the result that she at once became manageable, and was steered to a place of safety with her precious freight of human lives. For this noble act of self-devotion Mr. McDonell was duly decorated with the distinguishing honour.

William Martin Cafe,

Captain, 56th Bengal Native Infantry. This gallant officer was in the action at the Fort of Ruhya when with the assistance of Privates Thompson, Crowie, Spence and Cook, he bore away under a very heavy fire the body of Lieutenant Willoughby which was lying in the ditch near the fort. In the performance of this service Private Spence was severely wounded and would have been killed, but his heroic Captain rushed to his rescue and saved him. The date of the deed was the 15th of April 1858.

Francis David Millet Brown,

Lieutenant. This officer gained the cross for great

gallantry at Narrioue on the 16th of November 1857. At the imminent risk of his own life, and in the teeth of great difficulty he rushed to the assistance of a wounded soldier of the 1st European Bengal Fusiliers, whom he bore on his shoulders under a heavy and galling fire from the enemy, whose cavalry were only forty or fifty yards away. It was a splendid act of unselfish courage and noble devotion to a helpless comrade, and well merited the distinction with which it was marked.

Denis Dempsey,

Private, 10th Regiment, 1st Battalion. This brave Irishman performed valorous service on the 12th of August 1857, and again on the 14th of March 1858, while during the period between the two dates he nobly did his duty as a fearless and loyal soldier. On the 12th of August of the red letter year, Dempsey was the first man to enter the village of Jugdispore under a withering fire. His fearlessness set a splendid example, and inspirited the waverers, who rushed forward and drove the rebels out. In July of the same year Dempsey had already given evidence of his qualities, for during the retreat from Arrah he helped to carry Ensign Erskine of the 10th Regiment, the poor young fellow having been severely wounded.

On the 14th of March in the following year Dempsey was at Lucknow, when with extraordinary coolness and gallantry he carried a powder bag through a burning village for the purpose of mining a passage in the rear of the enemy's position. He performed this act while exposed to a very heavy fire from the enemy who was sheltered behind loopholed walls; and also while he and his dangerous burden were exposed to a rain of sparks which fell in all directions from the blazing houses. Had his bag of powder caught fire—and it was in imminent danger of doing so—Dempsey would have been blown to atoms. But he betrayed no fear. He moved as if he believed he bore a charmed life, and he not only escaped but he most satisfactorily carried out the duty assigned him.

Mr. George Bell Chicken,

of the Indian Naval Brigade, displayed great gallantry on the 27th of September 1858, at a place called Suhejnee near Peroo. He charged into the middle of a considerable body of the rebels who were preparing to rally and open fire upon the scattered pursuers. Had they done this there is no doubt the tables would have been turned, and the pursuers, would have become the pursued, while many a gallant life would have been sacrificed. But Mr. Chicken was there, and he saw the necessity of doing something. There was not a moment to be lost. Hesitation would have been fatal, and so without any regard for his own safety he bore down upon the enemy, who was surrounded on all sides but fighting with desperate energy. No fewer than five of then were killed by Chicken when he himself was cut down, and would have been hacked

"HE CHARGED INTO THE MIDDLE OF A CONSIDERABLE BODY OF THE REBELS."
[*page* 134.

to pieces, had not some of the men of the 1st Bengal Police and the 3rd Seikh Irregular Cavalry dashed into the crowd to his rescue. This threw the enemy into such confusion that they were completely routed and many of them were killed or wounded.

James Pearson,

Private, No. 1882, 86th Regiment. At the storming of Jhansi on the 3rd of April 1858, Pearson rendered yeoman service. He gallantly attacked a number of armed rebels, one of whom he killed, and bayonetted two others. In this scrimmage he was himself wounded. He also brought in at Calpee under a heavy fire, Private Michael Burns who had been terribly wounded. This act of devotion only prolonged Burns' life for a time as he died of his wounds, but his deathbed was smoothed and his anguish relieved as far as human skill could do it.

H. Hartigan,

Pensioned-Sergeant, 9th Lancers. This man was awarded the Cross for daring and distinguished gallantry in the following instances. At the Battle of Budle-Ke-Serai, near Delhi, on the 8th of June 1857, he went to the assistance of Sergeant H. Nelstone, who was wounded, dismounted and surrounded by the enemy. At the peril of his own life Hartigan picked up the wounded Sergeant and fighting his way through the rebels he bore the wounded man to a place of safety.

Again on the 10th of October of the same year at Agra.

he ran unarmed to the assistance of Sergeant Crews who was attacked by four rebels. Hartigan snatched a tulwar from one of them with his right hand, and with his left hand he gave him one on the mouth, straight from the shoulder, which sent the fellow reeling to the earth. Then with the tulwar he laid about him with such vigour that he killed one of the others and wounded two, but was himself disabled from further service by severe and dangerous wounds. But his plucky conduct brought its reward, and he had the satisfaction of knowing that his name would be duly enrolled on the list of his country's heroes.

Robert Grant,

Sergeant, 1st Battalion, 5th Regiment. For conspicuous devotion at Alumbagh on the 24th of September 1857, this brave man was awarded the Cross. He proceeded under a heavy and galling fire to save the life of Private E. Deveney, whose leg had been shot away; and eventually he succeeded with the assistance of Lieutenant Brown, who was killed, and some comrades in carrying the poor fellow to a place of safety.

Patrick McHale,

Private, 1st Battalion 5th Regiment, gained the Cross for conspicuous bravery at Lucknow on the 2nd of October 1857, when he was the first man at the capture of one of the guns at the Cawnpore Battery. Again on the 22nd of December 1857,

by a bold rush, he was the first to take possession
of one of the enemy's guns, which had sent several
rounds of grape through his company, which was
skirmishing up to it.

"On every occasion of attack"—so runs the
despatch—"Private McHale has been the first to
meet the foe, amongst whom he caused such consternation by the boldness of his rush, as to leave
little work for those who followed to his support.
By his habitual coolness and daring, and sustained
bravery in action, his name has become a household
word for gallantry amongst his comrades." This is
high praise indeed, but there is no doubt brave Mc-
Hale fully deserved it and Her Majesty never decorated a better soldier.

John Augustus Wood,

Captain, 20th Bombay Native Infantry. During the
war in Persia, Captain Wood was engaged on
active service, and led the Grenadier Company which
formed the head of the assaulting column sent against
Bushire. He was the first man on the parapet of
the Fort, where he was instantly attacked by a
large number of the garrison who suddenly sprang
upon him from a trench which had been artfully
cut in the parapet itself.

These men fired a volley at Captain Wood and
at the head of the storming party, when only a
yard or two distant from that officer; but though
Captain Wood was struck by no less than seven
musket balls, he at once threw himself upon the

enemy, passed his sword through the body of their leader, and being closely followed by the men of his company speedily overcame all opposition and established himself in the place. Captain Wood's energy and determined valour undoubtedly contributed in a high degree to the success of the attack. His wounds compelled him to leave the force for a time; but with the true spirit of a good soldier he rejoined his regiment, and returned to his duties at Bushire, before his wounds were properly healed. The date of the act of bravery which won him the Cross was the 9th of December 1856.

Lieutenant and Adjutant Arthur Thomas Moore } **3rd Bombay**
and } **Light**
Lieutenant John Grant Malcolmson } **Cavalry.**

These officers also served in Persia, and on the occasion of an attack on the enemy on the 8th of February 1857, led by Lieutenant-Col. Forbes C.B., Lieutenant Moore, who was the Adjutant of the Regiment, was perhaps the first of all by a horse's length. His horse leaped into the Square and instantly fell dead, crushing down his rider and breaking his sword as he fell amid the disordered ranks of the enemy. Moore speedily extricated himself by a supreme effort, and attempted with his broken sword to force his way through the soldiers who were surrounding him. In this attempt he would to a certainty have lost his life, had not his comrade, young Malcolmson, observed his peril, and rushed to his rescue, fighting for every inch of ground.

He then gave him his stirrups, and carried him through the astonished and howling foe out of his perilous position.

The thoughtfulness for others, cool determination, devoted courage, and ready activity shown in extreme danger by Lieutenant Malcolmson were most extraordinary, and attracted the attention of all with whom he came in contact.

James Travers,

Colonel, Late 2nd Bengal Native Infantry. For a daring act of bravery, in July, 1857, when the Indore Presidency was suddenly attacked by Holcar's troops, in having charged the guns with only five men to support him, and driven the gunners from the guns, thereby creating a favourable diversion, which saved the lives of many persons, fugitives to the Residency.

It is stated that officers who were present considered that the effect of the charge was to enable many Europeans to escape from actual slaughter, and time was gained which enabled the faithful Bhopal Artillery to man their guns. Colonel Travers' horse was shot in three places, and his accoutrements were shot through in various parts. He commanded the Bhopal Levy.

Samuel James Browne C.B.,

Lieutenant-Colonel, 46th Bengal Native Infantry. For having at Seerporah, in an engagement with the rebel forces under Khan, on the 31st of August 1858, whilst advancing upon the enemy's position at daybreak, pushed on with one orderly sowar upon a nine-pounder gun that was commanding one of the approaches to the enemy's position, and attacked the gunners, thereby preventing them from re-loading, and firing upon the infantry, who were advancing to the attack. In doing this, a personal conflict ensued, in which Captain, now Lieutenant-Colonel, Samuel James Browne, commandant of the 2nd Punjaub cavalry, received a severe sword-cut wound on the left knee, and shortly afterwards another sword-cut wound, which severed the left arm at the shoulder, not, however, before Lieutenant-Colonel Browne had succeeded in cutting down one of his assailants. The gun was prevented from being re-loaded, and was eventually captured by the infantry, and the gunner slain.

Herbert Taylor Reade,

Surgeon, 61st Regiment. During the siege of Delhi, on the 14th of September 1857, while Surgeon Reade was attending to the wounded, at the end of one of the streets of the city, a party of rebels advanced from the direction of the Bank, and having established themselves in the houses in the street, commenced firing from the roofs. The wounded were thus in very great danger, and would have fallen into the hands of the enemy, had not Surgeon Reade drawn his sword, and calling upon the few soldiers who were near to follow, succeeded, under a very heavy fire, in dislodging the rebels from their position.

Surgeon Reade's party consisted of about ten in

all, of whom two were killed, and five or six wounded.

Surgeon Reade also accompanied the regiment at the assault of Delhi, and, on the morning of the 16th of September 1857, was one of the first up at the breach in the magazine, which was stormed by the 61st Regiment and Belooch Battalion, upon which occasion he, with a sergeant of the 61st Regiment, spiked one of the enemy's guns.

NEW ZEALAND.

John Lucas,

Colour-Sergeant, 40th Regiment. On the 18th of March 1861, Colour-Sergeant Lucas acted as Sergeant of a party of the 40th Regiment, employed as skirmishers to the right of No. 7 Redoubt, and close to the Huirangi Bush, facing the left of the positions occupied by the natives. At about 4 o'clock p.m. a very heavy and well-directed fire was suddenly opened upon them from the bush, and the high ground on the left. Three men being wounded simultaneously, two of them mortally, assistance was called for in order to have them carried to the rear: a file was immediately sent, but had scarcely arrived, when one of them fell, and Lieutenant Rees was wounded at the same time. Colour-Sergeant Lucas, under a very heavy fire from the rebels, who were not more than thirty yards distant, immediately ran up to the assistance of this officer, and sent one man with him to the rear. He then took charge of the arms belonging to the killed and wounded men, and maintained his position until the arrival of supports under Lieutenants Gibson and Whelan.

Robert Montresor Rogers,
Lieutenant, 44th Regiment.

John M'Dougall,
Private, No. 220, 44th Regiment.

Edmund Henry Lenon,
Lieutenant, 67th Regiment. For distinguished gallantry in swimming the Ditches, and entering the North Taku Fort by an embrasure during the assault. They were the first of the English established on the walls of the Fort which they entered in the order in which their names are here recorded, each one being assisted by the others to mount the embrasure.

Nathaniel Burslem,
Lieutenant, 67th Regiment.

Thomas Lane,
Private, No. 612, 67th Regiment. For distinguished gallantry in swimming the Ditches of the North Taku Fort, and persevering in attempting during the assault, and before the entrance of the Fort had been effected by anyone, to enlarge an opening in the wall, through which they eventually entered, and, in doing so, were both severely wounded.

John Worthy Chaplin,
Ensign, 67th Regiment. For distinguished gallantry

at the North Taku Fort. This officer was carrying the Queen's Colour of the Regiment, and first planted the colours on the breach made by the storming party, assisted by Private Lane, of the 67th Regiment, and subsequently on the cavalier of the Fort, which he was first to mount. In doing this, he was severely wounded.

Arthur Fitzgibbon,

Hospital Apprentice, Indian Medical Establishment. For having behaved with great coolness and courage at the capture of the North Taku Fort, on the 21st of August 1860. On the morning of that day he accompanied a wing of the 67th Regiment, when it took up a position within 500 yards of the Fort. Having quitted cover, he proceeded, under a very heavy fire, to attend to a dooly-bearer, whose wound he had been directed to bind up; and, while the regiment was advancing under the enemy's fire, he ran across the open to attend to another wounded man, in doing which he was himself severely wounded.

Richard Harte Keatinge,

Major, Bombay Artillery. For having rendered most efficient aid at the assault of Chundairee, in voluntarily leading the column through the breach, which was protected by a heavy cross fire. He was one of the foremost to enter, and was severely wounded in the breach. The column was saved from a serious loss that would probably have resulted, but for Major Keatinge's knowledge of the small path leading across the ditch, which had been examined during the night by himself and a servant who declined, when required, to lead the column, without his master. Having cleared the breach, he led into the Fort, where he was struck down by another dangerous wound. The Commander-in-Chief in India states that the success at Chundairee was mainly owing to this officer, whose gallantry, really brilliant, he considers was equalled by his ability and devotion.

Major Keatinge was at the time a Political Officer with the 2nd Brigade of the Central India Field Force.

James Blair,

Captain, 2nd Bombay Light Cavalry. For having on two occasions distinguished himself by his gallant and daring conduct. First, on the night of the 12th of August 1857, at Neemuch, in volunteering to apprehend seven or eight armed mutineers who had shut themselves up for defence in a house, the door of which he burst open. He then rushed in among them, and forced them to escape through the roof; in this encounter, he was severely wounded. In spite of his wounds he pursued the fugitives, but was unable to come up with them, in consequence of the darkness of the night.

Second, on the 23rd of October 1857, at Teerum, in fighting his way most gallantly through a body of rebels who had literally surrounded him. After breaking the end of his sword on one of their heads, and receiving a severe sword cut on his right arm, he rejoined his troop. In this wounded condition, and with no other weapon than the hilt of his broken sword he put himself at the head of his men, charged the rebels most effectually, and dispersed them.

Charles George Baker,

Lieutenant, Bengal Police Battalion. For gallant conduct on the occasion of an attack on the rebels at Suhejnee, near Peroo, on the 27th of September 1858, which is thus described in this officer's own words. "The enemy" (at the time supposed to have mustered from 900 to 1000 strong in infantry, with 50 cavalry,) "advanced. Without exchanging a shot, "I at once retired slowly, followed up steadily by "the rebel line for 100 yards clear of the tillage or "jungle, when, suddenly wheeling about my divisions "into line, with a hearty cheer we charged into and "through the centre of the enemy's line, Lieutenant "Broughton, with his detachment, immediately "following up the movement with excellent effect, "from his position upon the enemy's left. The rebel "right wing of about 300 men, broke at once, but "the centre and left, observing the great labour of "the horses in crossing the heavy ground, stood, "and receiving the charge with repeated volleys, "were cut down, or broke only a few yards ahead "of the cavalry. From this moment, the pursuit "was limited to the strongest and best horses of "the force numbering some 60 of all ranks, who, "dashing into and swimming a deep and wide nul- "lah, followed the flying enemy through the village of Russowkee, and its sugar-cane khêts, over two

"miles of swamp, and 500 yards into the thick
"jungles near Peroo, when, both men and horses
"being completely exhausted, I sounded the halt
"and assembly, and collecting my wounded, returned
"to camp at Munjhaen about 6 p.m." The charge
ended in the utter defeat of the enemy, and is
referred to by Lord Clyde as deserving of the
highest enconium, on account both of conception
and execution. It is also described as having been
as gallant as any during the war.

William Francis Frederick Waller,

Lieutenant, 25th Bombay Light Infantry. For great
gallantry at the capture by storm of the fortress of
Gwalior, on the 20th of June 1858. He and Lieutenant Rose, who was killed, were the only Europeans
present, and, with a mere handful of men, they
attacked the fortress, climbed on the roof of a
house, shot the gunners opposed to them, carried
all before them and took the fort, killing every
man in it.

John Charles Campbell Daunt,

Lieutenant, 11th Bengal Native Infantry. Lieutenant
Daunt and Sergeant Dyson were recommended for
conspicuous gallantry in action on the 2nd of October
1857, with the mutineers of the Ramgurh Battalion
at Chota Behar, in capturing two guns, particularly
the last, when they rushed at and captured it by
pistolling the gunners, who were mowing down
with grape the detachment, one-third of which was
hors-de-combat at the time.

Lieutenant Daunt is also recommended for chasing, on the 2nd of November following, the mutineers of the 32nd Bengal Native Infantry across a plain into a rich cultivation, into which he followed them with a few of Rattray's Sikhs. He was dangerously wounded in the attempt to drive out a large body of these mutineers from an enclosure, the preservation of many of his party on this occasion, being attributed to his gallantry.

Denis Dynon,

Sergeant, No. 2165. Date of Act of Bravery, October 2nd 1857.

James Miller,

Conductor, Ordnance Department, Bengal. For having, on the 28th of October 1857, at great personal risk, gone to the assistance of, and carried out of action, a wounded officer, Lieutenant Glubb, of the late 38th Regiment of Bengal Native Infantry. He was himself subsequently wounded and sent to Agra.

Conductor Miller was at the time employed with heavy howitzers and ordnance stores attached to a detachment of troops, commanded by the late Colonel Cotton, C.B., in the attack on the abovementioned date on the rebels who had taken up their position in the Serai at Futtchpore Sikra, near Agra.

Arthur Mayo,

Midshipman, Indian Navy. For having headed the charge on the 22nd of November 1857, in the engagement between the Indian Naval Brigade and the mutineers of the 73rd Native Infantry and Bengal Artillery, when the former were ordered to charge two six-pounders which were keeping up a heavy fire. Mr. Mayo was nearly 20 yards in front of anyone else during the advance.

Thomas Cadell,

Lieutenant, the late 2nd European Bengal Fusiliers. For having, on the 12th of June 1857, at the Flagstaff Piquet at Delhi, when the whole of the Piquet of Her Majesty's 75th Regiment and 2nd European Bengal Fusiliers were driven in by a large body of the enemy, brought in from amongst the enemy under a most severe fire, a wounded bugler of his own regiment, who would otherwise have been cut up by the rebels. Also on the same day, when the Fusiliers were retiring, by order, on Metcalf's house, on its being reported that there was a wounded man left behind, Lieutenant Cadell went back of his own accord towards the enemy, accompanied by three men, and brought in a man of the 75th Regiment, who was severely wounded, under a most heavy fire from the advancing enemy.

Edward Talbot Thackeray,

Lieutenant, Bengal Engineers. For cool intrepidity and characteristic daring in extinguishing a fire in the Delhi Magazine enclosure, on the 16th of September 1857, under a close and heavy musketry fire from the enemy, at the imminent risk of his life from the explosion of combustible stores in the shed in which the fire occurred.

Cornelius Coghlan,

Colour-Sergeant, 75th Regiment. For gallantly venturing, under a heavy fire, with three others, into a Serai occupied by the enemy in great numbers, and removing Private Corbett, 75th Regiment, who lay severely wounded.

Also for cheering and encouraging a party which hesitated to charge down a lane in Subzee Mundee, at Delhi, lined on each side with huts, and raked by a cross fire; then entering with the said party into an enclosure filled with the enemy, and destroying every man.

For having also, on the same occasion, returned under a cross fire to collect doolies, and carry off the wounded; a service which was successfully performed, and for which this man obtained great praise from the officers of his regiment.

Charles Anderson,

Corporal (then Private) No. 875, 2nd Dragoon Guards,

Thomas Monaghan,

Trumpeter No. 1158, 2nd Dragoon Guards. For saving the life of Lieutenant-Colonel Seymour, C.B., commanding the regiment, in an attack made on him on the 8th of October 1858, by mutinous sepoys, in a dense jungle of sugar canes, from which an attempt was made to dislodge them. The mutineers were between 30 and 40 in number. They suddenly opened fire on Lieutenant-Colonel Seymour and his party at a few yards' distance, and immediately afterwards rushed in upon them with drawn (native) swords. Pistolling a man, cutting at him, and emptying with deadly effect at arm's length every barrel of his revolver, Lieutenant-Colonel Seymour was cut down by two sword cuts, when the two men above recommended, rushed to his rescue, and the trumpeter shooting a man with his pistol in the act of cutting at him, and both trumpeter and dragoon driving at the enemy with their swords, enabled him to arise, and assist in defending himself again, when the whole of the enemy were despatched. The occurrence took place soon after the action fought near Sundeela, Oudh, on the date above mentioned.

Edward MacKenna,

Colour-Sergeant (now Ensign) 65th Regiment.

For gallant conduct at the engagement near Camerontown, New Zealand, on the 7th of September 1863, after both his officers, Captain Swift and Lieutenant Butler, had been shot in charging through the position of an enemy heavily outnumbering him, and drawing off his small force consisting of two sergeants, one bugler, and thirty-five men, through a broken and rugged country, with the loss of but one man killed and another missing.

Lieutenant-General Cameron, C.B., commanding Her Majesty's Forces in the colony, reports that, in

Colour-Sergeant MacKenna, the detachment found a commander whose coolness, intrepidity and judgment, justified the confidence placed in him by the soldiers brought so suddenly under his command.

John Ryan,

Lance-Corporal, No. 261, 65th Regiment. For gallant conduct at the engagement near Camerontown above referred to. This non-commissioned officer, with Privates Bulford and Talbot, of the same regiment, who have been recommended for the medal for distinguished conduct in the field, for their behaviour on the same occasion, removed the body of the late Captain Swift from the field of action, after he had been mortally wounded, and remained with it all night in a bush surrounded by the enemy.

John Carstairs McNeill,

Lieutenant-Colonel, 107th Regiment. For valour and presence of mind which he displayed in New Zealand, on the 30th of March 1867, which is thus described by Private Vosper, of the Colonial Defence Force. Private Vosper states that he was sent on that day with Private Gibson, of the same force, as an escort to Major (now Lieutenant-Colonel) McNeill, aide-de-camp to Lieutenant Sir Duncan Cameron. Lieutenant-Colonel McNeill was proceeding to Te Awamutu on duty at the time. On returning from that place, and about a mile on this side of Ohanpu this officer, having seen a body of the enemy in front, sent Private Gibson back to bring up infantry from Ohanpu, and he and Private Vosper proceeded leisurely to the top of a rise to watch the enemy. Suddenly they were attacked by about 50 natives, who were concealed in the ferns close at hand. Their only chance of escape was by riding for their lives. And as they turned to gallop, Private Vosper's horse fell and threw him. The natives thereupon rushed forward to seize him, but Lieutenant-Colonel McNeill, on perceiving that Private Vosper was not following him, returned, caught his horse, and helped him to mount. The natives were firing sharply at them, and were so near that, according to Private Vosper's statement, it was only by galloping as hard as they could that they escaped. He says that he owes his life entirely to Lieutenant-Colonel McNeill's assistance, for he could not have caught his horse alone, and in a few minutes must have been killed.

Mr. Duncan Gordon Boyes,

Midshipman of Her Majesty's ship *Euryalus;* and

Thomas Pride,

Captain of the After-guard of Her Majesty's ship *Euryalus*.

For the conspicuous gallantry which, according to the testimony of Captain Alexander, C.B., at the time Flag Captain to Vice-Admiral Sir Augustus Kuper, K.C.B., Mr. Boyes displayed on the occasion of the capture of the enemy's stockade.

He carried the colour with the leading company, kept it in advance of all, in the face of the thickest fire, his Colour-Sergeants having fallen, one mortally, the other dangerously, wounded; and he was only detained from proceeding yet further by the orders of his superior officer. The colour he carried was six times pierced by musket balls.

Thomas Pride,

Captain of the After-guard, the survivor of the two Colour-Sergeants who supported Mr. Boyes in the gallant rush which he made in advance of the attack, was also recommended for the Victoria Cross for his conduct on the occasion.

William Seeley,

Ordinary Seaman of Her Majesty's ship *Euryalus*. For the intelligence and daring which, according to the testimony of Lieutenant Edwards, Commanding the Third Company, he exhibited in ascertaining the enemy's position, and for continuing to retain his position in front, during the advance, after he had been wounded in the arm.

George Vincent Fosbery,

Lieutenant, Late 4th Bengal European Regiment. For the daring and gallant manner in which, on the 30th of October 1863, acting as a volunteer at the time, he led a party of his regiment to re-capture the Crag Picquet, after its garrison had been driven in by the enemy, on which occasion sixty of them were killed in desperate hand to hand fighting.

From the nature of the approach to the top of the Crag amongst the large rocks, one or two men only could advance at one time; and "whilst I ascended one path" relates Lieutenant-Colonel Keyes, C.B., commanding the 1st Punjab Infantry, "I directed Lieutenant Fosbery, of the late 4th European Regiment, to push up another at the head of a few men. He led his party with the greatest coolness and intrepidity, and was the first man to gain the top of the Crag on his side of the attack."

Subsequently, Lieutenant-Colonel Keyes being wounded, Lieutenant Fosbery assembled a party with which he pursued the routed enemy in the direction of the Lalloo ridge, inflicting on them further loss and confirming the possession of the post.

Hugh Shaw,

Captain, 18th Regiment. For his gallant conduct at the skirmish near Nukumaru, in New Zealand, on the 24th of January 1865, in proceeding, under a heavy fire, with four privates of the regiment, who volunteered to accompany him, to within 30 yards of the bush occupied by the rebels, in order to carry off a comrade who was badly wounded. On the afternoon of that day, Captain Shaw was ordered to occupy a position about half a mile from the camp. He advanced in skirmishing order, and, when about 30 yards from the bush, he deemed it prudent to retire to a palisade about 60 yards from the bush, as two of his party had been wounded. Finding that one of them was unable to move, he called for volunteers to advance to the front to carry the man to the rear, and the four privates referred to accompanied him under a heavy fire, to the place where the wounded man was lying, and they succeeded in bringing him to the rear.

Timothy O'Hea,

Private, 1st Battalion, The Prince Consort's Own Rifle Brigade. For his courageous conduct on the occasion of a fire which occurred in a railway car containing ammunition, between Quebec and Montreal, on the 9th of June 1866. The sergeant in charge of the escort states that when at Danville Station, on the Grand Trunk Railway, the alarm was given that the car was on fire; it was immediately disconnected, and, whilst considering what was to be done, Private O'Hea took the keys from his hand, rushed to the car, opened it, and called out for water and a ladder. It is stated that it was due to his example that the fire was suppressed.

Samuel Hodge,

Private, 4th West India Regiment. For his bravery at the storming and capture of the stockaded town of Tubabecolony, in the kingdom of Barra, River Gambia, on the evening of the 30th of June 1866. Colonel D'Arcy, of the Gambia Volunteers, states that this man and another, who was afterwards killed— pioneers in the 4th West India Regiment—answered his call for volunteers, with axes in hand, to hew down the stockade. Colonel D'Arcy having effected an extrance, Private Hodge followed him through the town, opening with his axe two gates from the inside, which were barricaded, so allowing the supports to enter, who carried the place from east to west at the point of the bayonet. On issuing to the glacis through the west gate, Private Hodge was presented by Colonel D'Arcy to his comrades, as the bravest soldier in their regiment, a fact which they acknowledged with loud acclamations.

Charles Heaphy,

Major, Auckland Militia. For his gallant conduct, at the skirmish on the banks of the Mangapiko River, in New Zealand, on the 11th of February 1864, in assisting a wounded soldier of the 40th Regiment, who had fallen into a hollow among the thickest of the concealed Maories. Whilst doing so he became the target for a volley at a few feet distant. Five balls pierced his clothes and cap, and he was wounded in three places. Although hurt, he continued to aid the wounded until the end of the day.

Major Heaphy was at the time in charge of a party of soldiers of the 40th and 50th Regiments, under the orders of Lieutenant-Colonel Sir Henry Marshman Havelock, Bart., C.B., V.C., the senior officer on the spot, who had moved rapidly down to the place where the troops were hotly engaged and pressed.

THE "V. C."

Campbell Millis Douglas, M.D.,

Assistant Surgeon, 2nd Battalion, 24th Regiment.

Thomas Murphey
James Cooper
David Bell
William Griffiths
} Privates.

For the very gallant, and daring manner in which, on the 7th of May 1869, they risked their lives in manning a boat and proceeding through a dangerous surf to the rescue of some of their comrades, who formed part of an expedition which had been sent to the Island of Little Andaman, by order of the Chief Commissioner of British Burmah, with the view of ascertaining the fate of the commander and seven of the crew of the ship *Assam Valley*, who had landed there, and were supposed to have been murdered by the natives.

The officer who commanded the troops on the occasion reports: "About an hour later in the day, Dr. Douglas, 2nd Battalion, 24th Regiment, and the four privates, referred to, gallantly manning the second gig, made their way through the surf almost to the shore, but finding their boat was half filled with water, they retired. A second attempt made by Dr. Douglas and a party proved successful, five of us being safely passed through the surf to the boats outside. A third and last trip got the whole of the party left on the shore safe to the boats."

It is stated that Dr. Douglas accomplished these trips through the surf to the shore by no ordinary exertion. He stood in the bows of the boat, and worked her in an intrepid and seamanlike manner, cool to a degree, as if what he was then doing was an ordinary act of every-day life. The four privates behaved in an equally cool and collected manner, rowing through the roughest surf when the slightest hesitation or want of pluck on the part of any one of them would have been attended by the gravest results. It is reported that seventeen officers and men were thus saved from what must otherwise have been a fearful risk if not certainty of death.

William Spottiswood Trevor,

Major, Royal (late Bengal) Engineers.

James Dundas,

Lieutenant, Royal (late Bengal) Engineers. For their gallant conduct at the attack on the Blockhouse at Dewan-Giri, in Bhootan, on the 30th of April 1865, Major-General Tombs, C.B., V.C., the officer in command at the time, reports that a party of the enemy, from 180 to 200 in number had barricaded themselves in the Block-house in question, which they continued to defend after the rest of the position had been carried, and the main body was in retreat. The Block-house, which was loopholed was the key of the enemy's position. Seeing no officer of the storming party near him, and being anxious that the place should be taken immediately, as any protacted resistance might have caused the main body of the Blooteas to rally, the British force having been fighting in a broiling sun on very steep and difficult ground for upwards of three hours, the General in command ordered these two officers to show the way into the Block-house. They had to climb up a wall which was 14 feet high, and then to enter a house, occupied by some 200 desperate men, head foremost through an opening not more than two feet wide between the top wall and the roof of the Block-house.

Major-General Tombs states that on speaking to the Sikh soldiers around him, and telling them in Hindoostani to swarm up the wall, none of them responded to the call, until these two officers had shown them the way, when they followed with the greatest alacrity. Both of them were wounded.

George Nicholas Channer,

Captain, Bengal Staff Corps. For having, at Perak, with the greatest gallantry, been the first to jump into the enemy's stockade, to which he had been despatched with a small party of the 1st Ghoorkha Light Infantry, on the afternoon of the 20th December 1875, by the officer commanding the Malacca Column, to procure intelligence as to its strength, position, &c.

Major Channer got completely in the rear of the enemy's position, and finding himself so close that he could hear the voices of the men inside, who were cooking at the time, and keeping no look out, he beckoned to his men, and the whole party stole quietly forward to within a few paces of the stockade. On jumping in, he shot the first man dead with his revolver, and his party then came up, and entered the stockade, which was of a most formidable nature, surrounded by a bamboo palisade; about seven yards within was a log-house, loop-holed into two narrow entrances, and trees laid latitudinally, to the thickness of two feet. The officer commanding reports that if Major Channer, by his foresight, coolness, and intrepidity, had not taken this stockade, a great loss of life must have occurred, as from the fact of his being unable to bring guns to bear on it, from the steepness of the hill, and the density of the jungle, it must have been taken at the point of the bayonet.

Andrew Scott,

Captain, Bengal Staff Corps. For his gallant conduct at Quetta, on the 26th July 1877, whilst serving in the 4th Sikh Infantry, on the occasion of an attack by some Pathan Coolies on Lieutenants Hewson and Kunhardt, of the Royal Engineers.

On the evening of that day, Captain Scott, whilst on duty at the regimental parade ground of the 4th Sikh Infantry at Quetta, hearing an alarm that British officers were being killed, spontaneously rushed to the rescue, and finding Lieutenant Hewson cut down, and Lieutenant Runhardt retiring, hard-pressed and wounded, and only protected by Sepoy Ruchpal Singh, of the above-mentioned regiment, fell on the assailants, and with his own hand bayonetted two men, and closed with a third, who fell with him to the ground, and was killed by sepoys of the regiment.

This act of courage and devotion saved the life of Lieutenant Kunhardt.

John Cook,

Captain, Bengal Staff Corps. For a signal act of valour at the action of the Peiwar Kotal on the 2nd December 1878, in having, during a very heavy fire, charged out of the entrenchments with such impetuosity that the enemy broke and fled, when perceiving, at the close of the melée, the danger of Major Galbraith, Assistant Adjutant-General, Kurum Column Field Force, who was in personal conflict with an Afghan soldier, Captain Cook distracted his attention to himself, and aiming a sword cut which the Douranee avoided, sprang upon him, and, grasping his throat, grappled with him. They both fell to the ground. The Douranee, a most powerful man, still endeavouring to use his rifle, seized Captain Cook's arm in his teeth, until the struggle was ended by the man being shot through the head.

J. R. M. Chard,

Lieutenant, Royal Engineers,

G. Bromhead,

Lieutenant, 2nd Battalion, 24th Regiment. For their gallant conduct at the defence of Rorke's Drift, no the occasion of the attack by the Zulus on the 22nd and 23rd of January 1879.

The Lieutenant-General commanding the troops

reports that, had it not been for the fine example and excellent behaviour of these two officers under the most trying circumstances the defence of Rorke's Drift post would not have been conducted with that intelligence and tenacity which so essentially characterised it. The Lieutenant-General adds, that its success must, in a great degree, be attributable to the two young officers who exercised the chief command on the occasion in question.

John Williams,

Private, 2nd Battalion, 24th Regiment. Private Williams was posted with Private Joseph Williams, and Private William Horrigan, 1st Battalion, 24th Regiment, in a distant room of the hospital, which they held for more than an hour, so long as they had a round of ammunition left: as communication was for the time cut off, the Zulus were enabled to advance and burst open the door; they dragged out Private Joseph Williams and two of the patients, and assagaied them. Whilst the Zulus were occupied with the slaughter of these men a lull took place, during which Private John Williams, who, with two patients, were the only men now left alive in this ward, succeeded in knocking a hole in the partition, and in taking the two patients into the next ward, where he found Private Hook.

Henry Hook,

Private, 2nd Battalion, 24th Regiment. These two men together, one man working whilst the other fought and held the enemy at bay with his bayonet, broke through three more partitions, and were thus enabled to bring eight patients through a small window into the inner line of defence.

William Jones,

Private, 2nd Battalion, 24th Regiment, and

Private Robert Jones defended the post until six out of the seven patients had been removed.

Robert Jones,

Private, 2nd Battalion, 24th Regiment. In another ward, facing the hill, Private William Jones and Private Robert Jones defended the post to the last, until six out of the seven patients it contained had been removed. The seventh, Sergeant Maxfield, 2nd Battalion, 24th Regiment, was delirious from fever. Although they had previously dressed him, they were unable to induce him to move. When Private Robert Jones returned to endeavour to carry him away, he found him being stabbed by the Zulus as he lay on his bed.

William Allen,

Corporal, 2nd Battalion, 24th Regiment, and

Frederick Hitch,

Private, 2nd Battalion, 24th Regiment. It was chiefly due to the courageous conduct of these men that communication with the hospital was kept up at all. Holding together at all costs a most dangerous post, raked in reverse by the enemy's fire from the hill, they were both severely wounded, but their determined conduct enabled the patients to be withdrawn from the hospital, and when incapacitated by their wounds from fighting, they continued, as soon as their wounds had been dressed, to serve out ammunition to their comrades during the night. We may add that the defence of Rorke's Drift has long since taken its place amongst the splendid deeds which have added to

England's greatness. Scarcely anything in our "Rough Island Story" stands out in sharper outline as an example of splendid courage, and dauntless devotion, than that gallant fight of Chard and Bromhead with their handful of comrades against a host of pitiless savages. The only shelter our little force had was a hastily erected barrier of biscuit tins, but behind this frail barrier were English hearts of oak that nothing could daunt and though the struggle against the overwhelming hordes of Zulus that were hurled at them again and again seemed hopeless never a man of the little band quailed, but throughout those fearful hours with fire and death encompassing them they upheld the honour of England's flag, and added another leaf to her chaplet of glory. The defence of Rorke's Drift is worthy of being immortalised in an epic poem.

Reginald Clare Hart,

Lieutenant, Royal Engineers. For his gallant conduct in risking his own life in endeavouring to save the life of a private soldier.

The Lieutenant-General commanding the 2nd Division, Peshawar Field Force, reports that when on convoy duty with that Force, on the 31st of January 1879, Lieutenant Hart of the Royal Engineers, took the initiative in running some 1,200 yards to the rescue of a wounded sowar of the 13th Bengal Lancers in a river bed exposed to the fire of the enemy, and brought him under cover with the aid of some soldiers who accompanied him on his way.

Memorandum, May 2nd 1879.

Lieutenant Melville, of the 1st Battalion, 24th Foot, on account of the gallant efforts made by him to save the Queen's colours of his regiment after the disaster at Isandhwalha, and also Lieutenant Coghill, 1st Battalion, 24th Foot, on account of his heroic conduct in endeavouring to save his brother officer's life, would have been awarded with the Victoria Cross had they survived. But both these young officers laid down their lives in their country's cause, and the story of that desperate fight for the colours is one of the most heroic, as well as one of the most pathetic episodes in the record of England's heroes.

P. Brown,

Trooper, Cape Mounted Rifles. During the assault on Moirasis, on the 8th of April 1879, Brown with his comrades, lying under cover waiting for orders to recommence the advance, heard two men who had been wounded some time before, crying out for water. Brown could not resist this appeal. Fellow countrymen and soldiers like himself were in desperate strait, so up he rose, and leaving his safe shelter, he at once took his life in his hand, and carried his water bottle to the men, under a heavy fire. The men had crept under a rock for shelter, but while Brown was stooping down, giving the first man a drink he was wounded severely in the right thigh, and before he could complete his noble task a second bullet shattered his right arm the use of which he never recovered.

H. Buller, C.B.,

Captain and Brevet Lieutenant-Colonel, 60th Rifles. For his gallant conduct at the retreat at Inhlobana, on the 28th March, 1879, in having assisted, whilst hotly pursued by Zulus, in rescuing Captain C. D'Arcy, of the Frontier Light Horse, who was retiring on foot, and carrying him on his horse until he overtook the rear guard. Also for having on the same date and under the same circumstances, conveyed Lieutenant C. Everitt, of the Frontier Light Horse, whose horse had been killed under him, to a place of safety. Later on, Colonel Buller, in the same manner, saved a trooper of the Frontier Light Horse, whose horse was completely exhausted, and who otherwise would have been killed by the Zulus, who were within 80 yards of him.

William K. Leet,

Major, 1st Battalion, 13th Regiment. For his gallant conduct, on the 28th March 1879, in rescuing from the Zulus, Lieutenant A. M. Smith, of the Frontier Light Horse, during the retreat from Inhlobana.

Lieutenant Smith whilst on foot, his horse having been shot, was closely pursued by Zulus and would have been killed had not Major Leet taken him upon his horse and rode with him, under the fire of the enemy, to a place of safety.

James Henry Reynolds,

Surgeon-Major, Army Medical Department. For the conspicuous bravery, during the attack at Rorke's Drift, on the 22nd and 23rd of January 1879, which he exhibited in his constant attention to the wounded under fire, and in his voluntarily conveying ammunition from the store to the defenders of the Hospital, whereby he exposed himself to a cross fire from the enemy both in going and returning.

Edward S. Browne,

Lieutenant, 1st Battalion, 24th Regiment. For his gallant conduct, on the 29th March 1879, when the Mounted Infantry were being driven in by the enemy at Inhlobana, in galloping back and twice assisting on his horse (under heavy fire and within a few yards of the enemy), one of the mounted men, who must otherwise have fallen into the enemy's hands.

Wassall,

Private, 80th Regiment. For his gallant conduct in having, at the imminent risk of his own life, saved that of Private Westwood, of the same regiment.

On the 22nd of January 1879, when the camp at Isandhlwana was taken by the enemy, Private Wassall retreated towards the Buffaloe River, in which he saw a comrade struggling, and apparently drowning. He rode to the bank, dismounted, leaving his horse on the Zulu side, rescued the man from the stream, and again mounted his horse, dragging Private Westwood across the river under a heavy shower of bullets.

Lord William Beresford,

Captain, 9th Lancers. For gallant conduct in having at great personal risk, during the retirement of the reconnoitring party across the "White Umvolosi River" on the 3rd of July, turned to assist Sergeant Fitzmaurice, 1st Battalion, 24th Foot (whose horse had fallen with him), mounted him behind him on his horse, and brought him away in safety under the close fire of the Zulus who were in great force, and coming on quickly.

Lord William Beresford's position was rendered most dangerous from the fact that Sergeant Fitzmaurice twice nearly pulled him from his horse owing to weakness from loss of blood.

Walter Richard Pollock Hamilton,

Lieutenant, Bengal Staff Corps. For conspicuous gallantry during the action at Futtehabad, on the 2nd of April 1879, in leading on the Guide Cavalry in a charge against very superior numbers of the enemy and particularly at a critical moment when his commanding officer (Major Wigram Battye) fell, Lieutenant Hamilton, then the only officer left with the regiment, assumed command and cheered on his men to avenge Major Battye's death.

In the charge, Lieutenant Hamilton, seeing Sowar Dowlut Ram down, and attacked by three of the enemy, whilst entangled with his horse (which had been killed), rushed to the rescue, and followed by a few of his men cut down all three and saved the life of Sowar Dowlut Ram.

Cecil D'Arcy,

Captain, Frontier Light Horse. For his gallant conduct, on the 3rd of July 1879, during the reconnaissance made before Ulundi by the Mounted Corps, in endeavouring to rescue Trooper Raubenheim, of the Frontier Light Horse, who fell from his horse as the troops were retiring. Captain D'Arcy, though the Zulus were close upon them, waited for the man to mount behind him; the horse kicked them both off, and though much hurt by the fall and quite alone, Captain D'Arcy coolly endeavoured to lift the trooper, who was stunned, on to the horse, and it was only when he found that he had not strength to do so that he mounted and rode off.

His escape was miraculous as the Zulus had actually closed upon him.

Edmund O'Toole,

Sergeant, Frontier Light Horse. For his conspicuous

courage and bravery on several occasions during the campaign, and especially for his conduct, on the 3rd of July 1879, at the close of the reconnaissance before Ulundi, in assisting to rescue Sergeant Fitzmaurice, 1st Battalion, 24th Mounted Infantry, whose horse fell and rolled on him, as the troops retired before great numbers of the enemy. When lifted up behind him by Lord William Beresford, the man, being half stunned by the fall, could not hold on and he must have been left had not Sergeant O'Toole, who was keeping back the advancing Zulus, given up his carbine and assisted to hold Sergeant Fitzmaurice on his horse. At the time the Zulus, were rapidly closing on them, and there was no armed man between them and Sergeant O'Toole.

O'Moor Creagh,

Captain, Bombay Staff Corps. On the 21st of April, Captain Creagh was detached from Dakka with two Companies of his battalion to protect the village of Kam Dakka on the Kabul River, against a threatened incursion of the Mohmunds, and reached that place the same night. On the following morning the detachment, 150 men, was attacked by the Mohmunds in overwhelming numbers, about 1,500; and the inhabitants of Kam Dakka having themselves taken part with the enemy, Captain Creagh found himself under the necessity of retiring from the village. He took up a position in a cemetery not far off, which he made as defensible as circumstances would admit of, and this position he held against all the efforts of the enemy, repeatedly repusing them with the bayonet until three o'clock in the afternoon, when he was relieved by a detachment sent for the purpose from Dakka. The enemy were then finally repulsed—and being charged by a troop of the 10th Bengal Lancers, under the command of Captain D. M. Strong, were routed and broken, and great numbers of them driven into the river.

The Commander-in-Chief in India has expressed his opinion that but for the coolness, determination, and gallantry of the highest order, and the admirable conduct which Captain Creagh displayed on this occasion the detachment under his command would, in all probability, have been cut off and destroyed.

James Langly Dalton,

Acting Assistant (now Sub-Assistant) Commissary, Commissariat and Transport Department. For his conspicuous gallantry during the attack on Rorke's Drift Post by the Zulus, on the night of the 22nd of January 1879, when he actively superintended the work of defence, and was amongst the foremost of those who received the first attack at the corner of the hospital, where the deadliness of his fire did great execution, and the mad rush of the Zulus met its first check, and where by cool courage he saved the life of a man of the Army Hospital Corps by shooting the Zulu who having seized the muzzle of the man's rifle, was in the act of assegaing him.

This officer, to whose energy much of the defence of this place was due, was severely wounded during the contest, but still continued to give the same example of cool courage.

Schiess,

Corporal, Natal Native Contingent. For conspicuous gallantry in the defence of Rorke's Drift Post, on the night of January the 22nd 1879, when, in spite of his having been wounded in the foot a few days previously, he greatly distinguished himself when the Garrison were repulsing, with the bayonet, a series of desperate assaults made by the Zulus, and displayed great activity and devoted gallantry throughout the defence.

On one occasion when the Garrison had retired to the inner line of defence, and the Zulus occupied the wall of mealie bags which had been abandoned, he crept along the wall, without any order, to dislodge a Zulu who was shooting better than usual, and succeeded in killing him and two others, before he, the corporal, returned to the inner defence.

Edward Pemberton Leach,

Captain (now Major), Royal Engineers. For having in action with the Shinwarris near Maidanah, Afghanistan, on the 17th of March 1879, when covering the retirement of the Survey Escort, who were carrying Lieutenant Barclay, 45th Sikhs, mortally wounded, behaved with the utmost gallantry in charging, with some men of the 45th Sikhs, a very much larger number of the enemy.

In this encounter Captain Leach killed two or three of the enemy himself, and he received a severe wound from an Afghan knife in the left arm. Captain Leach's determination and gallantry in this affair, in attacking and driving back the enemy from the last position saved the whole party from annihilation.

Anthony Booth,

Colour-Sergeant, 80th Foot. For his gallant conduct, on the 12th of March 1879, during the Zulu attack on the Intombi River, in having, when considerably outnumbered by the enemy, rallied a few men on the south bank of the river, and covered the retreat of fifty soldiers and others for a distance of three miles.

The Officer Commanding the 80th Regiment reported that had it not been for the coolness displayed by this non-commissioned officer, not one man would have escaped.

Flawn and Fitzpatrick,

Privates, 94th Foot. In recognition of their gallant conduct during the attack on Sekukuni's Town, on the 28th of November 1879, in carrying out of action Lieutenant Dewar, 1st Dragoon Guards, when badly wounded.

At the time when he received his wound, Lieutenant Dewar had with him only Privates Flawn and Fitzpatrick, and six of the Native Contingent, and being incapable of moving without assistance, the natives proceeded to carry him down the hill, when about thirty of the enemy appeared in pursuit about 40 yards in the rear, whereupon the men of the Native Contingent deserted Lieutenant Dewar, who must have been killed but for the devoted gallantry of Privates Flawn and Fitzpatrick, who carried him alternately, one covering the retreat and firing upon the enemy.

Richard Kirby Ridgeway,

Captain, Bengal Staff Corps. For conspicuous gallantry throughout the attack on Konoma, on the 22nd of November 1879, more especially in the final assault, when, under a heavy fire from the enemy, he rushed up to a barricade and attempted to tear down the planking surrounding it, to enable him to effect an entrance, in which act he received a very severe rifle shot wound in the left shoulder.

Robert George Scott,

Sergeant, Cape Mounted Rifles. For conspicuous gallantry and devotion during an attack in Moirasi's Mountain, on the 8th of April 1879, in volunteering to throw time fuse shells, as hand grenades, over a line of stone barricades, from behind which, the enemy were bringing a heavy fire to bear on the colonial troops, and which it was impossible effectually to return.

After causing all the men of his party to retire under cover, lest the shell should burst prematurely, by which precaution many lives were in all probability saved—Sergeant Scott advanced in a most deliberate manner under a heavy fire, and having got under the wall, made two attempts to throw shells over it. At the second attempt, owing to some defect in the fuse, which he had just lighted, the shell exploded almost in Sergeant Scott's hands, blowing his right hand to pieces, and wounding him severely in the left leg.

William John Vonsden,

Captain, Bengal Staff Corps. For the exceptional gallantry displayed by him, on the 14th of December 1879, on the Koh Asmai Heights, near Kabul, in charging, with a small party, into the centre of the line of the retreating Kohistans force, by whom they were greatly outnumbered, and who did their utmost to close round them. After rapidly charging through and through the enemy, backwards and forwards, several times, they swept off round the opposite side of the village and joined the rest of the troop.

Arthur George Hammond,

Captain, Bengal Staff Corps. For conspicuous coolness and gallantry at the action on the Asmai Heights, near Kabul, on the 14th of December 1879, in defending the top of the hill with a rifle and fixed bayonet, against large numbers of the enemy, while the 72nd Highlanders and Guides were retiring; and again and again, on the retreat down the hill, with stopping to assist in carrying away a wounded sepoy, the enemy being not sixty yards off, firing heavily all the time.

THE "V. C." 177

William Henry Dick Cunyngham,

Lieutenant, The Gordon Highlanders. For the conspicuous gallantry and coolness displayed by him, on the 13th of December 1879, at the attack on the Sherpur Pass, in Afghanistan, in having exposed himself to the full fire of the enemy, and by his example and encouragement rallied the men who, having been beaten back, were, at the moment, wavering at the top of the hill.

George Sellar,

Lance-Corporal, Seaforth Highlanders (Ross-shire Buffs), for conspicuous gallantry displayed by him at the assault on the Asmai Heights, round Kabul, on the 14th of December 1879, in having in a marked manner led the attack, under a heavy fire, and, dashing on in front of the party up the slope, engaged in a desperate conflict with an Afghan who sprang out to meet him. In this encounter Lance-Corporal Sellar was severely wounded.

Henry Lysons,

Lieutenant, 2nd Battalion, The Cameronians (Scottish Rifles) and

Edmond Fowler,

Private. On the 28th of March 1879, during the assault of the Inhlobane Mountain, Sir Evelyn Wood ordered the dislodgement of certain Zulus (who were causing the troops much loss) from strong natural caves commanding the position in which some of the wounded were lying. Some delay occurring in the execution of the orders issued, Captain the Honourable Ronald Campbell, Coldstream Guards, followed by Lieutenant Lysons, aide-de-camp, and Private Fowler, ran forward in the most determined manner, and advanced over a mass of fallen boulders, and between walls of rock, which led to a cave in which the enemy lay hidden. It being impossible for two men to walk abreast, the assailants were consequently obliged to keep in single file, and as Captain Campbell was leading, he arrived first at the mouth of the cave from which the Zulus were firing, and there met his death. Lieutenant Lysons and Private Fowler, who was following close behind him, immediately dashed at the cave, from which led several subterranean passages, and firing into the chasm below, succeeded in forcing the occupants to forsake their stronghold. Lieutenant Lysons remained at the cave's mouth for some minutes after the attack, during which time Captain Campbell's body was carried down the slopes.

Alan Richard Hill,

Lieutenant, 2nd Battalion, the Northamptonshire Regiment. For gallant conduct at the action of Laing's Nek, on the 28th of January 1881, in having after the retreat was ordered, remained behind and endeavoured to carry out of action Lieutenant Baillie, of the same corps, who was lying on the ground severely wounded. Being unable to lift that officer into the saddle, he carried him in his arms until Lieutenant Baillie was shot dead.

Lieutenant Hill then brought a wounded man out of action on his horse, after which he returned and rescued another. All these acts being performed under a heavy fire.

John Doogan,

Private, Late 1st Dragoon Guards. For gallant conduct during the action of Laing's Nek, on the 28th of January 1881. During the charge of the mounted men Private Doogen, servant to Major Brownlow, 1st Dragoon Guards, seeing that officer (whose horse had been shot) dismounted and among the Boers, rode up and (though himself severely wounded) dismounted and pressed Major Brownlow to take his horse, receiving another wound while trying to induce him to accept it.

James Murray,

Lance-Corporal, Late 2nd Battalion, the Connaught Rangers,

John Danaher,

Trooper, Nourse's Horse.

For their gallant conduct during an engagement with the Boers at Elandsfontein, on the 16th of January 1881, in advancing for 500 yards under a very heavy fire from a party of about 60 Boers, to bring out of action a private of the 21st Foot who had been severely wounded; in attempting which Lance-Corporal Murray was himself severely wounded.

James Osborne,

Private, 2nd Battalion, Northamptonshire Regiment. For gallant conduct at Wesselstroom, on the 22nd of February 1881, in riding, under a heavy fire, towards a party of 42 Boers, picking up Private Mayes, who was lying wounded, and carrying him safely to camp.

Mr. Israel Harding,

Gunner, of Her Majesty's ship *Alexandre*. At about nine o'clock, on the morning of the 11th of July 1882, whilst Her Majesty's ship *Alexandre* was engaging the Forts at Alexandria, a 10-inch spherical shell passed through the ship's side and lodged on the main deck. Mr. Harding hearing the shout "There is a live shell just above the hatchway," rushed up the ladder from below, and, observing that the fuse was burning, took some water from a tub standing near, and threw it over the projectile, then picked up the shell and put it into the tub. Had the shell burst, it would probably have destroyed many lives.

William Mordaunt Marsh Edwards,

Lieutenant, 2nd Battalion, the Highland Light Infantry. For the conspicuous bravery displayed by him during the battle of Tel-el-Kebir, on the 13th of September 1882, in leading a party of the Highland Light Infantry to storm a redoubt. Lieutenant Edwards (who was in advance of his party) with great gallantry rushed alone into the battery, killed the artillery officer in charge, and was himself knocked down by a gunner with a rammer, and only rescued by the timely arrival of three men of his regiment.

"CAPTAIN WILSON THEN SPRANG TO THE FRONT AND ENGAGED IN SINGLE COMBAT WITH SOME OF THE ENEMY." [*page* 181

Frederick Corbett,

Private, 3rd Battalion, the King's Royal Rifle Corps. During the reconnaissance upon Kafr Dowar, on the 5th of August 1882, the mounted infantry, with which Private Corbett was serving, came under a hot fire from the enemy and suffered some loss, including Lieutenant Howard-Vyee, mortally wounded. This officer fell in the open, and there being then no time to move him, Private Corbett asked and obtained permission to remain by him, and though under a constant fire, he sat down and endeavoured to stop the bleeding of this officer's wounds, until the mounted infantry received orders to retire, when he rendered valuable assistance in carrying him off the field.

Arthur Knyvet Wilson,

Captain, Royal Navy. This officer, on the staff of Rear-Admiral Sir William Hewett, at the battle of El-Teb, on the 29th of February, attached himself during the advance to the right half battery, Naval Brigade, in the place of Lieutenant Royds, R.N., mortally wounded.

As the troops closed on the enemy's Krupp battery, the Arabs charged out on the corner of the square and on the detachment who were dragging the Gardner gun. Captain Wilson then sprang to the front and engaged in single combat with some of the enemy, thus protecting his detachment till some men of the York and Lancaster Regiment came to his assistance with their bayonets. But for the action of this officer Sir Redvers Butler thinks that one or more of his detachment must have been speared.

Captain Wilson was wounded, but remained with the half battery during the day.

Percival Scrope Marling,

Lieutenant, 3rd Battalion, King's Royal Rifle Corps, late Mounted Infantry. For his conspicuous bravery at the battle of Tamai, on the 13th of March 1884, in risking his life to save that of Private Morley, Royal Sussex Regiment, who, having been shot was lifted, and placed in front of Lieutenant Marling on his horse. He fell off almost immediately, when Lieutenant Marling dismounted, and gave up his horse for the purpose of carrying off Private Morley, the enemy pressing close on to them until they succeeded in carrying him about 80 yards to a place of comparative safety.

William Marshall,

Quartermaster-Sergeant, 19th Hussars. For his conspicuous bravery during the cavalry charge at El-Teb, on the 29th of February 1884, in bringing Lieutenant-Colonel Barrow, 19th Hussars, out of action. That officer having been severely wounded, and his horse killed, was on the ground surrounded by the enemy, when Quartermaster-Sergeant Marshall, who stayed behind with him, seized his hand and dragged him through the enemy back to the regiment. Had Lieutenant-Colonel Barrow been left behind he must have been killed.

THE "V. C."

Thomas Edward,

Private, 1st Battalion, Royal Highlanders. For the conspicuous bravery displayed by him in defence of one of the guns of the Naval Brigade, at the battle of Tamai, on the 13th of March 1884.

This man (who was attached to the Naval Brigade as mule driver) was beside the gun with Lieutenant Almack, R.N., and a bluejacket. Both the latter were killed, and Edwards, after bayonetting two Arabs, and himself receiving a wound with a spear rejoined the ranks with his mules, and subsequently did good service in remaining by his gun throughout the action.

Did good service in remaining by his gun throughout the action.

Albert Smith,

Gunner, Royal Artillery. At the Action of Abu Klea, on the 17th of January 1885, when the enemy charged, the square fell back a short distance, leaving Lieutenant Guthrie, Royal Artillery, with his gun, in a comparatively unprotected position. At this moment a native rushed at Lieutenant Guthrie with a spear and would in all probability have killed that officer, who had no weapon in his hand at the time (being engaged in superintending the working of his gun), when Gunner Smith with a gun handspike warded off the thrust, thus giving Lieutenant Guthrie time to draw his sword, and with a blow bring the assailant to his knees, but as the latter fell he made a wild thrust at the officer with a long knife, which Gunner Smith again warded off, not, however, before the native had managed to inflict a wound in Lieutenant Guthrie's thigh. Before the Soudani could repeat the thrust Gunner Smith killed him with the handspike and thus for the time saved the life of his officer though the latter unfortunately died some days afterwards of his wound.

John Crimmin,

Surgeon-Major, Bombay Medical Service. Lieutenant Tighe, 27th Bombay Infantry (to the Mounted Infantry of which Corps, Surgeon Crimmin was attached), states that in the action near Lwekaw, Eastern Karenni, on the 1st of January 1889, four men charged with him into the midst of a large body of the enemy who were moving off from the Karen left flank, and two men fell to the ground wounded. He saw Surgeon Crimmin attending one of the men about 200 yards to the rear. Karens were round the party in every direction, and he saw several fire at Surgeon Crimmin, and the latter joined the fighting line which then came up. Lieutenant Tighe further states that very shortly afterwards they were engaged in driving the enemy from small clumps of trees and bamboo, in which the Karens took shelter. Near one of these clumps he saw Surgeon Crimmin attending a wounded man. Several Karens rushed out at him. Surgeon Crimmin thrust his sword through one of them and attacked a second, a third Karen then dropped from the fire of a sepoy, upon which the remaining Karens fled.

Ferdinand Simeon Le Quesne,

Surgeon-Captain, Medical Staff, displayed conspicuous bravery and devotion to duty during the attack on the village of Tartan, by a Column of the Chin Field Force, on the 4th of May 1890, in having remained for the space of about ten minutes, in a very exposed position (within five yards of the loop-holed stockade from which the enemy were firing), dressing with perfect coolness and self-possession the wounds from which Second Lieutenant Michel, Norfolk Regiment, died shortly afterwards. Surgeon Le Quesne was himself severely wounded later on whilst attending to the wounds of another officer.

Charles James William Grant,

Lieutenant, Indian Staff Corps. For the conspicuous bravery and devotion to his country displayed by him in having, upon hearing on the 27th of March 1891, of the disaster at Manipur, at once volunteered to attempt the relief of the British captives, with 86 native soldiers, and having advanced with the greatest intrepidity, captured Thobal, near Manipur, and held it against a large force of the enemy.

Lieutenant Grant inspired his men with equal heroism, by an ever-present example of personal daring and resource.

Fenton John Aylmer,

Captain, Royal Engineers. For his conspicuous bravery in the assault and capture of the Nilt Fort, on the 2nd of December 1891.

The officer accompanied the storming party, burst open the inner gate with gun-cotton, which he placed and ignited, and though severely wounded, once in the leg and twice in the right hand, fired nineteen shots with his revolver, killing several of the enemy, and remained fighting, until fainting from loss of blood he was carried out of action.

Guy Hudleston Boisragon,

Lieutenant, Indian Staff Corps. For his conspicuous bravery in the assault and capture of the Nilt Fort on the 2nd of December 1891.

This officer led the assault with dash and determination, and forced his way though difficult obstacles to the inner gate, when he returned for reinforcements, moving intrepidly to and fro under a heavy cross-fire until he had collected sufficient men to relieve the hardly-pressed storming party and drive the enemy from the fort.

John Manners Smith,

Lieutenant, Indian Staff Corps, for his conspicuous bravery when leading the storming party at the attack and capture of the strong position occupied by the enemy near Nilt, in the Hunza-Nagar Country, on the 20th of December 1891.

The position was, owing to the nature of the country, an extremely strong one, and had barred the advance of the force for seventeen days. It was eventually forced by a small party of 50 rifles, with another of equal strength in support. The first of these parties was under the command of Lieutenant Smith, and it was entirely owing to his splendid leading, and the coolness, combined with dash he displayed while doing so, that a success was obtained. For nearly four hours, on the face of a cliff which was almost precipitous, he steadily moved his handful of men from point to point, as the difficulties of the ground, and showers of stones from above gave him an opportunity, and during the whole of this time was in such a position as to be unable to defend himself from any attack the enemy might choose to make.

He was the first man to reach the summit, within a few yards of one of the enemy's sungars, which was immediately rushed, Lieutenant Smith pistolling the first man.

William James Gordon,

No. 2829, Lance-Corporal, The West India Regiment. During the attack on the town of Toniataba 1892, Major G. C. Madden, West India Regiment, who was in command of the troops, was superintending a party of twelve men who were endeavouring with a heavy beam to break down the South Gate of the town, when suddenly a number of musket muzzles were projected through a double row of loop-holes which had been masked. Some of these were within two on three yards of that officer's back and before he realized what had happened Lance-Corporal Gordon threw himself between Major Madden and the muskets, pushing that officer out of the way, and exclaiming "Look out, Sir!" At the same moment Lance-Corporal Gordon was shot through the lungs.

By his bravery and self-devotion on this occasion the lance-corporal probably saved the life of his commanding officer.

Owen Edward Pennefather Lloyd,

Surgeon-Major, Army Medical Staff. During the attack on the Sima Post by Kachins, on the 6th of January 1893, Surgeon-Major Lloyd on hearing that the Commanding Officer, Captain Morton (who had left the fort to visit a picket about 80 yards distant) was wounded, at once under a close and heavy fire, ran out to his assistance, accompanied by Subadar Matab Singh.

On reaching the wounded officer, Surgeon-Major

Lloyd sent Subadar Matab Singh back for further assistance, and remained with Captain Morton till the subadar returned with five men of the Magwe Battalion of military police, when he assisted in carrying Captain Morton back to the fort, where that officer died a few minutes afterwards. The enemy were within ten or fifteen paces keeping up a heavy fire which killed three men of the picket and also Bugler Purna Singh. This man accompanied Captain Morton from the fort, showed great gallantry in supporting him in his arms when wounded, and was shot while helping to carry him back to the fort.

(The native officer and five sepoys above alluded to have been awarded the Order of Merit).

William Odgers

was a leading seaman of her Majesty's Ship *Niger*, and on the 28th of March 1860, he was on active service in New Zealand. At the storming of a Pah during the operations then being carried on against the natives he displayed the utmost gallantry. He was the first to enter the Pah under a heavy fire, and assisted in hauling down the enemy's colour. His bravery and coolness contributed in a large measure to the success of the attack.

Henry Evelyn Wood,

Lieutenant, 17th Lancers. During the action at Sindwaho, on the 19th of October 1858, this now well-known officer was in command of a troop of the 3rd Light Cavalry, when he attacked, almost single-handed, a body of rebels who had made a desperate stand, and by his prowess and valour he routed them.

Subsequently near Sindhora, he gallantly advanced with a Duffadar and Sowar of Beatson's horse, and rescued from a band of robbers a Potail, by name Chemum Singh, whom the robbers were in the act of hanging.

Samuel Morley,

Private, No. 201, 2nd Battalion, Military Train. On the evacuation of Azimgurh by Koer Sing's Army, on the 15th of April 1858, a squadron of the military train, and half a troop of horse artillery were sent in pursuit.

Upon overtaking them, and coming into action with their guard, a squadron of the 3rd Seikh Calvalry (also detached in pursuit) and one troop of the military train were ordered to charge, when Lieutenant Hamilton, who commanded the Seikhs, was unhorsed, and immediately surrounded by the enemy, who commenced cutting and hacking him whilst on the ground. Private Samuel Morley observing the predicament and peril of the Lieutenant, although his own (Morley's) horse had been shot from under him, immediately and without a moment's hesitation rushed to the officer's assistance, and in conjunction with Farrier Murphy (who had already received the Victoria Cross) cut down one of the sepoys and fought over Hamilton's body, and thereby saved the officer from being killed on the spot.

Charles Crawfurd Fraser,

Major, 7th Hussars. The Major was decorated with the Cross for conspicuous and cool gallantry on the 31st of December 1858, in having volunteered at great personal risk, and under a sharp fire of musketry, to swim to the rescue of Captain Stisted, and some men of the 7th Hussars, who were in imminent danger of being drowned in the River Kaptee, while in pursuit of the rebels.

Major Fraser succeeded in this gallant service although at the time he was partially disabled, as he had not recovered entirely from a severe wound received while leading in a charge against some fanatics in the action of Nawatgunge on the 13th of June 1858.

James Munro,

Colour-Sergeant, 93rd Regiment, was decorated for devoted conduct and conspicuous bravery at Secunderabagh on the 16th of November 1857, when he promptly rushed to the rescue of Captain E. Walsh of the same corps, who was desperately wounded and in peril of his life. Munro, however, succeeded in carrying him to a place of comparative safety, to which place the sergeant himself was brought in very shortly afterwards, badly wounded.

Michael Magner,

Drummer, No. 3691, 33rd Regiment,

James Bergin,

Private, No. 949, same Regiment. During the assaults on Magdala, on the 13th of April 1878, these two men greatly distinguished themselves. Lieutenant-General Lord Napier reports that while the head of the column of attack was checked by the obstacles at the gate, a small stream of officers and men of the 33rd Regiment, and an officer of Engineers, breaking away from the main approach to Magdala and climbing up a cliff, reached the defences and forced their way over the wall and thorny fence, thus turning the defenders of the gateway.

The first two men to enter Magdala were Drummer Magner, and Private Bergin. During the whole of the trying time they showed extraordinary coolness and the most dauntless courage.

Joseph Gee, C.B.,

Surgeon, 78th Regiment. The Cross was awarded in this instance for most important services, and remarkable gallantry, on the entry of Major-General Havelock's force into Lucknow on the 25th of September 1857. During heavy fighting, when the 78th Highlanders, then in possession of the Char Bagh captured two 9-pounders at the point of the bayonet, he by great exertion and devoted exposure, attended to the large number of those wounded in the charge, and he succeeded in getting them removed in cots, and on the backs of their comrades, until he collected the dooly bearers who had fled. Subsequently on the same day in endeavouring to reach the Residency with the wounded men, Surgeon

Gee became besieged by an overwhelming force in the Mote-Mehal, where he remained during the whole of the night, and following morning, voluntarily and repeatedly exposing himself to a heavy

He attended to the large number of those wounded.

fire in proceeding to dress the wounded men who fell while serving a 24-pounder in a most exposed situation. He eventually succeeded in taking many of the wounded through a cross fire of ordnance and musketry, safely into the Residency, by the river bank, although repeatedly warned not to make the perilous attempt.

Lord Gifford,

Lieutenant, 24th Regiment. Lord Gifford won the Cross by his gallant conduct during the operations at, and especially during the taking of Becquah. 1873—74, February 1st. The officer commanding the expeditionary force reports that Lord Gifford was in charge of the scouts, after the army crossed the Prah, and that it is no exaggeration to say that since the Adansi Hills were passed he daily carried his life in his hands in the performance of his most dangerous duty. He hung upon the rear of the enemy, discovering their position and ferreting out their intentions. With no other white man with him, he captured numerous prisoners, but Sir Garnet Wolseley brings him forward for the mark of Royal favour most, especially for his conduct at the taking of Bec,quah into which place he penetrated with his scouts before the troops carried it, when his gallantry and courage were most conspicuous.

Samuel McGaw,

Lance-Sergeant, 42nd Regiment. This man greatly distinguished himself during the operations in Ashanti. At the battle of Amoaful he led his section through the bush in most excellent style, continuing to do so throughout the whole of the day, although he was badly wounded at the beginning of the engagement. Nevertheless he would not retire, but enduring without a murmur he set a splendid example of devotion and courage which greatly inspirited his men. The date was January 31st, 1874.

Reginald William Sartorius, C.M.G.,

Major, 6th Bengal Cavalry. During the attack on Abogoo (Ashanti), on the 17th of January 1874, Major Sartorius removed from under a heavy fire Sergeant-Major Braimah Doctor, a Houssa non-commissioned officer, who was mortally wounded, and placed him under cover.

Mark Sever Bell,

Lieutenant, Royal Engineers. This officer was awared the Cross for his distinguished bravery, and zealous, resolute, and self-devoted conduct at the battle of Ordahsu (Ashanti), on the 4th of February 1874, whilst serving under the immediate orders of Colonel Sir John Chetham McLeod, K.C.B., of the 42nd Regiment who commanded the advanced guard. Sir John McLeod was an eye-witness of his gallant and distinguished conduct on the occasion, and considered the Lieutenant's fearless and resolute bearing, he being always in the front, in urging on and encouraging an unarmed working-party of Fantee labourers, who were exposed not only to the fire of the enemy, but to the wild and irregular fire of the native troops in the rear, contributed very materially to the success of the day. By his example he made these men do what no European party was ever required to do in warfare, namely to work under fire in face of the enemy without a covering party.

THE STORY OF THE INDIAN MUTINY OF 1857.

As the Indian Mutiny period was rich in deeds of heroism, and a large proportion of the awards of the Victoria Cross was made during that time, a brief sketch of the great revolt can hardly fail to be interesting. For since that fatal Sunday, the 10th of May, 1857, when the streets of Meerut ran red with blood, a new generation of men has sprung up, and it is proverbial of the public memory that it is short. Lord Bacon, the great historian, says:—

"The causes and motives for reaction are innovation in religion, taxes, alteration of laws and customs, breaking of privileges, general oppression, advancement of unworthy persons, strangers, death, disbanded soldiers, factions grown desperate, and whatever in offending people joineth and knitteth them in a common cause."

All the items which Bacon so ably classified two hundred and fifty years before, were doing their deadly work in India in 1857. It had long been known that a spirit of discontent and restlessness was making itself manifest amongst the native races; but with a strange, even criminal indifference, the rulers allowed this to go on and strengthen, and any suggestion of real danger, was not only pooh-poohed, but those making it were stigmatised as "Alarmists", "Faddists". And even a worse term than these was in some cases applied. At Vellore in the Madras Presidency in 1856, two sepoy battalions had risen and attacked the European soldiers, killing one hundred and thirteen of them in cold blood. A terrible revenge was exacted, for the 19th Dragoons under Colonel Gillespie, attacked the native troops in return and eight hundred of them were slain. This incident ought to have been taken to heart as an object lesson; and if the Government had only put themselves to the trouble to ascertain the causes which had led to this upleaping of the flames, they would have found them to be absurd regulations in regard to the dress of soldiers, an equally absurd order which compelled the Sepoys to shave, and to their wearing marks of caste. Trifling as these things might have seemed to an onlooker who knew nothing of the workings of the native mind, they had a very serious importance indeed to the natives themselves who felt that they were being barbarously treated by their foreign masters.

The lesson of the Vellore rising, however, was disregarded, and the officers and men who by their devotion, energy, and courage prevented the fire from spreading were not even thanked for their services. Indeed, in certain quarters it was openly stated that they had exceeded their duty. So matters were allowed to drift, but the natives looked forward to a day of redemption, and during 1856, small cakes, known as chupatties were mysteriously circulated throughout India. These cakes were carried to the head man of every village, and he at once sent similar ones to the next village. It came to the knowledge of the authorities that this secret sign was being passed through the land, and it was urged upon them that it foreboded ill and that very serious trouble indeed was brewing. Still they declined to take any notice of it. They said it was merely a superstitious rite and had no significance; the idea that it was the beginning of a vast conspiracy which was to knit Hindoos and Mussulmans together in a common cause, never entered the heads of those who were responsible for the safety of our great dependency. No one now who looks back to those dark days can doubt for a moment that the government of the time committed a grave blunder in being blind to all the signs, and deaf to all the warnings. The moan of the rising wind was making itself manifest over the land, but those who ought to have taken means to prepare for the storm remained supremely indifferent.

The immediate cause which led to the great outbreak, was attributed to the incident of the greased cartridges. The Enfield rifle which was a tremendous stride in the improvement in arms of precision, had been introduced into India. The Enfield necessitated an alteration in the old-fashioned cartridge which had so long been in use, and the cartridge had to be bitten open before being used. This fact at once offered to the enemies of England a tremendous power wherewith to sway the native mind, and they were not slow to avail themselves of it. Far and wide amongst the soldiery, upon whom our hold on India seemed to depend, the report was spread that we had greased these cartridges with hog's fat and cow's fat; and that our object in so doing was to break the caste of the Hindoos and degrade them to a common level, for Hindoos are specially prohibited by their creed from eating animal fat. The belief that their religion was being interfered with made the natives furious, and neither a proclamation of the Governor-General, nor the withdrawal of the offending cartridge served to calm the fury. At Dum-dum, Barrackpore and other places open acts of mutiny took place, and executions and disbandments were resorted to; nevertheless with a supineness that seems now truly wonderful the authorities refused to believe in any widespread discontent. But the fatal day was fast approaching when tocsin-like the alarm was to ring through the land that England was in real danger; and those who were responsible for the well being of our fellow subjects were to be rudely shaken out of their apathy.

It was the 23rd of April 1857, and on the parade ground at Meerut. The 3rd Bengal Cavalry—that is a native regiment—were drawn up for instruction in platoon exercise. Meerut was one of our most important military stations, and the barracks and cantonments were all on an extensive scale. Its distance from Delhi is 34 miles in a N.E. direction. It has played an important part in the history of India for in 1819 it offered a desperate resistance to Mahmud of Ghizni who was then conducting military operations against Kunäoge. In the early part of the 13th century it was invested by the army of Jurma-Kuorin Khan, a descendant of Gheius Khan. The defenders, however, offered such a determined front to their foes that the besiegers were worn out and withdrew suffering fearful loss. In 1399, when the name of Timor was ringing through India, and when he had carried fire and sword into the proud Mogul city of Delhi itself, he called upon the garrison of Meerut to lay down their arms. They not only declined to do this but laughed the conqueror's ambassadors to scorn. Timor at once laid siege to the city, and after a fearful and protracted struggle it fell into his hands. He thereupon, out of revenge, gave it over to the plunder of his troops and a frightful massacre ensued. It is said that Timor himself fired the place on the windward side, and the flames spreading rapidly reduced the town to ashes with the exception of the citadel and fortifications which being built of solid masonry defied the ravages of the flames. When the English conquered India they recognised the importance of Meerut as a military station, and at the time of the outbreak of the mutiny a very large force of troops—principally of natives—was stationed there.

The 3rd Bengal Light Cavalry had already shown some signs of insubordination. The regiment was in command of Colonel Carmichael Smith who seems to have had thorough faith in his men. He knew that ninety of them were armed with muzzle loading carbines, and with a view to putting their loyalty to the test he harangued them on that now historical parade day and pointed out to them the groundlessness of their fears as regarded the greased cartridges. Then he gave orders to them to load their carbines with the suspected cartridge. Five out of the ninety did this but eighty-five of them stood sullen and silent with scowling looks on their dark faces. The order was repeated but without effect, and the parade was dismissed. Of course a court-martial followed immediately, and the eighty-five mutineers were put upon their trial. It stood to reason that only one result of the court-martial was possible. That result was a verdict of "guilty" and each man was sentenced to ten years' imprisonment.

General Hewett was then in command of the Meerut Division, and this gallant officer being strongly of opinion that the native regiments as a body were as stanch as steel, and that the mutinous eighty-five were a mere handful of malcontents who by no means represented the opinions of their fellows, considered the sentences too severe, and in the case of the younger men he reduced the sentences to five years. Rightly or wrongly it has been said that this leniency confirmed the native opinion that we were weak and afraid. But looking at all the circumstances now dispassionately—as we are able to do at this point of time—it is highly probable that the reduction of the punishment had little to do with subsequent events which were the outcome of a long period of supineness, and a fatuous belief in our own greatness. The fire had long been smouldering and gathering strength, and the insubordination at Meerut on the 24th of April was but part of a settled plan, for there was hardly a native regiment in India that was not more or less affected, and the work of preparing them for the great crisis had proceeded slowly but surely. All that was wanted was a little vent to let the fire burst forth. That vent was made at Meerut; and the erstwhile confined forces broke free with one appalling upheaval.

On the 9th of May, the whole garrison of Meerut was paraded to hear the sentences of the Court-Martial read out and to witness the degradation of the eighty-five mutineers. It was a Saturday morning and the scene was one which was not likely to be ever forgotten by those who took part in it. There wasn't a white man there who didn't feel that a supreme crisis had arrived and that our fate trembled in the balance. Besides the disgraced regiment, there were two native infantry corps present, namely the 11th and 20th, while the European artillery were drawn up in readiness and in addition there were Her Majesty's 60th Foot, the 6th Dragoon Guards, and the carabineers. All the white troops were provided with service ammunition, and they were so posted that the native regiments were at their mercy. This will serve to show that the authorities had at last awakened to the fact that there was real danger.

When the sentence had been duly read out the eighty-five mutineers were ordered to step forward. Native blacksmiths then proceeded to fit each man with a pair of leg irons. For two long hours in the broiling sun the troops stood motionless, their nerves strung to the highest pitch, while the felon-shackles were being rivetted on, and the miserable criminals were crying aloud to their comrades to help them. But never a response came; never an arm was raised. The stern British troops who were ready on the slightest sign to spring to action, overawed the native soldiers and the native crowd alike. It was a splendid lesson of what determination and a bold front can do even against long odds. But now comes the most remarkable part of the tragic drama. The ceremony being over, the felons were marched off to a jail two miles distant, and there left entirely in charge of their own countrymen. It seems difficult now to understand how such stupendous folly could have been possible after the imposing ceremony of degradation, and the display we made of our power. But so it was, and from the moment that the men were left the plot began. On the following day, Sunday, the 3rd Bengal Cavalry resolved to rescue their comrades. Collecting a number of native smiths they rode over to the jail, broke into the cells, released the prisoners, ordered the smiths to strike off their fetters, and then they rushed to the quarters of the other two native regiments who at once joined them and rose in rebellion. With a great cry of vengeance they made their way to the European quarters thinking to find the greater number of the English at church. In this they were mistaken, for a warning had already gone forth that something was about to happen. Colonel Finnis, who rode out to try and pacify the men, was shot dead. He was the first victim of the mutiny, and the sight of his blood inflamed the rebels to madness. A cruel massacre followed. Unarmed men and defenceless women and children were barbarously slaughtered; no pity was shown. Invalid ladies were dragged from their beds and butchered; and little children were brained and tossed into the gutters. The streets literally ran red with blood, and from various quarters flames broke out as the houses were fired, until the scene resembled a pandemonium. The telegraph wires were cut; all rascaldom turned out, and everyone seemed bent on shedding blood and securing plunder. But even in that dark hour if there had been no wavering on the part of the authorities, and if the English regiments had at once been let loose on the rabble, the local riot would have been crushed out and there would have been no mutiny. There were 1,500 European troops in garrison. They were all splendidly armed. All were seasoned men. Yet for some inscrutable reason they were held in check during the time that the rebels were burning and slaughtering. Late in the evening General Hewett, and General Archdale Wilson, moved their men over the open plain of the infantry parade ground, and ordered a few rounds to be fired. But the night was pitch dark and the soldiers did not know what they were firing at. The only result was that an English officer, Lieutenant Galloway, who had sought shelter in an outhouse that was in the line of fire was nearly killed. After this little display of resolution the force was withdrawn to the European lines again. Having committed all the havoc they could, the rebels cleared out and went as hard as they could to Delhi.

Delhi as most people know is situated on the Ganges and the Jumna. The great city had for centuries been the capital of India, and the metropolis of the great Mogul empire. Gradually decaying, it had nevertheless kept up an outward semblance of strength under the successors of Aurungzebe, who was the last of the great emperors of the house of Timor.

At the time of the outbreak in Meerut there was living in Delhi in the precincts of the magnificent palace an old and withered man nearly ninety years of age. He was in receipt of a handsome pension from the East India company, and had been allowed to keep up some theatrical show of state and greatness. This old man was the Mogul; a direct descendant of Aurungzebe and in the eyes of the natives of Upper India he was the rightful ruler of Hindustan. Many years before this period Macaulay, the historian, writing of this very man, said, "There is still a Mogul, a pensioner of the company, who is allowed to play at holding courts and receiving petitions within the confines of the palace of Delhi, where he might boast of possessing some of the outward attributes of royalty, but who has less power to help or to harm than the youngest official in the company's service."

When Macaulay wrote these words he was in ignorance of the latent power that was pent up in the old man, who was to all intents and purposes a puppet; but whose name was one to conjure with amongst the natives, and who was still regarded by them as a mighty ruler, a king of kings, although fallen from his high estate and ruling nothing but his own household. The Oriental mind, however, must not be gauged by the same standard as that which is used to measure the European with. The natives of Hindustan looked upon this Mogul descendant as a great personage still; and as one whose power might be temporarily eclipsed but not destroyed. What was wanted was a shibboleth, an opportunity to proclaim their king, a king again; and if once he grasped the sceptre, they believed the company's Raj would be over for ever and the accursed Fernighees would be driven out of the country. This shibboleth, this opportunity was found when the Meerut mutineers were allowed, by a fatuous error, to gallop from Meerut to Delhi without being pursued and cut to pieces as they might easily have been, if the splendid battalions of rifle and artillery who were panting to be let loose, but were kept inactive, had been hurled after them. It is generally agreed now that had that been done, not a rebel would have entered the Mogul city to tell the tale. But it was not to be. As the morning dawned they clattered through the gates of Delhi with a great crowd of cut-throats and ruffians in their train. With shouts and cries they swarmed around the palace and awakened the old puppet from his sleep. They bowed down before him and paid him homage; and then with a roar of fierce joy they proclaimed him Emperor of India; and reared the standard of a revolutionary war on the battlements of the palace shouting themselves hoarse with the cry of, "Tamerlane, Tamerlane. Restoration of the Royal House of Tamerlane. Death to the Feringhees."

The palsied old greybeard was shaken for a moment from his lethargy and forgetting his impotence he believed that the hour of triumph had come, and so he accepted the homage of the fanatics. He smiled when they proclaimed him emperor, and in his feeble voice he echoed the cry of "Death to the Feringhees."

Nevertheless he played the hypocrite for a time, and summoned to his presence, Captain Douglas who was in charge of the palace guards. The palsied and tottering old man met the captain in what was known as the Hall of Audience, and said he was afraid something had happened and that he thought there had been a mutiny. On hearing this, Douglas said he would go and talk with the mutineers, but the king forbade him to do this. In the mean time the rebels were not standing idle. They scattered themselves through the town, and a terrible scene ensued. Every European they met fell a prey to their ferocity; and as they went an enormous Mahometan rabble gathered about them, and the air was rent with cries of "Glory to the Padishah and Death to the Feringhees." Having run amuck through the town, setting fire to houses and shops they doubled back to the Calcutta gate where somebody had informed them, Douglas and other Englishmen had gathered, amongst them being Commissioner Frazer. As the rebels rushed up with the shout of "Deen, Deen", Frazer suddenly seized a musket from one of the guard and shot the foremost trooper dead. He then sprang into his buggy in which he had hastily driven to the palace on hearing the uproar, and drove off to the Lahore gate. At the same time Douglas sprang into the ditch of the Fort, and though severely injured by the fall, he crept towards the palace gate. Some *chuprassies* of the Palace Guard lifted him up, for he was almost powerless from the injuries he had received in his leap, and they bore him into the palace. He was taken to a room where the chaplain and a number of Englishmen and women had gathered in affright, not knowing exactly what had happened, and before they could decide on any plan of action, the cowardly ruffians who had been clamouring for admission were admitted by some traitor, and rushing up the stairs guided by a native servant they burst into the room where the unhappy English people were gathered, and every soul there was murdered in the most brutal manner. And not content with slaying the hapless people, the murderers mutilated their bodies, slashing some of them out of all chance of recognition. Their brutal work completed, and worn out with excitement and fatigue, they stabled their horses in the courts of the palace, while the splendid Hall of Audience was turned into a barrack, and straw being scattered about, they threw themselves down to sleep. Thus the great city made common cause with the mutineers. The regiments in garrison rose and put many of their officers to death. The English residences were looted and fired. A band of Hindoo gipsies lay in wait to kill every European who was found abroad. In the town the scenes of Meerut were re-enacted; a wholesale massacre began. Hundreds fell, and the rest who could do so made their escape.

There were clergymen, officials, officers, men, women and children, who, broken-hearted and ruined, sought to reach some haven of safety. But many fell into the hands of the bloodthirsty gipsies; others perished from exhaustion and fright. A party of about fifty men, women and children were brought together to the palace where they were confined in an underground apartment, with what object is not known, for at the end of a few days, they were butchered in cold blood.

Not very far from the palace was situated the

great Delhi magazine, with all its vast supplies of munitions of war. At that time it was in charge of Lieutenant George Willoughby of the Ordnance Commissariat Department. He was supported by Lieutenant Forrest and Lieutenant Raynor both of the Bengal Artillery. In addition there were six European conductors and commissariat sergeants. The European magistrate of the city was Sir Thomas Metcalfe, and when he heard of the outbreak he rushed to the magazine to obtain a couple of guns in order that he might defend the bridge over the river, but he soon learned that it was too late, for the rebels had already swarmed in. Thereupon he called upon the little band in the magazine to defend it to the last. This they had resolved to do, and rather than let it fall into the hands of the mutineers, they would blow it up and bury themselves in the ruins. The outer gates were at once closed and barricaded. Guns were then brought out, loaded with double charges of grape and posted so as to command the gates. These arrangements hurriedly completed, a train was laid from the powder magazine and it was preconcerted, that should the magazine be attacked, and defence become hopeless, a match was to be applied to the train, and the enormous stores were to be blown up. While this noble little band, were thus heroically determined to thwart the rebels, messengers came from the king to say that the arsenal was to be given up. These messengers were soon packed about their business, and then the rebels began to swarm towards the magazine, armed with scaling-ladders and other appliances. Then all the natives in the magazine, the gun lascars, artificers and others, threw off their allegiance and making a bolt sprang over the walls, and joined the rabble. A desperate attempt was now made by the mutineers to take the place, and the gallant Englishmen plied them with grape, but though they reeled and recoiled they came on again, and many of the sepoys climbed the walls, and kept up a rolling fire of musketry. For hours the terrible fight was sustained, until the garrison had exhausted all their ammunition, and could not descend from their posts for more. Then came the supreme act in this splendid defence. Willoughby gave the signal, and Conductor Scully fired the train. A tremendous explosion ensued. Hundreds of the rebels were hurled to destruction, and a large section of the city was shaken down as by an earthquake. Strangely enough, four out of the band of nine gallant fellows escaped the effects of the explosion.

The news of the revolt soon spread, and when the people of Calcutta heard it they were highly indignant, for they thought the mutiny ought never to have been allowed to go to the length it had gone to. No worse time for the rising could have been chosen as far as the English were concerned, than this. The number of available European troops in India was about 38,000 only, while opposed to them were 200,000 sepoys, all trained and drilled in the European modes of warfare. Moreover, they were comparatively well armed and supplied with ammunition. Most of the European forces were posted either on the Afghan or the Pegu frontiers, and between them and Calcutta lay 1,200 miles, over which space was scattered the vast native army. At this time Lord Canning was Governor General of India, and he at once took active steps to meet the awful danger that threatened us. An expedition had been fitted out for a campaign in China, and the troops destined for that work were at once recalled. England had also been at war with Persia, but that war had come to a close just before the outbreak of the mutiny, and Sir James Outram who had conducted it with such brilliant success was, together with his war-seasoned army, available for service in India. In Calcutta the excitement and agitation were tremendous, as day after day, news reached the city that the revolt was spreading like wildfire. The whole of Northern India seemed involved, and it was pretty certain that unless energetic measures were at once taken to check the spread, the Madras and Bombay Presidencies would also rise. Lord Canning in spite of much opposition, and a great deal of personal abuse, as it was thought at the time that he showed too much sympathy with the natives, persevered in his course, and he called to his aid every man available who was capable of giving advice or wielding a sword. Amongst them were the two splendid soldiers, Sir John, and Sir Henry Lawrence. The Lawrences proved a host in themselves, and to them was due to a very large extent, the measures which prevented the revolt spreading south. The way in which they disarmed the native regiments at Meean Meer who were about to mutiny, cannot be told too often. Meean Meer is in the Punjaub. It was known that a very dangerous temper was manifesting itself amongst the sepoys, so a parade was ordered for daybreak. When the troops assembled they were put through certain military movements which brought the heads of four columns of the native soldiers in front of twelve guns charged to the muzzle with grape. Behind the guns stood silent and grim the British artillerymen with their port fires lighted in their hands. Behind these again was a line of Queen's soldiers standing ready with loaded rifles. Having thus decoyed the sepoys into a trap they were ordered to pile their arms. They stood literally at the cannon's mouth and they would have been swept off the face of the earth by the fire of those twelve guns. Sullenly they obeyed the order and as the arms were piled, they were collected by European soldiers, thrown into carts that were in readiness, and borne away. By this masterly movement, mutiny was prevented and the Punjaub was saved.

Everyone who knew anything at all of the situation recognised that the re-capture of Delhi was of paramount importance and an army was at once prepared for that desperate duty. General Anson was placed in command of it, but unhappily before he could try conclusions with his foe he fell a victim to cholera which was committing more ravages even than the natives were. Although poor Anson died on the march he was severely criticised by people who seemed to have lost their heads and were incapable of understanding what a stupendous undertaking the recapture of Delhi was. This important city is situated in the centre of a sandy plain upon a rocky ridge which rises to an altitude of 120 feet on the right bank of the Jumna, which is here a deep and broad river at all seasons of the year. The city proper was about five miles in circumference at the time of the mutiny. It was built on a range of rocky hills surrounded by walls constructed of large blocks of grey granite and fortified with a loopholed parapet. At intervals in the wall were gateways and bastions, and the whole place was one of considerable strength, and capable of withstanding a protracted siege. The mutineers, who had shut themselves up there, were at least thirty thousand strong; and they were assisted by the huge population who hated the British rule. The work, therefore, of taking the city was not likely to be a military promenading. It promised, in fact, to prove the most desperate undertaking the English had been engaged in for a very long time.

Sir Henry Barnard was appointed successor to General Anson, but this unfortunate officer's mind suddenly gave way under the tremendous strain put upon it. His very anxiety to fulfil his duty hastened his end, and early in July he, too, fell a victim to cholera after an illness of only six or seven hours. General Reed succeeded to the command, but he suffered so much in health that he had to return to the Punjaub. Then Brigadier General Wilson essayed the task, and he conducted the siege operations with great skill and gallantry.

There is little doubt that when the rebels found themselves in possession of Delhi they had an idea that all was won, though that belief showed a very poor opinion indeed of England's power. But after the cruel massacre, and when so many days were allowed to pass without any show of force being made, it really seemed as if the Feringhees had been wholly destroyed. The exultant pride of the rebels, however, was soon to receive a shock. They had established themselves in force in a village about six miles from the great city. It was known as Budlee-Ka-Serai. It was full of groups of old houses and walled gardens, having once been the country seat of members of the imperial family. The houses although old, were well built, and they and the walled gardens rendered it very suitable for a military outpost where a watch could be kept. In this place the mutineers established themselves in strength, for until this village was taken, no force could sit down before Delhi. They threw up earth works, planted guns in them, and made it a formidable position. On the 8th of June, however, that was a little less than a month after the outbreak, a small English force was sent against that village; a tremendous fight took place, but our arms were triumphant, and the saucy enemy was shattered and broken; and such of them as survived the onslaught fled in all haste to the city. That was the first effective blow struck, and it created a deep impression, for the sepoys realised that the Feringhees had not been wiped out altogether. But though this village had been taken with comparative ease, the humblest drummer-boy realised that the reduction of the huge city would be a long and laborious process. For some time great difficulty was experienced in getting up a siege train, and anything like a thorough investment was out of the question, while no attempt could be made to stop the various streams of mutineers who poured in from the south, and ceaselessly harassed the little army which held its ground gallantly, and waited patiently for the expected reinforcements, and the necessary material for carrying on the work. It was weary waiting, however, for disease and casualties diminished our force, while the enemy's was increased by brigades and regiments who marched into the city almost daily, their arrival being greeted with cheers and gun firing. But in spite of misery, suffering and death, the small army made up of English, Sikhs and Gurkhas clung to their ground and refused to be driven away. In the early part of August, the rebels made a desperate attempt to cut off the communication of the besiegers. Not far off was a canal known as the Najufgush canal spanned by a bridge which our troops had destroyed. The enemy took possession of this, re-established the bridge, and were then able to threaten the communications.

But on the 14th of August, General Nicholson led into the Delhi camp the moveable column which had already done splendid service in disarming the mutineers at Plullour, and Umritsar, and in destroying a brigade at Trimmoo Ghat. Eleven days later he marched out again with a small force of all arms, fell upon the enemy at Najufgush, swept them away with heavy loss to themselves, and cleared the road for the approach of the siege train, which was slowly making its way from Ferozepore Arsenal. But not until the 4th of September did the huge guns and mortars, drawn by colossal elephants roll through the camp on to the Ridge. On the 6th a final batch of reinforcements, the 60th Rifles from Meerut entered the camp, and preparations were at once begun for the great assault. From that moment there was little rest for anyone. It was work, work. Engineers, sappers and miners toiled with a heartiness and will beyond all praise, and as fast as the monster guns were mounted they vomited forth their iron hail against the doomed city.

On the night of the 13th of September a tremendous fire was kept up on Delhi, and an order flew through the camp that the long-prepared-for assault would be delivered at three in the morning. The whole force was divided into four columns, and a "Rescue." The first was to storm the breach that had been made at the Cashmere bastion; the second was to hurl itself against the water bastion where there was also a breach, the third was to blow open the Cashmere gate, and the fourth whose position was on the extreme right was told off to clear Kissengunge and enter by the Lahore gate, while the reserves were to follow up in the wake of the first three columns, and throw in supports wherever necessary. The post of honour and danger was claimed by General Nicholson. The morning of the 14th dawned. It was big with the fate of the mutineers. The sun sprang up in the sky and gilded the domes of the mosques and minarets of the Mogul city which had so often in its history withstood storm and siege, and had witnessed blood poured out like water. But on this day a scene was to be enacted compared with which all the others sank into insignificance. The British camp was early astir and every man was eager and burning for the fray. Quietly but rapidly the troops were got into their respective positions, and then the great struggle began. The cavalry brigade was under the command of Sir Hope Grant, and they had to stand almost powerless under a fierce hurricane of grape and musketry. The 4th column had unfortunately been driven back. They had failed to force an entrance into the city by the Lahore gate partly owing to the want of artillery. Then fell upon the cavalry brigade the stern duty of keeping the enemy from pouring out and pursuing the retreating infantry. The brigade was small. All told it was only about six hundred horse, while the rebels numbered thousands. An awful rain of lead was poured on the devoted brigade from the walls of the city and from Kissengunge. Men and horses went down, but there was no flinching; the ranks were closed up, and the noble few refused to yield an inch of ground although they were unable to return the fire or do anything but remain as targets for the enemy's fire. It was an awful but honourable position, and not until the success of the column at the Cashmere gate had drawn the rebels off from the Lahore, was the crippled and shattered brigade able to retire from their post of honour. They had sacrificed themselves to save their infantry comrades.

When our troops gained a footing in the city the carnage that ensued was dreadful. The native soldiers fought, so to speak, with a rope round their necks. From street to street and house to house the maddened defenders went. No quarter was given on either side, none was asked for. To such a pitch of fury were the besiegers wrought by the memory of their murdered countrymen and women that it was only with difficulty they were restrained from reducing the whole city to ashes.

As showing how enormous were the odds against us, it may be stated that the strength of the four assaulting columns was only 3,660 men; the reserves numbered 1,500, making a total of 5,160. "Opposed to them was a fortress seven miles in circumference, filled with an immense fanatical Mussulman population, garrisoned by fully 30,000 soldiers armed and disciplined by ourselves, with 114 heavy pieces of artillery mounted on the walls, with the largest magazine of shot, shell and ammunition in the upper provinces at their disposal, besides some 60 pieces of field artillery, all of our own manufacture, and manned by artillerymen drilled and taught by ourselves."* The result of the day's tremendous fighting was, that with a loss of 1,145 on our side in killed and wounded, we were only able to get a grip of a very small corner of the city, but it was the grip of the British bulldog, and all the efforts of the desperate defenders were powerless to dislodge us. So the roar of conflict continued and for some hours, as is now well known, it was a question whether after all we should not have to beat a retreat from sheer weakness. If such had been the case it would have been a disaster, but fortunately our hard-won gains were kept.

On the 16th an important advance was made. An assault was delivered upon the magazine which was taken with a trifling loss. There were still great stores of artillery munitions in it, and without a moment's waste of time, mortars were got into position and turned against the palace which was only a quarter of a mile distant, and where a strong body of the rebels were still posted and defiant. On the night between the 18th and 19th, the besiegers steadily worked their way from house to house and enclosure to enclosure, during which many a hand-to-hand encounter took place, for the enemy died hard, and when the morning came we were

* Extract from Colonel Wilson's letter to Colonel Baird Smith, dated 30th August 1857.

in possession of the Lahore Bastion, before which Sir Hope Grant's Cavalry Brigade had made such a magnificent stand.

It was found that the old King, his son and his household had fled, and inquiries led to its being known that he was concealed in a place known as Hunundyoon's Tomb, about five miles outside of the city. Captain Hodson of "Hodson's Horse," a body of irregular cavalry which had performed excellent service, rode out with a number of his men, and reaching the King's refuge, he found the courtyard occupied by a number of troops. Boldly going in amongst them he commanded them to lay down their arms. Either because they were demoralised by the recent events, or because they didn't know that he had only a handful of men with him, they sullenly obeyed the command. Then he sent a peremptory message to the King to surrender, and presently he tottered forth, a pitiable wreck, yet still pleading for his life, which Hodson promised should be spared. He was placed in a bullock waggon, conveyed as fast as possible to the town and confined as a prisoner in the palace, where he remained in close captivity until his death. On the following morning, Hodson, on learning that the King's sons, and some relatives were still in the tombs, rode out again, and seized two younger sons of the King, and a grandson, the Shahzada or heir-apparent. They gave themselves up unconditionally, and were driven away in a bullock gharry, Hodson following them. When within a couple of miles of Delhi, they were met by an enormous crowd who were evidently bent on rescuing the prisoners. Hodson, in the face of the odds against him, halted, made the princes alight, and having taxed them with having taken part in the massacres at Delhi, which they strenuously denied, he shot them dead one after the other. For this act he has been very much criticised, and even friends have said that he committed a grave error. But he knew and saw that the slightest wavering on his part would be fatal, and had the princes been rescued and got out of the city as they assuredly would have been the mutiny beyond all doubt would have been, prolonged. That Hodson was a brave man and excellent soldier no one will deny, and it is a great pity that a charge of having exceeded his duty should rest upon his memory; for he did what any man of resource and energy would have done. It was not a time to halt between two opinions, and recognising the hopelessness of trying to convey his captives through the angry and excited mob, he slew them rather than let them escape.

Perhaps the most ghastly page in the history of the great revolt is the story of the massacre of Cawnpore. For terrible ferocity and fiendish cruelty it has not many parallels in the world's story. Cawnpore at the time of the mutiny was a great and important military station. It is on the high road to Oude, and about fifty miles from Lucknow. In 1857 its population was something like 60,000 natives, 1000 Europeans and Eurasians mostly engaged in trade, a large garrison of native soldiers, and 300 English officers and soldiers who were under the command of a veteran, Sir Hugh Wheeler. In addition there was a considerable number of women and children, the wives and families of the officers and soldiers.

A few miles up the river Ganges which waters Cawnpore was the small town of Bithoor, which years before had been appointed as the residence of the Peishwa of Poonah, Bagee Rao. This man had formerly been ruler over an extensive territory which had been annexed by the East India Company who allowed him a very handsome income, and to keep up a show of royal state, as some compensation for his loss. He was the last of his race, a powerful Mahratta family who had for ages terrorised and ruled with a pitiless and iron hand. Having no children of his own he had adopted as his son and heir one, Seereck Dhoordoo Punth, who was destined to live in history for ever more as Nana Sahib of Bihoor. On the death of his foster father Nana Sahib expected that the handsome pension which Bagee Rao had enjoyed would be continued to him in accordance with oriental custom. But Lord Dalhousie and the John Company made the fatal error of cutting off the pension. Nana Sahib, although a wealthy man, was greatly incensed at this cheese-paring economy, and he made frequent applications that the pension might be restored. Failing to get a favourable response, he sent in 1854, a young man of low origin, who was known as Azimoolah Khan, as his agent to London, to advocate his claim there. Azimoolah had by some means or other become a great favourite with the Nana who regarded him somewhat in the light of a brother. He was clever, unscrupulous, and in many respects brilliant. He spoke English well, and was plausible, fluent and persuasive, although he failed in his mission. But in England he was lionised, and fêted, and society petted him for the time, for he was "a novelty." Although this, however, failed to win his good opinion, as an oriental he knew how to conceal his true feelings, and few of the many great ladies who fawned upon him dreamed of the deadly hatred that had been called into being in his black heart by the refusal of the authorities to grant his prayer for the restoration of the pension to his master.

Wearied at last with the fulsome flattery, Azimoolah took his departure smarting with disappointment and dangerously embittered. It was the time of the Crimean war, with its sad story of disaster and suffering, and Azimoolah gathered from this that the power of England was waning and her influence was no longer worth anything. At any rate he represented to his master, Nana Sahib, that it was so, and there is no doubt now that the Nana was inflamed with a fierce desire for vengeance for insulted pride and wounded dignity. But at that time he saw no opportunity of gratifying that vengeance. He had the oriental's patience, however, and he knew how to wait. So he kept up an outward semblance of great friendliness for the English and often entertained the officers and others with princely hospitality, and with an apparent sincerity of purpose which left nothing to be desired.

The city or town of Cawnpore at the time of the mutiny was purely a commercial town, and had never figured in history. Its trade was in leather, and its leatherwork was renowned. It was washed by the broad waters of the Ganges, on which floated vessels of all sizes and shapes, from the venetianed pinnace to the humble dinghy. Cawnpore had long been used as a military station. It was a long straggling place six or seven miles in extent. The British lines stretched along the southern bank of the Ganges which was spanned by a bridge of boats about midway between the two extremities of the cantonment. This bridge led from a point opposite the city to the Lucknow road on the other bank. The private dwellings, houses and public offices of the English were scattered in the most promiscuous manner. There were theatres, churches, meeting houses, fashionable promenades and public gardens. It had always been regarded as one of our greatest Indian stations and there were few military officers whether of the Queen's or the Company's army but had their quarters there during some period of their eastern service. When the mutiny broke out the place was still the head quarters of the Division, and the commanding General resided there with the Division staff. But there were no longer European regiments, or even a European regiment in its barracks. A great strength of native soldiers garrisoned the station, with some sixty men of Her Majesty's 84th Regiment and a few Madras Fusiliers whom Tucker and Ponsonby had sent on from Benares.

The Cawnpore Division was commanded by General Sir Hugh Wheeler, an old and distinguished officer of the company's army. He was seventy years of age but bore the burden of his years well. Short in stature and light in weight he was an excellent horseman, as well as a most efficient soldier. When the outbreak occurred there were a large number of invalids, women and children of the 32nd Queen's Regiment quartered in the town, and the responsibility of protecting these people fell upon the aged general. In carrying out this duty he threw up some earthworks, within which all the Christian population were to assemble. The spot selected was about six miles from the river to the north east, and not far from the sepoys' huts. There were quarters of a kind for the people within two long hospital barracks. One was built wholly of masonry. The other had a thatched roof. They were single storied buildings with verandahs running round them, and the usual outhouses attached. As soon as danger threatened, the general began to entrench this spot, to fortify it with artillery, and to provision it with supplies of various kinds. The fortifications so-called were so paltry that a boy might have ridden over them. The earthworks were little more than four feet high; and not even bullet proof at the crest. The apertures for the artillery exposed both guns and gunners, whilst an enemy in adjacent buildings could find cover on all sides. But no better place could be fixed upon and no better defence made. The weather was excessively dry, with the result that the earth was so hard it was difficult to dig it; and so friable was it when it was dug that there was no cohesion in it. At the request of General Wheeler eighty-four men of the 32nd Queen's were sent from Lucknow by Sir Henry Lawrence. A detachment of the 84th was also sent from Benares.

So the days wore on and when June came and there was no outbreak Wheeler thought all danger had passed, and being under the impression that other places needed assistance more than he did, he ordered part of the detachment of the 84th to proceed to Lucknow. It was a fatal error, but one that was easily excusable. Scarcely had they got clear of the city when an outbreak occurred. The gaol was burst open, the treasury sacked, and the magazine seized by the rebels with all its supplies of ammunition, and the priceless wealth of heavy artillery. These things were piled on elephants and in carts, the first intention of the mutineers being to make straight for the Mogul city. But the crafty, cunning and treacherous Nana Sahib—who had promised to help the English—did not like the idea of centralising the mutiny. The restoration of the Mogul might be all very well. But he too wanted to be restored and he wanted to be revenged. The rebels had already begun their march accompanied by the

Nana, and had reached a place called Killianpore where they halted. Here the Nana harangued them until they succumbed to his influences and turning their backs on the imperial city they marched to Cawnpore again.

With the Nana were Balla Rao, and Baba Bhut, his brothers; the Rao Sahib his nephew, and Tantia Topee who had been his playfellow in former days, and was then his counsellor and his guide and possessed great influence over him. At the command of this proud, ambitious and cruel Mahratta were four disciplined native regiments, besides all his Bithoor retainers. He had great stores of ammunition, guns of various calibre, and abundance of treasure. With these things, aided by determination, what could he not accomplish, and ever by his side, walking with him like his shadow, and whispering promises of greatness in his too ready ears, was the fiendish Mahomedan Azimoolah, upon whom English women had fawned, but who hated the English with a hatred passing words. So the Nana threw in his influence, his power and his sword against Wheeler, and on the 6th of June he wrote a letter to the general to say he intended to attack the entrenchments. The little garrison did all they could to strengthen their position and about noon the booming cannon told that the attack had begun.

"Then commenced a siege the miseries of which have seldom been exceeded. The June sky was little better than a canopy of fire; the summer breeze that blew was like the blast of a furnace.

To touch the barrel of a gun was to recoil as from red hot iron. But even under the fierce meridian sun the little band of brave men were ever straining to sustain the strenuous activity of constant battle against fearful odds. Our weary, over-worked, under-fed people labouring in the trenches, ever under fire, with the clothes rotting on their backs, and the grime from the guns caking on their hands and faces. Amongst them was one man ever conspicuous in the front of the battle, inspiring and animating all who served under him by his lustrous example. This was Captain Moore of the 32nd—a soldier of a commanding presence, light-haired and blue-eyed, whom no toil could weary, no danger could daunt. Wounded at the very commencement of the siege he went about with his arm in a sling, but the strong spirit within him defied pain. Day and night he laboured on, now in the trenches, now heading desperate sorties against the enemy; and even when he ceased to hope he neither fainted nor failed. There was no greater heroism than this English captain's in all the war; from first to last no name more worthy than his to be recorded on the roll of English chivalry.

"There were other heroes too. Whiting, captain of the Bengal Engineers, who commanded at the north-west point of the entrenchments. He was a man of stout heart and clear brain. Then there was Jenkins, captain of the second Cavalry, described as one of the bravest and best of the party, who held the outposts beyond the trenches with unflinching gallantry, till a bullet through the jaw from the musket of a sepoy who was feigning death brought his services to an agonising end. There was Mowbray Thomson, subaltern of the 56th, who had the satisfaction, such as it was, of avenging his friend's death on the spot—a gallant soldier ever to be found where danger was hottest. He exposed himself to death in every shape, but seemed to bear a charmed life. And there was his friend and comrade to the last, Delafosse of the 53rd, a young hero, equal to any feat of heroic daring. One day a shot from the enemy's battery had blown up a tumbril and set fire to the woodwork of the carriage in the place where the ammunition was stored. It was clearly seen both by the insurgents and the defenders that if the fire was not extinguished there would be a most disastrous explosion. So the sepoys poured in a deadly stream of eighteen and twenty-four pound shot. But unmoved by these messengers of death, Delafosse went forth, threw himself down beneath the burning carriage, tore off the burning wood with his hands, and throwing dry earth upon the fire, stifled it before it could spread. Then there was Sterling the 'dead shot', who perched up in a sort of crow's nest on the barrack wall which Delafosse had improvised for him, he picked off single sepoys with unerring aim. Jervis of the Engineers, who with the indomitable pride of race refused to run from a black fellow and was shot through the breast whilst walking across the open in stern composure."

And never since war began; never in the "brave days of old" of which poets delight to sing, when women turned their hair into bow strings, has the world seen nobler patience and fortitude than clothed the lives and shone forth in the deaths of the wives and daughters of the fighting men of Cawnpore.

When the missiles fell short by reason of damage done to our pieces by the heavy artillery fire of the enemy, and the canister could not be driven home, the women gave up their stockings, and the canister having been tapped the stockings were charged with the contents of the shot cases. It is related that the wife of a private of the 32nd, Bridget Widdowson by name, stood sentry, sword in hand, over a batch of prisoners tied together by a rope, and the captives did not escape until the feminine guard was relieved by one of the opposite sex.

A terrible misfortune for the little band of heroic defenders was it when the thatched roofed barrack was burned down and the poor women and children had to turn out and lie on the bare ground. But all undaunted by their misfortunes and their awful sufferings, no word of surrender was uttered. The men fought on, and the women cheered them. At last a message was brought by a Christian woman to General Wheeler from the Nana. It was written on a single slip of paper in Azimoolah's handwriting, and it ran:—

"To the subjects of Her Most Gracious Majesty Queen Victoria. All those who are in no way connected with the acts of Lord Dalhousie, and are willing to lay down their arms shall receive a safe passage to Allahabad."

Next morning an armistice was proclaimed and Azimoolah and a subordinate presented themselves near the entrenchments. Captains Moore and Whiting accompanied by Mr. Roche, the Postmaster, went out with full powers to treat with the emissaries of the Nana. It was then proposed that the British should surrender their fortified position, their guns, their treasure, and that they should march out with their arms and sixty rounds of ammunition in the pouch of every man. The Nana was to afford them safe conduct to the river, provide carriages for the women and children, and provisions of flour, sheep and goats for the voyage to Allahabad. The proposals were committed to paper and given to Azimoolah. The same afternoon a horseman from the rebel camp brought back word that the terms were agreed to and the garrison were to move that night. To this Wheeler objected, saying it would be impossible to march until the morning. This was at last agreed to, and though some of the sorely tried band were not very confident that all would be well, there was a general feeling of relief, and hostilities being suspended for the night, the poor worn out people got some sleep and rest. They had hoped against hope for reinforcements and succour, but none had come; and though it broke their pride to have to capitulate to the rebels, for the sake of the women and the little ones who were all in such a fearful plight, they would yield. So the morning dawned and preparation for the exodus was made; and now was enacted a crime which no Englishman can read without the profoundest emotions of both pity and pride.

Forth from their wretched entrenchments, which they had held with such lion-hearted bravery, went the remnants of the garrison, with such of the women and children who had lived through the horrors of the siege, gaunt and ghastly, in tattered garments, emaciated and enfeebled by want, worn by long suffering, some wounded and scarred with the indelible marks of the battle upon them.

"The wounded were borne in palanquins. The women and children went in rough native bullock carts, or on the backs of elephants, while the able-bodied marched on foot, but with little semblance of martial array. The veteran Wheeler with his wife and daughters walked down to the boats. With what faith and hope within him the poor old man turned his face towards the Ghauts, He alone who reads the secrets of all hearts ever knew. But there were many in that woebegone train, although there was no sunshine in their faces, had glimmerings in their hearts of a peaceful future, and who were fain to carry with them as they went, such of their household gods as they had saved from the great wreck, to be treasured in after years in their dear homes beyond the seas.

"The beautiful had left their beauty, the young had left their youth in those battered barracks, and even the children had old and wizened faces which told that they had lived long years in those few terrible weeks.

"The place of embarkation was known as the Suttee Chowra Ghaut, so called from a ruined village close by. The road ran over a wooden bridge painted white. Across this bridge they defiled down into a ravine which led past the compounds of some of the English residences to the Ghaut. Near the Ghaut was a Hindoo Temple known as the Temple of Hurdes, or the Fisherman's Temple, a structure of somewhat fanciful and not unpicturesque design. When the procession reached the point of embarkation the uncouth vessels that were to convey them to their destination, were seen in the stream in shallow water, for it was the close of the dry reason, and the water was at its lowest. The boats were the ordinary, eight oared budgerows of the country; ungainly structures with thatched roofs, looking at a distance like haystacks.

"Every boat that was prepared was intended to be a human slaughter house. The people had not gone down to the banks of the river that was to float them to safety. They had been lured to the appointed shambles, there to be given up to a cruel death. So foul an act of treachery the world has never before seen.

"Tantia Topee, who had been appointed master of the ceremonies, sat enthroned on a 'chaboutree', or platform of the Temple, and issued orders to his dependents. Azimoolah was also there and Teekha Singh. It looked like a holiday show. All the natives lined the banks of the river to see the exodus of the English. The soldiers had gone out in force, horse, foot, and artillery. The troopers sat their horses with their faces turned towards the river.

"No sooner were the people on board than the foul design became apparent. The sounds of a bugle were heard. Then a murderous fire of grape shot and musket balls, opened upon the wretched passengers, from both sides of the river. And presently the thatch of the budgerows, cunningly ignited by hot cinders burst into flame. The men leapt overboard and strove with might and main to push the boats into mid-channel. The bulk of the fleet remained immovable, and the conflagration was spreading; the sick and wounded were burnt to death, or mercilessly suffocated by the smoke, while the stronger women took to the water with their children in their arms to be shot down or sabred in the stream by the troopers who rode in after them, to be bayonetted on reaching land, or made captive and reserved for a later and more cruel immolation.

"The Nana waited in his tent on the cantonment plain. He paced about uneasily, and at last sent orders that no more women and children were to be slain; but not an Englishman was to be left alive.

"Above a hundred women, about one hundred and twenty, some sorely wounded, some half-drowned, all dripping with the water of the Ganges, and begrimed with its mud, were carried back in custody to Cawnpore.

"One boat did manage to get away, and drifted down the dark waters of the river without boatmen, without oars, without a rudder, but it was not destined to go far.

"Soon a blazing budgerow was sent after it, and burning arrows were discharged at its roof. Still the boat was true to its occupants, and made slow progress between the banks. At sunset a pursuing boat came down from Cawnpore with sixty armed natives on board, and they had been ordered to destroy the English. But the pursuer grounded on a sandbank. Then ensued one of those last grand spasms of courage even in death which are seldom absent from stories of British heroism. Exhausted, famishing, sick and wounded as they were, the pursued would not wait to be attacked. A little party of officers and soldiers armed to the teeth fell upon the people who had come to destroy them, and very few of the pursuers lived to tell of their pursuit.

"This was the last victory of the heroic martyrs of Cawnpore. They took the enemy's boat and found in it good stores of ammunition. Sleep fell upon the survivors and when they woke the wind had risen and they found themselves drifting down the stream. But with the first glimmer of morning, despair came upon them, for they discovered that their craft had been carried out of the main stream into a creek where the enemy discovered them and poured in a deadly shower of musketballs. Then Vibart, who lay helpless with both his arms shot through, issued his last orders. It was a forlorn hope but whilst there was a sound man amongst them the great game of the English was to go to the front and smite the enemy, as a race that seldom waits to be smitten. Fourteen rushed forward; charged the natives, and then rushed back to their boat, but it had drifted away and the fourteen were left upon the pitiless land, whilst their doomed comrades floated down the pitiless water. As they retreated along the banks of the river they made for a Hindoo Temple which they had spied. Reaching it, they defended the door with fixed bayonets. After a little time they stood behind a rampart of black and bloody corpses, and fired with comparative security over this rampart of human flesh. A little putrid water found in the temple gave the men new strength, and they held the doorway so determinedly and so gallantly that there seemed no chance of the enemy expelling them by force of arms. So while word was carried to the Nana that the little remnant of the broken army could not be conquered, the assailants brought leaves and faggots which they piled up against the walls and strove to burn out the little garrison. Then Providence came to their help in their sorest need. The wind blew the smoke and fire away from the temple, but the enemy threw bags of powder on the burning embers. So there was nothing left for the people but flight. Precipitating themselves into the midst of the enemy they fired a volley, then charged with the bayonet. Seven of the fourteen carried their lives with them to the banks of the river. There they took to the stream, but presently two of the survivors were shot through the head, whilst a third, making for a sandbank, had his skull battered in as soon as he landed. But the other four being strong swimmers, and with heroic power in doing and suffering, struck down the stream and aided by the current, evaded their pursuers.

"Since the days of early Rome when the three kept the bridge; there have been none more worthy of all the honour that a sovereign or a nation could bestow, than those who held the temple on the banks of the Ganges, and fought their way through an armed multitude thirsting for their blood, until from village to village ran the cry that the English could not be beaten.

"The boat which had escaped was brought back. It contained about eighty men, women and children. The Nana went out to gloat his eyes upon the scene. The men were doomed at once to death. The women and children with greater refinement of cruelty, were reserved for a second death.

"This done Dundoo Punt, the Nana Sahib, went off to his palace at Bithoor. Next day in all the pride and pomp of power he was publicly proclaimed Peishwah. No formality, no ceremony was omitted that could give dignity to the occasion.

"He took his seat upon the throne. The sacrament of the forehead mark was duly performed. The cannon roared out its recognition of the new ruler, and when night fell the darkness was dispelled by a general illumination and showers of fire-works.

He tried to drown the cares of state with music, dancing and buffoonery, and when these things failed to still his conscience he sought oblivion in strong drink."

"In the meantime the captive women and children were moved to a small house known as the "Bubei-Ghur". It had recently been used as the residence of a Eurasian clerk. In this scanty accommodation were penned over two hundred women and little ones. The place lay between the native city and the river, and within the shadow of the improvised palace of the Peishwah.

"In a very short time a fifth of their number were dead of cholera, dysentry and other diseases. The rest were reserved for the insatiable vengeance of Nana Sahib. Baffled and despairing at last, for news had been brought to him that General Havelock was marching rapidly towards the city, he determined nevertheless to satisfy his lust for revenge. The survivors were told that they would be massacred, and the manner in which that was carried out has scarcely a parallel in history. Five men— two of them said to be butchers from the shambles, two were Hindoo peasants, and the fifth was a servant of the Nana's — were sent to the prison house one evening. Then ensued a scene which is too horrible even to read. The hapless women and children were literally hacked to pieces and their shrieks and screams were heard at a great distance. When all was at last still in this house of bitter death the accursed butchers emerged from the horrible scene locking the door behind them. The next day all the bodies were dragged out and thrown into a dry well where they were found in a festering heap when Havelock's troops entered the city."

When he saw that all was lost, and his short-lived glory but a mockery, Nana Sahib fled in the direction of Nepaul, and is supposed to have taken shelter in the deadly jungles of the Terai. Every effort was made to capture him, but he was never heard of more, and probably his end will for ever remain a mystery in this world. It is more than likely that he fell a prey to the fierce beasts that have their home in the Terai or to the poisonous exhalations from the swamps. But whatever his end was it must have been a fearful one, and it is easy to imagine his being tortured with the cries of his victims ringing in his ears as he passed from worldly scenes, to a judgment greater than man's.

While the dreadful scenes recorded were being enacted in Cawnpore the residents in Lucknow were no better off. Sir Henry Lawrence, the Governor, struggled with determined valour, and excellent judgment against the mutineers. But the overwhelming odds brought to bear compelled him to retreat to the Residency, which he fortified to the best of his ability as a refuge for the Europeans under his care. Here he had to withstand a determined siege; but he conducted the defence so skilfully and magnificently that the rebels were repulsed again and again. But at last he was mortally wounded by the bursting of a shell, and he expressed a desire that his only epitaph should be—

"Here lies Henry Lawrence, who tried to do his duty."

Meanwhile, tremendous efforts were being made to relieve Lucknow and Cawnpore. General Havelock was marching by forced marches to raise the siege, and in a series of engagements with the mutineers who tried to hold him in check he beat them time after time.

Sir Henry Havelock, who during the mutiny so indelibly wrote his name on the pages of history, was a quiet, modest man, without any influential connections. Although not generally known he had greatly distinguished himself as a soldier, his career dating from before the Burmese war of 1824. He had been educated at the Charterhouse School in London, where his grave and studious nature earned for him the nickname of "Old Phlos" or philosopher. When he entered the army his deeply religious mind attracted a good deal of attention and subjected him to no little ridicule. He was indifferent to it all, however, and he and "his saints" were found to be as efficient soldiers as those who made no outward display of their religious feelings. At any rate the valour of Havelock and his men during the mutiny earned for them an undying reputation amongst their countrymen in far off England, where the movements in India were watched with such intense and anxious interest.

Sir James Outram, who had been appointed chief commissioner in Oudh, hastened to join his force to

Havelock's little army; and with splendid generosity he declined to take the position of commander, to which post his seniority and his official rank clearly entitled him. He declared he would merely act in his civil capacity as commissioner and would place himself and his men at Havelock's disposal, for a soldier who had made such gallant efforts to relieve Lucknow should have all the honour of completing the work. The march up from Calcutta had truly been a tremendous feat of arms. The country was swarming with foes, and the heat was terrific. Battle after battle had been fought, but the onward march could not be stopped. The tired and disease worn soldiers died by the wayside but their comrades were never daunted, though they knew they must face fearful odds and that their steps were dogged by cholera, dysentry, and other kindred diseases. Often they were reduced to terrible straits for commissarlat, and their only drink at times was the stinking water from the nullahs.

On reaching Allahabad, Havelock and his splendid soldiers took a short rest; then the general pushed on again with a little army of only 1,400 men. At Futtipoor he gained a brilliant victory which was acknowledged to be one of the achievements of the year. By the 13th of July he was before Cawnpore, and Nana Sahib and his huge army came out to give him battle, feeling confident of victory. It seemed absurd to suppose that such a handful of men, British though they were, could stand against the tremendous forces the Nana had at his back. But he reckoned without his host. Every white man there was equal to a dozen natives at least. At any rate the treacherous Nana and his troops were scattered and crushed, and he disappeared into the darkness from which he has never emerged. When the British troops got into Cawnpore and saw with their own eyes the awful slaughter-house and the ghastly well, all feelings of mercy fled from their hearts and they wreaked a terrible vengeance.

Fearful that a second massacre might be enacted at Lucknow, General Havelock did not pause in Cawnpore a moment longer than was necessary. He pressed on to the beleaguered city with his brave soldiers in spite of hardship, want and disease. In nine different battles on the way he beat the enemy, and gained Lucknow towards the end of September. Then even with the reinforcements Outram was able to give him, his little army only amounted to 5,600 men, while the enemy around them had 50,000. Yet in spite of the odds they fell upon the rebels, and cut their way through them with heavy loss, to the Citadel, where they were received with the wildest joy and delight by the sorely pressed garrison, who as may be supposed had been reduced to sore straits and had suffered terribly, especially the women and children.

As in Cawnpore, so at Lucknow there had been magnificent instances of individual valour, and many a time were the rebels taught the lesson that it is dangerous to attack lions at bay. If all the brave deeds which were performed by men and even women, during that period of India's agony could be minutely chronicled, we should have some splendid examples of devotion and unselfishness which would go far to elevate human nature to a much higher standard than is generally accorded it.

After the death of Sir Henry Lawrence, Colonel Inglis became responsible for the defence of Lucknow and right well does he seem to have performed his duty. But as may be supposed his resources were severely taxed, and his losses by casualities, and disease were very heavy. But during this trying period when women were suffering agony in silence, and children were crying for bread, no one ever breathed the word "surrender". To fight while there was a gun to fire, a cartridge left, and a man to wield a sword was the feeling that actuated everyone; and young and old alike, the feeble and the strong, men and women united to present a bold front to the pitiless enemy and defy him. And that he was pitiless, cowardly, treacherous, the records of the time too surely prove! Generally, a brave foe respects and admires bravery, and will display generosity when he triumphs. The sepoys unhappily were incapable of anything of this kind. They were maddened with implacable hatred which wreaked itself on the heads of even defenceless babes and helpless women. Everyone in Lucknow therefore knew that it was better far to die than fall into the hands of their foes.

When Havelock got into the city the first intention was to transport the wounded, the sick, and the women and children to Cawnpore, where it was thought they would be safer and better cared for, but it was soon found that even the two military forces combined were too weak to undertake such a task. Havelock himself had lost 535 men out of his little army during the fierce fighting between the 19th and 25th of September. That represented more than a fifth of his available force. So all that could be done was to add their strength to that of the exhausted and suffering garrison and still keep the foe at bay till more reinforcements should arrive, for it did not seem probable that the devoted defenders could be left long without succour.

As soon as Havelock had passed into the beleaguered city the enemy closed up behind him, and their number was strengthened by thousands who came from goodness knows where. Smarting from the blow that had been inflicted upon them they renewed the siege with increased vigour and seemed determined to break through the cordon of steel and carry death to every member of the sorely pressed community. Day and night they harassed the unhappy people, and attempt after attempt was made to gain an entrance. But, like waves that hurl themselves against granite rocks only to be shattered and beaten back, so were those dense masses of yelling sepoys beaten back. Again and again did they recoil before the dauntless few, but their ranks never seemed to thin. Death and disease made great havoc amongst them, but if thousands fell, thousands more were ready to take their place.

And so for days and days, and nights and nights, did the unequal struggle go on. The unhappy garrison suffered terribly, and famine began to increase their woes. And yet they fought as heroes fight. The story of that noble defence of Lucknow against fearful odds is but another splendid page added to the stirring history of England's valour. But to those suffering people it seemed as if help would never come. Often must they have turned their weary eyes to the burning horizon for some sign that would give them hope, but never a sign was there. The blistering sun rose in the morning in the flaming sky, and it set in the evening in a flood of gold and red. Day after day it was the same. The monotony was maddening, and the relentless foe never slept. At every point he tried to break in; and at every hour the clock struck, he was scattering his missiles of death amongst the devoted garrison. To that garrison as the bitter nights passed without bringing a cessation of their heart-rending misery, it must have appeared as if they were neglected and forgotten. Of what was going on in the outer world they knew nothing. No news ever reached them. But the help they wanted and the help they prayed for was coming.

Sir Colin Campbell who had so distinguished himself at the battle of the Alma had been appointed commander-in-chief of the Indian Army, and had received orders to proceed to the east with all possible despatch. As showing that he allowed no time to be lost he commenced his journey the very day after he received his command. As soon as he set foot in India the news flew from lip to lip, and was flashed over the wires wherever they reached; and from the moment of his arrival the fate of the mutiny was sealed. His magnificent little army was fresh, able and burning with a desire to revenge the awful cruelties that had been practised on their hapless countrymen and women. On swept that avenging band; nothing could stand against them, and on the 14th of November, the grim old Scot and his band of heroes had burst through the beleaguering army of Lucknow, and relieved the famine stricken garrison which had bravely held Alum Bagh. This was a group of houses with a surrounding garden to the south of Lucknow. Here Havelock on his arrival had placed four hundred men with his sick and wounded. And at that time he never anticipated that he himself was going to be shut up in the city.

Sir Colin at this time had about 5,000 men under his command. They had performed prodigies of valour, nevertheless it was but a small army compared with the enemy's, and the general was too wary a soldier to allow himself to be taken at a disadvantage, or to throw a chance away. His march up to this point had been a march of triumph; he had rolled every obstacle out of his way; the bands of rebels who had pitted themselves against him, had been practically swept to destruction. Before him flew the news of his advance, and no doubt with the tendency to oriental exaggeration, those who bore it magnified his army into enormous proportions.

This was all in his favour for it demoralised the rebels, and there were unmistakable signs that they were growing despondent. He saw clearly enough therefore that it would never do to weaken the impression his advance had made. A defeat would probably mean for him, disaster; for if the enemy discovered how few in number his army was, they would gain heart, and he too, might find himself beleaguered and reduced to sore straits. But he prevented this by splendid skill and strategy. The grip of the foe was loosened; Havelock and Outram were set free, and it was decided to abandon Lucknow for the time. So with all possible speed, the sick, the wounded, the women and the children were removed to a palace called Dilkoosha five miles from the Residency, and which he had taken before entering Lucknow. And when this had been effected he established himself with the main body of his army at the Alum Bagh.

And now a cruel and terrible blow fell upon the garrison in the death of brave Havelock. The incessant toil of months, the tremendous responsibility, the cankering care, the sleepless nights, the harassing days told upon his iron frame until he was worn out, and dysentery seized him. For some days he lay in the Alum Bagh, suffering much, but uttering no complaint, until merciful death quietly and gently closed his weary eyes, and stilled for ever his aching heart. He had lived as a soldier and died as a soldier; and there was no one amongst that sorely-stricken band who did not feel that in

Sir Henry Havelock he had lost a personal friend. Throughout England his praises had rung. His Queen had acknowledged his splendid services by bestowing upon him a pension, a baronetcy, and the K.C.B. But before this could be made known to him, he had passed from this vale of strife and tears, and was taking his well-earned rest in a soldier's grave beneath a tree in the garden of the Alum Bagh, and on the tree had been carved the single letter "H". The news of his death came like a shock to his countrymen, and never was hero more sincerely mourned than he was. It is not too much to say that in palace and hut alike, there was genuine regret that he had not survived to enjoy his well-earned honours.

This narrative of those distressful days in Lucknow would hardly be complete without a passing reference to the act of heroism and devotion performed by a civilian, a Mr. Kavanagh, who was shut up with the garrison. This gentleman had performed yeoman service during the siege, but he was to make himself famous by still another act of courage which entitles him to be ranked amongst England's roll of heroes. It became known to the beleaguered garrison that Sir Colin Campbell was on his way to their relief; but to such sore straits had they been reduced that it seemed doubtful if they would be able to hold out until he arrived. In these circumstances it was deemed expedient that information should be conveyed to him of their awful plight, so that his march might be accelerated if that were possible. But then arose the question; how was the information to be conveyed? Mr. Kavanagh was equal to the occasion. "I will take it," he said. "But how?" was naturally asked. For a white man to show his face in the enemy's lines meant a cruel death. He would be mercilessly tortured and butchered. No one who knew the temper of the rebels could doubt that. Therefore it seemed that for anyone to go forth was to go to certain destruction. Kavanagh, however, was not to be deterred. He spoke the language of the country fluently, and he would go disguised as a native.

In his letter to the *Times*, Dr. Russell, the war correspondent, thus described Kavanagh whom he met in Lucknow. "He is a square-shouldered, large-limbed, muscular man, a good deal over the middle height, with decided European features; a large head, covered with hair of—a reddish auburn, shall I say? Moustaches and beard still lighter; and features and eyes such as no native that ever I saw possessed. He has made himself famous by an act of remarkable courage—not in the heat of battle, or in a moment of impulse or excitement, but performed after deliberation, and sustained continuously through a long trial."

From this description the difficulty of an effectual disguise will be easily gathered. But Kavanagh did it and made his way through the native lines, conveyed the information, and returned to Lucknow without having been detected. Yet the risk was enormous and he literally carried his life in his hands.

Kavanagh's act has passed into history where our children's children shall read it in the days to come, and it may serve to stimulate many a youth yet unborn to similiar deeds of daring. But as we have said the mutiny years were rich in personal valour. Some of it has been chronicled, but far more has never seen the light of publicity. In a campaign conducted as this one necessarily was, something of the rigid discipline of grim warfare was relaxed, for very frequently a handful of men, probably under the command of a subaltern, would find themselves surrounded in a position where it was every man for himself. On such occasions, hand-to-hand encounters brought out all the qualities of swordsmanship, and many a desperate fight took place between a British soldier and a sepoy, and the records go to prove that the Britisher proved himself the better man. Not but what many of the sepoys were most excellent swordsmen, but somehow they lacked the coolness and steadiness indispensable to a horseman who finds himself pitted against another mounted man. The frenzied excitement which the natives so frequently displayed in their encounters with their enemies was the means of their undoing, and many a man went to earth, who had he been more collected might have lived to tell his grand-children how with a mighty sweep of his tulwar he had claved in twain the skull of some English fighting man.

There is one good story of dare-devilry which

so far as I know has not been generally recorded. A certain officer, well-known for his recklessness and courage, obtained permission of his commander to reconnoitre a village where a considerable body of the enemy was supposed to be concealed. With only about fourteen or fifteen men at his back he started off, and having galloped for many miles he drew rein in front of a gateway in a wall which ran round a village. There were indications that behind the wall a number of sepoys were posted. The number might have been a thousand or it might have been a hundred for aught the officer knew, and for aught he cared. Calling out to his men in Hindustani he said "Fifteen of you only will follow me in; the rest of the regiment will remain in readiness outside." Then this bold officer rode through the gateway, and found eighty or ninety sepoys in the act of cooking their dinner. But at the sound of his voice they had started to their arms, and were prepared to give battle. "Pile your arms" he cried to the startled soldiers, and they, actually believing that an English regiment was outside, did pile their arms. Then he ordered the young men to drive the old ones out, as the old ones had no doubt led them astray, and this being done he shot the greybeards; and having disposed of them, he killed the young fellows for their cowardice in giving up their comrades. This remarkable and summary execution of the rebels having been carried out to the officer's entire satisfaction he and his men proceeded to feast on the dinner which the luckless sepoys had commenced to cook but were destined never to partake of.

This little anecdote is in keeping with many others of a like nature which would serve to fill a volume, and which want of space alone prevents my making a selection from but here is one other which is so good, that I take the liberty of transcribing it verbatim from the interesting pages of Colonel Mackenzie's "Mutiny Memoirs."

"A company of native Infantry was performing an uncommonly rapid movement to the rear, to get away from an undesirable neighbourhood, when a British officer roared after it: 'Halt! Halt! Halt!' At this a fat old subadar, who was doing his best to keep up with his command, indignantly spluttered out as he scuttled along puffing and blowing, "Kaun guddha halt bola hai? Yih halt ka wakt nahin hai! (What ass says halt! This is no time to halt!)"

It will thus be seen that even the stern duties of warfare are sometimes relieved by a little humour; and the slaughtering of one's fellowman has its ludicrous side.

To continue the narrative of the great rebellion it seems fitting to make a passing reference to a mode of punishment that was found necessary and which undoubtedly struck terror into the native heart. That is the blowing away from the guns. The moral effect of this form of execution could not be overrated, however dreadful it may seem to those people who are disposed to judge all nations and all things by one common standard. As I, who write this, had the opportunity of witnessing an execution of the kind, perhaps it will not be uninteresting if I venture to describe it:

On or about the 4th of October 1857, that was nearly five months after the outbreak at Meerut, a seditious meeting took place somewhere in Bombay at which it was proved, two native soldiers were present, and sought to inflame the minds of their fellows by inflammatory language, and violent denunciations of England generally, and the East India Company in particular. One of these men was a drill sergeant by name Syed Hossein, of the Marine Battalion, Native Infantry. The other man was a private, named Mongol, or Mungul Guddred. He belonged to the 10th Regiment of Native Infantry. Both these men were exceedingly intelligent and able fellows, and had generally been accounted good soldiers. For some time, however, before they fell into disgrace their loyalty had been suspected, and as they were known to have considerable influence in their respective regiments a watch was kept upon them, and by this means their defection became known. So violent was the language they used, and so strenuous the efforts they put forth to promote a rebellion, calling upon their fellows to rise in their might and emulate "the splendid deeds" of their countrymen in Oude and elsewhere by driving the accursed Feringhees into the sea, and thus destroy the foreign yoke that had been placed on India, that it was deemed necessary to bring them to a

European court martial. During the trial everything in their favour was said that could be said, but the evidence of their guilt was so conclusive that only one verdict was possible under military law. That verdict was Death, and the mode of death, it was decided, should be by blowing away from the muzzle of a gun.

The sentence was a terrible one, and there were those who thought that it erred on the side of severity, and that a life sentence of imprisonment would have answered the purpose. But it must be remembered that India was passing through a crisis and England's sons and daughters had been foully massacred by men whose passions and hatred had been aroused by false statements and seditious language. Stern and repressive measures, therefore, were required, and the object aimed at was to make such an impression on the native mind, as to reduce the chances of an outbreak to a minimum. Imprisonment or hanging would not have had this effect. Therefore the more terrible form of death was decided upon because that carried with it a moral weight which nothing else could.

The date fixed for the execution was the 13th of October, the time five o'clock in the afternoon, the place the general parade ground of Fort George, Bombay. Up to the fatal day the sentence had not been allowed to become generally known, for the native temper was very irritable; a seething discontent was smouldering in the army, and the lower orders of the population were yearning for the opportunity to loot and pillage. It was known that the garrison was weak, and scattered in and around Bombay were a large number of white people all of whom were more or less wealthy. All the conditions favourable to an outbreak were there save one; there was no leader, no one capable of being a leader of men. Fear kept the soldiers in subjection, as fear confined the budmashes to their hovels and dens. But had the tocsin been sounded, and the standard of revolution unfurled by some daring and resolute man, thousands would have rallied around him, and for a time success would probably have attended the effort to throw off the yoke. The European residents might have been murdered, and the garrisons reduced to fighting for bare life in the fortress. But Bombay's position on the sea made it impossible for a rabble to hold it for many days as the men of war in the harbour would have played havoc with them.

On that fatal 13th of October a garrison order made it known at all the government offices about noon, that the execution was to take place in the evening, and as it was thought probable that there might be a rising amongst the incensed natives, and a rescue might even be attempted, every precaution was taken and a requisition was made upon most of the ships in the harbour to send as many of their crews ashore as could be spared. Amongst the Europeans there was intense excitement, and they flocked by hundreds to the parade ground, while from every hole and corner of the native city the population poured forth. It may be imagined how uneasy the minds of the officials were, for it was only too evident that a spark would cause an explosion, and if the regiments mutinied and the rabble rose in their strength, there would be a deluge of blood. What was to prevent the mutiny and the rising? There was a mere handful of white soldiers, so to speak, and a few sailors. But from one end of India to the other it was known what a handful of the dominant race was capable of doing. Britons could die, but they couldn't be beaten, nevertheless had a shibboleth been raised in Bombay on that 13th of October, the scenes of Meerut might have been enacted over again. The population of the city and its suburbs at that time was nearly a million. As the hour of doom drew near the bugles spoke and the troops marched on to the parade ground and drew up so as to form three sides of a hollow square. The base of the square consisted of 500 men of the 95th; and about an equal number of sailors in the East India Company's service. The sides of the square were composed of three sepoy regiments including Mungul Guddred's own regiment the 10th Native Infantry. It was a daring thing to bring the men of that regiment on to the ground to witness the execution of one of their own comrades. But it was this very, apparently, reckless boldness which tended to win from the natives such an opinion of the prowess of Englishmen.

From the base line two guns pointed, and to these

guns the culprits were to be attached. In addition to these, three guns on each side were so placed as to command the sides of the square which as already stated were composed of native regiments. The six guns were loaded with double charges of grape, and they were placed in charge of men of the Royal Artillery who stood with lighted torches in their hands. At the same time all the European soldiers and sailors stood with their Enfield rifles loaded, and it had been prearranged that at the slightest sign of mutiny on the part of the native regiments, soldiers, sailors and artillerymen were to pour a deadly fire into them. It was an exciting moment and the nerves of all were strung to a pitch of great tension, for it was not known whether the sepoys would remain steady when their comrades were brought out for execution.

In a little while, all being in readiness the drums rolled, then ceased, and amidst a death-like silence the two condemned men were escorted on to the ground by artillery men, who in obedience to an order stripped them of their regimental jackets, and bound them by means of ropes to the muzzles of the guns, their backs being to the muzzle, and their hands fastened behind them.

Syed Hoossein was a man of splendid physique, with a stern, determined-looking face which betrayed no emotion during the terrible ordeal; but his great chest heaved and fell with spasmodic breathing, and in his dark eyes was an expression of pitiable despair. When the men had been bound, the commanding officer read out the sentence, and the doomed men were asked with cruel formality if they had anything to urge against that sentence being carried out.

Guddred mumbled something, but Syed Hoossein, drew himself up, and every muscle of his body seemed to work with some masterful emotion, while his face became a study in defiance and hatred. It was a terribly painful moment and something like a groan and a shudder ran through the assembled multitude. Then for an instant there was a solemn silence. The air was palpitating with heat; a hot breeze blew up from the sea, and the sun was declining in the western sky which was filled with vivid greens, with burning gold, and scarlet red. Suddenly the silence was broken by a clear ringing voice giving the order "Fire!" There was the roar of an explosion. From two guns burst forth belching flame; two huge clouds of dense smoke rolled upward, and then there fell on to the parade ground a pattering hail of human remains.

The native soldiers witnessed this horrible scene with an apparent indifference. But if the thoughts their stolid faces concealed could have been read, we might have understood how tremendous an effort was required to conceal them. But never a man stirred, never an arm was raised, never a word was uttered. The six grape loaded guns, and the Enfield rifles of the white troops awed them into silence.

Before the smoke had cleared away native sweepers

with brooms and buckets came forth and proceeded to gather up the fragments of the two unhappy beings who had been so effectually disintegrated. When this ghastly work was completed, the drums rolled, the bugles blared, the native troops were marched back to their quarters, and the Europeans returned to their residences with a feeling that a great crisis had passed, and if the punishment inflicted had been terrible, it had also been exemplary, and now it was probable Bombay would escape the horrors of Oude, of Lucknow, of Cawnpore, of Delhi. Many a white mother pressed her child more closely to her heart that night, and muttered an unusually fervent " Thank God ", and there wasn't a white man in the island who didn't go to his bed with a sense of greater security.

The action of stern retribution, which was carried out on that memorable 13th of October, did not escape criticism in certain quarters, but no unbiassed person can come to any other conclusion than that the salutary lesson inflicted was absolutely necessary to awe the sepoys into subjection. The two men who had forfeited their lives—it was clearly proved in the evidence—had associated themselves with an organised conspiracy which had for its object the massacre of every European man, woman and child; the seizure of the magazine and the fort, and the destruction of every bungalow residence. Other conspiracies of a like kind had been nipped in the bud by the vigilance and promptness of the authorities, who were capable of knowing what was going on, and how to deal with the natives better than those who sat at home at ease. One thing is pretty certain that had a rising taken place in Bombay, Madras and Calcutta would have followed suit and the southern Presidencies would have been in flames. Fortunately there were men in Bombay who knew their duty, and performed it with a determination and a courage beyond all praise.

To return once more to the north. Although the fall of Delhi was a tremendous blow to the rebels, it by no means brought the mutiny to an end. Sir Colin Campbell had moved to the relief of General Windham who had been placed in command at Cawnpore, and Sir James Outram was left at Alum Bagh with instructions to closely watch the rebels in Lucknow. During this time large reinforcements from Calcutta and other places were making their way up country with all speed, and when 1858 dawned, hope grew strong amongst the Europeans that a few weeks more would see the flames of insurrection stamped out. This hope was greatly strengthened when it became known that Sir Hugh Rose had captured Jhansi and Kalper and inflicted terrible punishment on the insurgents. On the 5th of May Sir Colin Campbell—then Lord Clyde—won a great victory at Bareilly; and at the 19th of June Sir Hugh Rose was able to once more hoist the British flag in Gwalior. With the fall of Gwalior the mutiny might be said to have come to an end; although here and there the rebels made last despairing rallies. The villain Tantia Topee was fortunately captured, but instead of being blown from a gun he was hanged, which was far too good a death for him.

About this time the Governor-General issued a proclamation granting an amnesty to all the rebels who had not taken active part in the murder of British subjects, and it was also proclaimed throughout the length and breadth of India that the Queen of England had annulled the charter of the East India Company, and that henceforth the country would be placed under a Viceroy instead of a Governor-General. This change was due to the "India Bill" of August 2nd 1858.

Since that period of its agony India has undergone a wonderful change, and no one with any knowledge of the subject would dare to say that the native population is not infinitely better off than at any other period in the history of the country. Wise reforms have been introduced, and there is a free press, just laws, equitable taxation. Schools have been established for the teaching of native children. Caste prejudices are respected, and competitive examinations for government positions are open to natives of all classes. The country is covered with a network of railways, and the telegraph goes everywhere. India is prospering and will continue to prosper so long as men are allowed to rule there who understand something of the native temper, and who sternly set their faces against fads and fancies.

THE ZULU WAR.

THE story of the events that led up to the Zulu War, as well as the conduct of the war itself is not pleasant reading. To some extent it reflects upon our honour, and also upon the general management of the campaign. As in all British battles there were magnificent examples of individual heroism, of devotion, of suffering patiently borne, of men sacrificing their lives to save their brother men. These are the redeeming features of a story which otherwise is a dismal record of bungling and disaster.

The causes that brought about the war may be briefly recapitulated. Previous to 1879 we had had some minor troubles with certain tribes known as Gaikas and Gallekas, who occupied a strip of country on the south-eastern coast. They had shown themselves very hostile to another tribe termed Fingoes whom we had deemed it desirable to take under our protection. Having thus thrown the aegis of British majesty around them we could not very well sit still and see them "eaten up", for they were quite unable to hold their own against their warlike neighbours. So we carried on desultory skirmishes with the Gallekas and the Gaikas, but they proved harder nuts to crack than we had anticipated, and we discovered, as we have frequently discovered on similar occasions when dealing with savage races, that they were not to be wiped out by merely military promenades. But what was perhaps still more serious at the time was the jealousies that were aroused on the part of the colonists against the regular officers of the British troops which had been sent out to help the colonial troops. It appears that colonial officials claimed the exclusive right of commanding their own volunteers, and they insisted on conducting the little squabbles without any reference to the British Commander-in-chief. Into the merits of this unfortunate difference I do not propose to enter. Suffice it to say that after some very undignified wrangles it was decided by the Governor that Sir Alexander Cunnyngham should have supreme command of colonial and British troops alike. This cementing of differences was productive of good results. The fiery tribes of Gaikas and Gallekas were convinced that it would be useless to prolong a struggle, the end of which for them would be absolute extermination. This was well as far as it went, but our troubles had led to a belief in other quarters that we were not quite so invincible as we would have it believed. It will be remembered that we annexed the Transvaal in 1877. At this period there was a piece of territory on the left bank of the Blood River, and extending into Zululand which had been filched from the

Zulus by the Boers who had established themselves thereon. A Boer colony had sprung up consisting of farms and stations, and the invaders seemed to be prosperous. But the luckless Zulu King, Cetewayo, distinctly objected to be robbed of his birthright, and he ordered his suzerain, Sekukuni, to take up arms and expel the dominant Boers. Sekukuni was not only a very intelligent savage but a very warlike one and capable of giving a very great deal of trouble. The result of his action was a declaration of war between the Boer Republic and himself, and in a short time the Boers enlisted on their side the services of a tribe known as the Swazis, and together they carried fire and slaughter into Sekukuni's territory. They had, however, underrated the power of their enemy, and they were driven out much quicker than they went. In spite of this defeat, the Boers not only stuck to the territory they had filched, but actually had the audacity to lay claim to the whole of Sekukuni's country. The poor savage chief, however, soon found himself between two stools, for when Great Britain annexed the Transvaal it was declared that the whole of his country was included in that annexation. Why that should have been so does not appear to be very clear, unless it was on the pretext that we wished to protect Sekukuni from being gobbled up by the Boers who were hungering for his land. But however good our intentions were, unhappily they were not appreciated by Sekukuni, nor by his sovereign lord and master Cetewayo.

Now let it not be forgotten that the king was at the head of the Zulus, who were the most warlike race of savages in the world and trained to a standard in the art of war such as had rarely before been attained by any savage race. The chief was head of the Basutos who were also powerful and warlike people, second only to the Zulus whose supremacy they acknowledged. Somewhere about February in 1878, unfortunately for himself, some of his tribe trespassed on the territory of another chief named Pokwana with whom we deemed it policy to keep on friendly terms. Of course there was bloodshed, and in the end the Basutos were beaten. Notwithstanding this, the British commissioner who had been placed in power in the Transvaal sent a strong remonstrance to Sekukuni, with a hint possibly that if he didn't keep quiet he would very likely be gobbled up. The dignity of the unhappy chief was no doubt wounded by this, for first of all he had seen the Boers settle in his country without asking permission, and when he had thrashed them, the English walked in and told him they were going to be owners from that time onward. It is scarcely to be wondered at that he smarted and groaned under his affliction, for he preferred white men at a distance. He knew from tradition and bitter experience that whenever they came into a savage land they generally came to stay. The result of it all was that he did not receive the commissioner's remonstrance in the spirit of humility which he ought to have done according to the invaders' ideas, and instead of showing funk, he returned a haughty answer to the effect that he was Sekukuni, that the country was his, that the white man had no business there and he must clear out.

This imperious answer was practically the gage of war, and Sekukuni was declared to be a rebel. Measures were at once taken to bring him into subjection, but we made the fatal mistake that the Boers had done. We despised our enemy, underrated his power, and were beaten back. It must have been a proud moment for the savage chief. He had beaten the Boers, and now even the invincible English had succumbed to him. He was supreme ruler in his country again. Naturally enough Cetewayo was not indifferent to the doings of his suzerain; and that he had not interfered up to this period was owing no doubt to a belief that Sekukuni was capable of taking care of himself. But he was shrewd enough to perceive, that unlike the Boers, the English were not likely to humbly accept their defeat and say no more about it. They bore the reputation of being a nation to whom the meaning of defeat was unknown. It is scarcely to be wondered at therefore, that he got uneasy, and councils of war were held by him and the suzerain, the consequence being that Natal became alarmed, and the colonists declared that they were in fear of an invasion of the Zululand Basutos, and that England ought to take measures to protect them. In response to this request preparations were made to break the power of the Zulus, and Lieutenant-

General, the Honourable F. Thesiger—better known as Lord Chelmsford, he having succeeded to the title on the death of his father—was charged with this onerous duty. At this time Sir Alexander Cunnyngham had returned home. Lord Chelmsford lost no time in taking steps in accordance with the decision of the authorities, and he massed his troops in Pretoria, the Transvaal, and on the borders of Natal. Having done this, he applied to England for more troops to be sent out. The force at his disposal at that time all told was about 13,000 men, of whom only about half were whites. Opposed to them were at least 50,000 superb fighting men, many of whom were armed with rifles, while the country they inhabited was something like 10,000 square miles in extent.

During the lull that took place previous to the arrival of reinforcements from England various negotiations were carried on between the High Commissioner, the Lieutenant-Governor of Natal, and the British Administrator of the Transvaal, and these gentlemen decided that Cetewayo should be left in undisturbed possession of certain territory which was clearly defined, subject to his agreeing to a set of conditions. These conditions were of a very arbitrary character, or at any rate they seemed so to Cetewayo. One of them stipulated that the Zulu army should be disbanded, and only brought together with permission of the Great Council of nations assembled, and by consent of the British Government. Another, that every Zulu on arriving at man's estate should be free to marry without having to seek the king's permission as heretofore. A third demanded that a British Resident should be allowed to be stationed in the capital of Zululand.

Had these conditions been accepted, Cetewayo and his suzerain would have had to be very different men to what they were. The answer made by the king's representatives was to this effect— " The condition as to the disbandment of the army is inacceptable. The Zulu nation has as much right to keep up an army as England has." Other clauses in the conditions were strongly objected to. But the envoys were peremptorily informed by the British High Commissioner that no alterations whatever would be made, and the representatives took their leave, returning to Ulundi with all speed, where the king anxiously awaited their return.

When he heard what they had to say he saw clearly enough that he had nothing to hope for from the great white power which had resolved to crush him, and so he resolved that his splendidly organized army should measure strength with the invader.

By this time Lord Chelmsford had received his reinforcements, and began to make preparations for the war which had now become inevitable. It was quite thought that, comparatively speaking, the invasion of Zululand would be an easy matter. Battles with Cetewayo's army were of course looked for, but the common belief was that the savage warriors would be wiped out, and in a few weeks the fat king would be crawling in the dust craving for mercy. It was this self-confident air, this contempt for the power of the enemy which led to all the disastrous results.

At first the arrangement was that the country should be invaded by five columns. On this point, however, there were differences of opinion, and it was ultimately decided that the force in command of Lord Chelmsford should be divided into three columns only. One of these columns under the command of Colonel Glyn marched to Rorke's Drift which was on the banks of the Buffalo River in Natal. The column was made up of 1,700 British regulars, 2,500 natives, and 320 colonial volunteers. A second column consisting of 1,600 regulars, 200 volunteers, and 250 natives, under the command of Colonel Evelyn Wood, was sent to a place called Bembas Kop which is in the Transvaal, on the Upper Blood River. The third column was placed under the command of Colonel Pearson. Its strength was 1,500 regulars, 300 volunteers, and 2,400 natives. Its position was near the mouth of the Tugela River which forms the boundary between Natal and Zululand. The invading force included 1,300 cavalry and 20 guns, and the total strength was under 11,000. But in addition there were two other columns. One under Colonel Rowlands had orders to occupy Luneburg as a post of observation and keep a sharp eye on the suzerain. The other under the command of Colonel Durnford was to guard the Natal Frontier at Rorke's Drift, and render assistance to Colonel Glyn should he need it.

The three columns, roughly speaking, occupied the base of a triangle; one being placed at each end of the base, the other in the centre. The base line was probably about 135 miles in length. At the apex of the triangle was the objective point of the military operations; that was Ulundi, the capital.

When all was ready a crossing was made at Rorke's Drift. Here the river is broad, deep and very rapid, but the infantry was passed over in safety by means of hastily constructed pontoons, and the cavalry crossed by means of a ford some distance away. It was anticipated that the passage would have been disputed by the Zulus who were known to be in strength in the neighbourhood, and the wonder to this day is why the invaders were allowed to cross so peacefully. However, cross they did without a shot being fired or an assegai being thrown, and towards the close of the day the column had encamped; a company of the 24th had been left at Rorke's Drift, to take charge of a mission house which was there, and which for the purposes of the invasion had been converted into a commissariat store, and a field hospital. Lord Chelmsford who had personally superintended the passage of the river at the Drift, rode with an escort, as soon as the column was in Zululand, to meet Colonel Wood who was under orders to effect the passage of the Blood River the same morning. The two met at a distance of about twelve miles from Rorke's Drift, as Colonel Wood was on his way to meet the Commander-in-chief, and having consulted for some time each returned to his respective post.

The next day Lord Chelmsford, with Colonel Glyn, and part of the column, started on a reconnoitring expedition; the remainder of the column remained in camp. When the reconnoitring party had proceeded a few miles they suddenly came upon a large number of cattle quietly grazing in a valley through which flowed a river known as the Bashee. On the hills above, a force of Zulus was observed, and while a portion of the soldiers were told off to seize the cattle, the other portion were to dislodge the enemy. A fight ensued and the first blood was drawn. A kraal a little higher up the valley was burnt; thirty Zulus were killed, four were wounded, and ten prisoners were taken. The invaders then returned to their camp driving before them oxen, sheep, goats and horses.

Twelve days later the camp on the Buffalo river where the soldiers had been very comfortable and had the advantage of good water and abundance of provisions, without being molested, broke up and marched to Isandhlwana hill, which had already been reconnoitred and fixed upon as the site of the new camp. It is not necessary to dwell upon all the details of the next few days. Lord Chelmsford seemed to have committed an error of judgment in dividing his small force, and leaving one portion in camp at Isandhlwana while he went forward with the other portion to reconnoitre.

It was known all this time that the enemy was in force in the neighbourhood. And while the broken and hilly country was difficult for British troops to move over, it was peculiarly favourable to the wily Zulus, whose agility and fleetness on precipitous slopes were simply marvellous. The fatal error on the part of the British Commander was that division of his force, and in not discovering that every movement he made was being watched by the enemy whose military tactics would not have disgraced civilized troops. Having seen one part of the little army well away, a large force of Zulus crept down stealthily, and like a whirlwind swept upon the camp, and then began that massacre which has written Isandhlwana in letters of blood on history's page. An urgent message, when the camp was first attacked, was sent to Lord Chelmsford. It ran as follows; "For God's sake come back; the camp is surrounded, and things, I fear, are going badly." This message was received from Captain Develin, who was entrusted with it by Commandant Browne, who was in charge of a native detachment. With this detachment he had been out exploring and was returning to the camp when he noticed that it was surrounded, and he immediately sent off that despairing message. Unfortunately Lord Chelmsford does not seem to have attached the importance to it, it deserved. He rode to the brow of a hill which commanded a view of the camp, and not being able to discern anything unusual, he considered that some mistake had been made or that matters were not as urgent as reported. But in the meantime a fearful scene was being enacted in the camp. The Zulus had come down in their thousands, and nothing could stop their impetuous rush. The native levies of course broke up and fled; the British soldiers fought as British soldiers always do; but their courage, their devotion, their desperation availed them nothing; the pitiless enemy shot and assegaied them until they fell in heaps; and any who attempted to escape were pursued by hundreds of the savages, and when overtaken slain until not a man was left alive, with the exception of Captain Essex, a staff officer, and a Basuto. He and the native by some strange chance had escaped the massacre, and sending the Basuto with all speed to Rorke's Drift to tell them to prepare to defend it to the uttermost, he himself galloped as fast as his horse would take him to a ford on the Buffalo, succeeded in crossing it and reaching Helpmaker, a station a little beyond the river, and putting the garrison on their guard.

The sad and pitiable story of this dreadful disaster is relieved by some splendid deeds of daring. It is told how one solitary Englishman of the 24th regiment escaped to a low hill above the camp. But let it not be supposed that he turned his back to the foe. Slowly he went, keeping up a deadly fire on the yelling Zulus who followed him. At the top of the hill was a cavern and into this he crept. A piece of rock in front served him as a rest for his rifle, and as the men rushed forward to shoot or spear him he dropped them with unerring aim until they thought he bore a charmed life.

He knew of course, that he must die, but he resolved that while he had a cartridge he would hold the foe at bay. This strange duel was kept up for some time and the wary savages were afraid to expose themselves to the deadly fire of this hero; until at last, maddened by seeing so many of their number fall by his single gun, they massed themselves together, made one wild rush, reached the cavern and fired a volley at the brave fellow who fell dead.

To the same regiment, the luckless 24th, belonged Lieutenant Teignmouth Melville, who was an adjutant of his regiment. When he saw that all was lost, he resolved to try and prevent the crowning dishonour and save the colours. Seizing them, he grasped the reins of a horse which was near, leapt on its back, and galloped towards the Buffalo river. Finding that the track that led to Rorke's Drift was impassable, owing to the enemy swarming over it, he turned his horse's head in the direction of Helpmaker. A few mounted men who had managed to get clear of the camp joined him and forward they sped over a fearfully hilly country. For nearly six miles a number of the Zulus on foot kept almost abreast of them, and poured in a galling fire. At last weary and worn, Melville reached the river, and without a moment's hesitation he plunged his charger into the rushing water. The colours, as soon as they were wet, clung about him, and the impetuous stream swept him from his horse, and carried him to a rock in the centre, where Lieutenant Hugginson who had been one of the party that had got out of the camp, was clinging for dear life. Melville called upon him to take the colours, which he did, but at that moment he and the colours were swept away by a rush of the torrent, which at that spot was particularly strong. While this pathetic scene was being enacted, Lieutenant Coghill, also of the 24th, rushed up. He had injured his knee, but notwithstanding this when he saw the others go off, he had seized a charger, flung himself into the saddle and followed in their track. Reaching the river he dashed in and gained the opposite bank. Looking back he observed Melville in the water still trying to save the colours, so he immediately sprang to his assistance. At this point a crowd of Zulus who had been in pursuit come up and pouring in their fire, succeeding in killing Coghill's horse, and he was thus left struggling in the water, while the colours for which they had made such a bold bid were carried down the stream. Seeing the absolute hopelessness of trying to recover them the two young men battled with the seething current until they gained the opposite bank up which they scrambled half dead with fatigue. Up the steep ascent they painfully made their way and behind them like ravening wolves followed the cruel enemy who was not moved to pity by the magnificent courage and devotion of the two brave men. Many days later, as Lord Chelmsford had received no news as to their fate, he sent out a search party, and on the crest of the hill upon which they had climbed, their dead bodies were found, and around them were a pile of dead Zulus, who had fallen before the two heroes themselves fell pierced with dozens of assegai wounds.

When Lord Chelmsford became aware that a disaster had overtaken his camp, he waited until Colonel Glyn, to whom he had sent an urgent message, came up with reinforcements, and then he hurried back to the camp. It was dark when he reached it, not a light was seen, not a voice heard. The silence of death was there. Fifteen hundred dead, natives and English, were strewn about, with dead horses, and all the wreck of the camp. The troops who had returned with him were so exhausted that the commander ordered them to rest; but before daylight came to reveal the ghastly scene which they had not been able to fully realise, he sounded the reveille and led them towards Rorke's Drift which was already the centre of a deadly conflict.

The previous afternoon about three o'clock, Lieutenant Chard, of the Royal Engineers, was in charge of the pontoon and raft which had served for the crossing of the troops. Suddenly two mounted men were seen galloping excitedly down the opposite bank, and as they came near they shouted wildly to be taken across. Chard at once had them brought to his side, and he then learnt from them, that the camp had been taken, its defenders massacred, and that the enemy was advancing rapidly to Rorke's Drift. A very few minutes later he received a hasty message from Lieutenant Bromhead, who was in command of the men who had been left at the mission house to protect the stores. This message asked him to return at once. So Chard ordered his men to reach the stores with all speed, and he galloped forward in advance of them. He found that Bromhead, with the assistance of Commissary Dalton, who had once been a sergeant-major in the British army, had already made considerable progress in putting the place into a state of defence. A bulwark of bags of mealie or corn had been raised so as to connect the two buildings, that is the hospital and store house. There was also a garden, which was walled round. Loopholes had also been made in the walls of the building. The ammunition was so disposed as to be easily got at, and every man received special instructions as to what he was to do; moreover he was emphatically given to understand that the lives of the whole garrison depended on the individual efforts the men themselves made.

At this time Captain Stephenson with some native levies was at the Drift but for some reason or other, late in the afternoon he started out with his men to Helpmaker, and the little garrison was thus further weakened. It then occurred to Chard that it would be impossible to hold effectually the extended line of defence with the few men at his command, so he set to work to construct an inner line, by piling up biscuit boxes. Before the task was completed an officer who had been keeping watch at the river galloped in with the information that the enemy was approaching rapidly. Very soon a considerable body of Zulus, numbering several hundreds, appeared in sight, and with a wild yell they rushed towards the first or outer defence which then faced them. They were met by a withering fire from the soldiers who sprang to their posts, and many a savage fell prone upon the earth never to rise again.

Gathering themselves together the survivors made another rush but again a volley checked them, and fearing to again face the deadly and determined fire of the defenders they scattered, taking shelter in the scrub and bush, and the military field ovens a little way off. An hour later a compact army of 3,000 more Zulus appeared. They were astonished to find the place being defended, and, seeing so many of their slain companions lying about, they had a hurried consultation, and then spread themselves over the hillside, at a distance of something like four hundred yards, and from their sheltered positions they poured in a galling fire. Presently they crept down in small bodies and taking advantage of every projection or bit of scrub they gradually worked their way near until with a rush many of them gained the wall of mealie bags, but bayonet and bullet played havoc amongst them and they recoiled. Unfortunately for the defenders, fire from the hills in the rear wounded several of their number, and being thus at a disadvantage in having the enemy both before and behind, Lieutenant Chard ordered his men to retire to the inner line of defence, that is the biscuit-boxes. This movement was admirably performed while a withering shower of bullets was poured on the enemy from the loopholes. The Zulus now made the most frantic endeavours to break into the hospital, the doors of which had been barricaded. Failing in their attempt they scrambled to the roof which unhappily was composed of thatch, and tearing great holes in it, and firing the rest, they succeeded in getting into the building. In the mean time those in charge of the hospital lost not a moment in trying to get the invalids into a place of safety. The Zulus were kept at bay while the sick men one by one were passed through a window which looked on the square formed by the mealie bags, the opposite end from the window being the inner line of defence which enclosed the commissariat stores. The removal of the sick was a splendid achievement, for the few men upon whom the onerous duty fell had to protect themselves from the assegais, keep the maddened savages at bay and convey the sick from room to room until the window was gained. Every inch of the way was disputed with such determination and energy that the black bodies were piled up in heaps. But still the enemy poured in through the holes in the roof. Some of the unfortunate invalids who were too weak and ill to help themselves in any way were stabbed to death with assegais as they lay in bed, while others were suffocated by the smoke from the burning rafters.

At last the Zulus gained possession of the hospital, and the light from the flaming building revealed to Chard that the position was desperate indeed, for the enemy was also swarming over the outer defences. But not for a moment did the gallant defenders slacken their efforts. The wounded who could not take any active part in the defence kept their comrades supplied with ammunition, and Chard and Bromhead by voice and example encouraged the men in every possible way. As the Zulus got closer to the biscuit-boxes they were met with such a withering fire that they fell back, leaving a great pile of their dead in front of them. Again and again did they try to rush the defences but each time they were shattered by the leaden hail, until at last dismayed and appalled by their awful losses they began to withdraw, but for some time kept up a pattering fire on the noble garrison. At last the welcome daylight dawned; then the tired and weary soldiers to their joy saw that not a Zulu save the dead ones was in sight. But the dead lying everywhere bore ghastly evidence to the stubbornness of the defence and the heroism which had saved the garrison of Rorke's Drift from being wiped out as the poor fellows of Isandhlwana had been.

Very soon afterwards redcoats were observed on the hills at the Zulu side of the river.

These redcoats were Lord Chelmsford's soldiers who had spent the night in the camp of death at Isandhlwana. It was then a little after eight in the morning, and as his lordship saw the flames and smoke rising from the burning buildings at the Drift his worst fears that the garrison had been slaughtered and the stores destroyed seemed to be realized. But as he and his men descended the declivity, they saw that hats were being waved in the entrenchments, and this welcome signal was greeted with tremendous British cheers which told how great was the sense of relief all experienced as they gathered that the noble little band under Chard and Bromhead had upheld the honour of England during that terrible night and had kept a host at bay. It was a fight that England may well be proud of for there are not many parallels to it in our history.

Where all were heroic alike it seems somewhat insidious to particularize, but mention must be made of the service rendered during that memorable night by Joseph Williams, William Horrigan, and John Williams, all humble privates of the 24th regiment. They were in charge of one of the rooms of the hospital, which for more than an hour they defended against the Zulus, and only retired when their last cartridge had been expended. Then they discovered that their communication with their comrades behind the biscuit-boxes was cut off by the Zulus, several of whom at this moment burst open a door, and seizing Joseph Williams they stabbed him to death together with three of the invalids. Nothing daunted John Williams smashed in a portion of the partition, and through the hole thus made he carried two sick patients into another room, where a comrade, one private Hook, was stationed. The two brave fellows quickly decided on a line of action. One kept the foe at bay with his bayonet; the other set to work to break a way through three more partitions, and he succeeded in getting eight invalids through the holes thus made into the inner defences, and thus saved their lives.

In another room of the hospital, William Johns and Robert Johns, presumably brothers, defended their charges which consisted of seven men. Six of these men they got away. The seventh was raving with fever, and utterly helpless, and before they could carry him off he was assegaied.

Frederick Hitch, a private, and his comrade Corporal William Allen were charged with the perilous duty of keeping open the communications between the hospital and the inner line of defence. It was a post not only of great difficulty, but great danger because they were subjected to a cross fire. We will give an idea of the relative position of Rorke's Drift, and the defences.

The distance from the window at the inner side of the hospital to the biscuit-boxes would be about twenty yards. It was this open space that was held by Allen and Hitch.

Allen and Hitch performed their duty nobly. Each of them was severely wounded so that they were unable to use their rifles. But when their wounds had been attended to by the surgeon they employed themselves in keeping their comrades supplied with ammunition.

There is another act of splendid devotion which must be chronicled here. Amongst the few who managed to effect their escape from the carnage at Isandhlwana, was a mounted infantry man named Wassal who was a private in the 80th regiment. He reached the Buffalo river where he saw a comrade struggling for his life in the water. Wassal, without a thought about himself, sprang from his horse which he left on the Zulu side of the river: then he jumped into the boiling rapids and helped the drowning man to the bank where the horse was. He got him out, put him on the horse, sprang up behind, and jumped the horse into the river just as a number of Zulus came up and sent a shower of bullets after him, but happily he succeeded in gaining the opposite bank.

Amongst the gallant defenders of the Drift was Assistant Commissary Dalton who did splendid work and rendered special service. He was severely wounded in the early part of the fight, but nevertheless he stuck to his post, encouraging the men and displaying marvellous coolness himself, and he was particularly active in handing out the cartridges as the soldiers' pouches became emptied.

When the curtain fell upon the first act of the sanguinary Zulu campaign there was indignation and sorrow in England. Lord Chelmsford sent an urgent demand for reinforcements which were at once got ready, and forwarded to Africa with all possible despatch.

In the mean time Colonel Pearson, who was at the head of the first column, had crossed the lower Tugela river not far from the sea. He had with him a troop of British seamen from some of the men-of-war, and the passage of the river having been effected, the column commenced its march into the enemy's country, and on the 22nd of January, the fatal Isandhlwana day, it reached the Inyezani river on the road to Ekowe. His first action was fought on this day; and as numerous Zulus were observed on the hills, a company was ordered to clear them out. In performing this operation one officer, four European non-commissioned officers, and three native soldiers lost their lives. Later in the day another fight occurred in which a number of the column were killed and wounded. After a rest the troops marched to Ekowe where there was a half-ruined mission station. It was placed in order and an entrenched camp prepared, and in this place the unfortunate column was doomed to stay for about three months, cut off from all communication with the rest of the world by a large force of the enemy who harassed them night and day. The garrison suffered terribly from privations and sickness, and it must have seemed to them that relief would never come. But Lord Chelmsford did not remain inactive; his army had already suffered so terribly that it would have been an irreparable disaster, and a stain upon the British arms if the unfortunate contingent at Ekowe were wiped out.

And yet another bitter blow was still in store for Lord Chelmsford. Colonel Wood's column erected a fort on the Kambula Hill which served as a base of operations against the enemy. Here a good deal of desultory fighting took place, without any decided gain to either party. A garrison was placed in Luneberg, and supplies for the place were forwarded from Derby. Early in March the garrison having been made aware of the approach of the convoy, Captain Moriarty with a company of the 80th regiment went out to meet it, and fell in with it on the banks of the Intombi river. A halt was made, and a laager constructed but not until some days later did the last of the convoy arrive. In the mean time there had been exceedingly heavy rains, and the river was so swollen that further progress could not be made, and the force of armed men was divided between the two banks of the river. There were seventy-one men in tents and under waggons on the left bank, and on the opposite side were thirty-five men in tents, who were charged with the duty of guarding the supply waggons. There was also a guard on each bank. Moriarty was on the left bank, and Lieutenant Harward occupied the right. In the early morning of the 12th of March a sentry on the left bank gave a signal of alarm by firing his rifle. The soldiers on the other side jumped up at once and stood to their arms. Orders were also given for the men on the left bank to do the same, but for some inscrutable reason the order was not obeyed. An hour later a powerful Zulu force which had crept up in the fog which hung over the scene, fell upon them and slaughtered nearly the whole of them as they rushed out of their tents. Captain Moriarty was one of the first victims. The men on the opposite side of the river under Lieutenant Harward commenced firing on the Zulus, nevertheless a considerable number got across the river, and seeing that his life was in danger the gallant Lieutenant put spurs into his horse, and galloped off as fast as the horse would take him to Luneberg, leaving his men to take care of themselves. Sergeant Booth was the senior non-commissioned officer and he at once took charge of the company, and they made a plucky fight, as they retreated for three miles. Not a man fell of the British but the Zulus suffered so severely that at last they retired. But they secured all the stores and ammunition, and destroyed the camp.

The noble Harward was tried by Court Martial for his cowardice but acquitted on some technical point. In acting as he did, he evidently had in his mind the heroic sentiment—

> "He who fights and runs away
> May live to fight another day."

His defence was that he went to Luneberg for assistance. Sergeant Booth who had saved the company from slaughter was very properly awarded the Victoria Cross. The *Gazette* in chronicling the award added, "Had it not been for the coolness displayed by this non-commissioned officer not one man would have escaped."

Space forbids my dwelling further on the details of the war which from first to last reflected no great credit on our arms, and which brought nothing but misfortune to us from the fatal day of Isandhlwana to the final act in the tragedy when the wretched fugitive Cetewayo was captured by Major Marter and a body of dragoons.

As is well known the young Prince Imperial of France went out to Zululand where, while on a reconnaissance, he and his party were suddenly surrounded by Zulus who so frightened his horse that he was unable to mount and fell pierced with numerous wounds. That in itself was a very dark page in the history of the war, and Lieutenant Carey who accompanied the Prince and deserted him in the moment of peril, could not certainly be held up as a bright example of a British officer. But if the story of the invasion of Zululand is marred by such acts as those of Harward and Carey, the deeds of daring it tells may well beget a sense of pride; while the fight for the colours on the Buffalo River when Lieutenants Melville and Coghill perished, and the defence of Rorke's Drift, when all through the dreadful night a handful of British soldiers entrenched behind some biscuit-boxes kept a host at bay, will go down to posterity as bright spots in our splendid military history.

INDEX.

	PAGE
ARTHUR, Thomas	231
Ablett, Alfred	26
Alexander, John	42
Aikman, Frederick Robertson	79
Anson, The Hon. Augustus Henry Archibald	88
Anderson, Charles	149
Allen, William	164
Aylmer, Fenton John	186
BUCKLEY, Cecil William	1
Burgoyne, Hugh Talbot	2
Bythesed, John	14
Berryman, John	20
Bell, Edward W. D.	33
Beach, Thomas	39
Byrne, John	41
Bouchier, Claude Thomas	45
Bradshaw, Joseph	49
Boulger, Abraham	68
Bradshaw, William	72
Buckley, John	73
Blair, Robert	74
Bambrick, V.	87
Butler, Thomas Adair	107
Brennan, Joseph	119
Byrne, James	120
Brown, Francis David Millet	132
Browne, C.B., Samuel James	139
Burslem, Nathaniel	142
Blair, James	144
Baker, Charles George	145
Boyes, Duncan Gordon	152
Bell, David	157
Bromhead, G.	161
Brown, P.	166
Buller, C.B., H.	167
Browne, Edward S.	168
Beresford, Lord Wm.	169
Booth, Anthony	174
Boisragon, Guy Hudleston	186
Bergin, James	191
Bell, Mark Sever	195

	PAGE
COOPER, Henry	3
Commerell, John Edmund	6
Curtis, Henry	13
Connors, John	30
Coffey, William	35
Coleman, John	44
Clifford, Hon. Henry H.	45
Cuninghame, William James	45
Craig, James	56
Crowe, Joseph P. H.	65
Connolly, William	80
Cochrane, Hugh Stewart	99
Carlin, P.	102
Cook, Walter	111
Cubitt, William George	112
Clogstoun, Herbert Mackworth	116
Cameron, Alymer Spicer	119
Champion, James	125
Cafe, William Martin	132
Chicken, George Bell	134
Chaplin, John Worthy	142
Cadell, Thomas	148
Coghlan, Cornelius	149
Cooper, James	157
Channer, George Nicholas	159
Cook, John	161
Chard, J. R. M.	161
Creagh, O'Moor	171
Cunyngham, Wm. Henry Dick	177
Corbett, Frederick	181
Crimmin, John	184
DAY, George Fiott	4
Daniels, Edward St. John	9
Dowell, George Dare	17
Dunn, Alexander Robert	19
Dixon, Matthew Charles	22
Duffy, Thomas	70
Diamond, Bernard	79
Dunley, J.	91
Donohoe, P.	95
Davis, James	110
Dowling, William	122

INDEX.

	PAGE
Divane, John	128
Dempsey, Denis	133
Daunt, John Charles Campbell	146
Dynon, Denis	147
Douglas, Campbell Millis	157
Dundas, James	158
D'Arcy, Cecil	170
Dalton, James Langly	172
Doogan, John	179
Danaher, John	179
ELTON, Frederick C.	39
Esmonde, Thomas	54
Elphinstone, Howard Crawford	61
Edward, Thomas	183
FARRELL, John	54
Forrest, George	73
Fitzgerald, Richard	79
Ffrench, Alfred Kirke	86
Freeman, J.	95
Flinn, Thomas	105
Farquharson, Francis E. Henry	111
Fitzgibbon, Arthur	143
Fosbery, George Vincent	153
Flawn	174
Fitzpatrick	174
Fowler, Edmond	177
Fraser, Charles Crawfurd	191
GORMAN, James	12
Grieve, John	18
Graham, Gerald	23
Goodlake, Gerald Littlehales	27
Gardiner, George	59
Gill, Peter	83
Gardner, William	83
Goat, W.	85
Guise, John Christopher	89
Graham, P.	90
Grant, P.	91
Gough, Hugh Henry	94
Green, Patrick	102
Gough, Charles John Stanley	114
Garvin, Steven	126
Grant, Robert	136
Griffiths, William	157
Grant, Charles James William	186
Gordon, William James	188
Gee, C.B., Joseph	192
Gifford, Lord	194

	PAGE
HEWETT, W. Nathan Wright	9
Henry, Andrew	22
Hughes, Matthew	30
Hamilton, T. De Courcy	40
Humpston, Robert	48
Holmes, Joel	68
Hollowell, James	68
Home, Anthony Dixon	71
Hills, James	77
Hawthorne, Robert	78
Harrison, John	84
Hill, S.	90
Hawkes, David	92
Harrington, Hastings Edward	93
Hewage, Clement Walker	103
Hollis, George	103
Hall, W.	104
Hackett, Thomas Bernard	104
Heathcote, Alfred Spencer	122
Hartigan, H.	135
Hodge, Samuel	155
Heaphy, Charles	156
Hook, Henry	162
Hitch, Frederick	164
Hart, Reginald Clare	165
Hamilton, Walter Richard Pollock	169
Hammond, Arthur George	176
Hill, Alan Richard	178
Harding, Israel	180
INGOUVILLE, George	14
Irwin, C.	87
Innes, J. McLeod	100
JOHNSTONE, William	16
Jones, Henry Mitchell	52
Jones, Alfred Stowell	74
Jennings, E.	93
Jarrett, Hanson Chambers Taylor	112
Jerome, Henry Edward	118
Jones, William	163
Jones, Robert	164
KELLAWAY, Joseph	3
Knox, John	46
Kerr, William Alexander	77
Kenry, J.	87
Kells, R.	96
Kavanagh, Thomas Henry	113

INDEX.

Name	Page
Kirk, John	130
Keatinge, Richard Harte	143
LUCAS, Charles D.	16
Lennox, D.	24
Lendrim, William J.	25
Lindsay, Robert James	28
Lyons, John	33
Lumley, Charles Henry	43
Leitch, Peter	62
Lambert, George	67
Laughnar, J.	93
Leith, James	97
Lyster, Harry Hammon	116
Lawrence, Samuel Hill	121
Lucas, John	141
Lenon, Edmund Henry	142
Lane, Thomas	142
Leet, Wm. K.	167
Leech, Edward Pemberton	173
Lysons, Henry	177
Le Quesne, Ferdinand Simeon	185
Lloyd, Owen Edward Pennefather	188
McKECHNIE	28
Maule, Frederick Francis	29
Mognihan, Andrew	32
Madden, Ambrose	36
McWheeney, William	37
McDermond, John	38
McCorrie, Charles	41
McGregor, R.	47
Malone, Joseph	51
Monat, C.B., James	60
McDonald, Henry	68
Miller, Frederick	63
Maude, C.B., F. Cornwallis	66
Macpherson, Herbert Taylor	66
McMaster, Valentine Munbee	67
Mahoney, Patrick	67
McManus, James	69
Mylott, P.	88
Mackay, D.	91
McBean, William	92
McInnes, H.	93
McGuire, J.	101
Monger, George	105
McPherson, Stewart	105
Murphy, Michael	108
Miller, Duncan	111
McGovern, John	112
Mangles, Ross Lowis	114
McQuirt, Bernard	120
McDonell, William Fraser	131
McHale, Patrick	136
Moore, Arthur Thomas	138
Malcolmson, John Grant	138
M'Dougall, John	142
Miller, James	147
Mayo, Arthur	147
Monaghan, Thomas	149
MacKenna, Edward	150
McNeill, John Carstairs	151
Murphey, Thomas	157
Murray, James	179
Marling, Percival Scrope	182
Marshall, William	182
Morley, Samuel	190
Munro, James	191
Magner, Michael	191
McGaw, Samuel	194
NORMAN, William	31
Newell, R.	85
Napier, W.	98
OLPHERTS, William	66
Oxenham, William	121
O'Hea, Timothy	155
O'Toole, Edmund	170
Osborne, James	179
Odgers, William	189
O'Connor, Luke	34
Owens, James	39
PEEL, William	8
Prettyjohn, John	17
Parkes, Samuel	19
Perie, John	25
Palmer, Anthony	26
Prosser, Joseph	29
Park, John	41
Probyn, Dighton Macnaghten	75
Pye, Charles	86
Paton, J.	90
Park, J.	93
Pearson, John	103
Prendergast, Harry North Dalrymple	116
Pearson, James	135
Pride, Thomas	152

INDEX.

	PAGE
ROBERTS, John	2
Richard, William	8
Reeves, Thomas	12
Raby, Henry James	13
Ross, John	24
Russell, Sir Charles, Bart.	26
Reynolds, William	29
Rowlands, Hugh	36
Ramage, Henry	57
Ryan, John	70
Raynor, William	73
Rosamond, M.	82
Robinson, A.B., Edward	84
Rushe	86
Roberts, Frederick Sleigh	94
Roberts, J. R.	96
Rennie, William	99
Ryan, M.	101
Renny, George Alexander	105
Roddy, Patrick	106
Richardson, George	120
Rodgers, George	121
Reade, Herbert Taylor	140
Rogers, Robert Montresor	142
Ryan, John	151
Reynolds, James Henry	168
Ridgeway, Richard Kirby	175
SULLIVAN, John	11
Shepherd, John	11
Scholefield, Mark	12
Stanbock, William	27
Strong, George	28
Smith, Philip	33
Shields, Robert	35
Sims, John J.	35
Symons, George	55
Sylvester, Henry Thomas	57
Smith, John	78
Smith, Henry	78
Salunor, Nowel	84
Spence	85
Sinnott	89
Stewart, Wm. George Drummond	90
Smith, J.	93
Shaw, Same	102
Simpson, John	109
Shebbeare, Robert Haydon	115

	PAGE
Sleavon, Michael	119
Sutton, William	127
Seeley, William	153
Shaw, Hugh	154
Scott, Andrew	160
Schiess	173
Scott, Robert George	175
Sellar, George	177
Smith, Albert	184
Smith, John Manners	187
Sartorius, C.M.G., William Reginald	195
TREWAVAS, Joseph	3
Taylor, John	13
Teesdale, C.B., Charles	49
Tombs, C.B., Henry	77
Tytler, John Adam	82
Thomas, J.	100
Thompson, Alexander	109
Thompson, James	129
Turner, Samuel	130
Travers, James	139
Thackeray, Edward Talbot	148
Trevor, Wm. Spottiswood	158
VONSDEN, William John	176
WILKINSON, Thomas	18
Walters, George	38
Wright, Alex.	42
Wheatley, F.	46
Walker, Mark	59
Wooden, Charles	65
Ward, Henry	70
Watson, John	75
Wilmot, Henry	92
Wadeson, Richard	98
Ward, Joseph	103
Whirlpool, Frederick	117
Waller, George	126
Wood, John Augustus	137
Waller, Wm. Francis Frederick	146
Williams, John	162
Wassall	168
Wilson, Arthur Knyveh	181
Wood, Henry Evelyn	189
YOUNG, Thomas James	104

www.ingramcontent.com/pod-product-compliance
Lightning Source LLC
Chambersburg PA
CBHW032100090426
42743CB00007B/184